L. N. Gadodia
Chairman

Sri Ram

Mathra Das

Shiv Narain

Chairman

Pirare Lal

Har Prasad

S. K. Sen

Din Dayal Sharma

Bisheshar Nath Zutshi

Chairman

Bisheshar Nath Zutshi
Hon Secretary

Sri Ram

Jagannath

Kanhaiya Lal
President
19/3/12

A. V. ... Principal Hindu College
Delhi

HINDU COLLEGE
DELHI

HINDU COLLEGE DELHI

A PEOPLE'S MOVEMENT

Kavita A. Sharma
W.D. Mathur

Foreword
Dr Kapila Vatsyayan

NIYOGI BOOKS

Published by

NIYOGI BOOKS

D-78, Okhla Industrial Area, Phase-I
New Delhi-110 020, INDIA
Tel: 91-11-26816301, 49327000
Fax: 91-11-26810483, 26813830
Email: niyogibooks@gmail.com
Website: www.niyogibooksindia.com

Editor: Shaurya Shaukat Sircar
Cover Design: Shashi Bhushan Prasad
Design: Nabanita Das

ISBN: 978-93-83098-28-6
Publication: 2014

Printed at: Niyogi Offset Pvt. Ltd., New Delhi, India

CONTENTS

University of Delhi

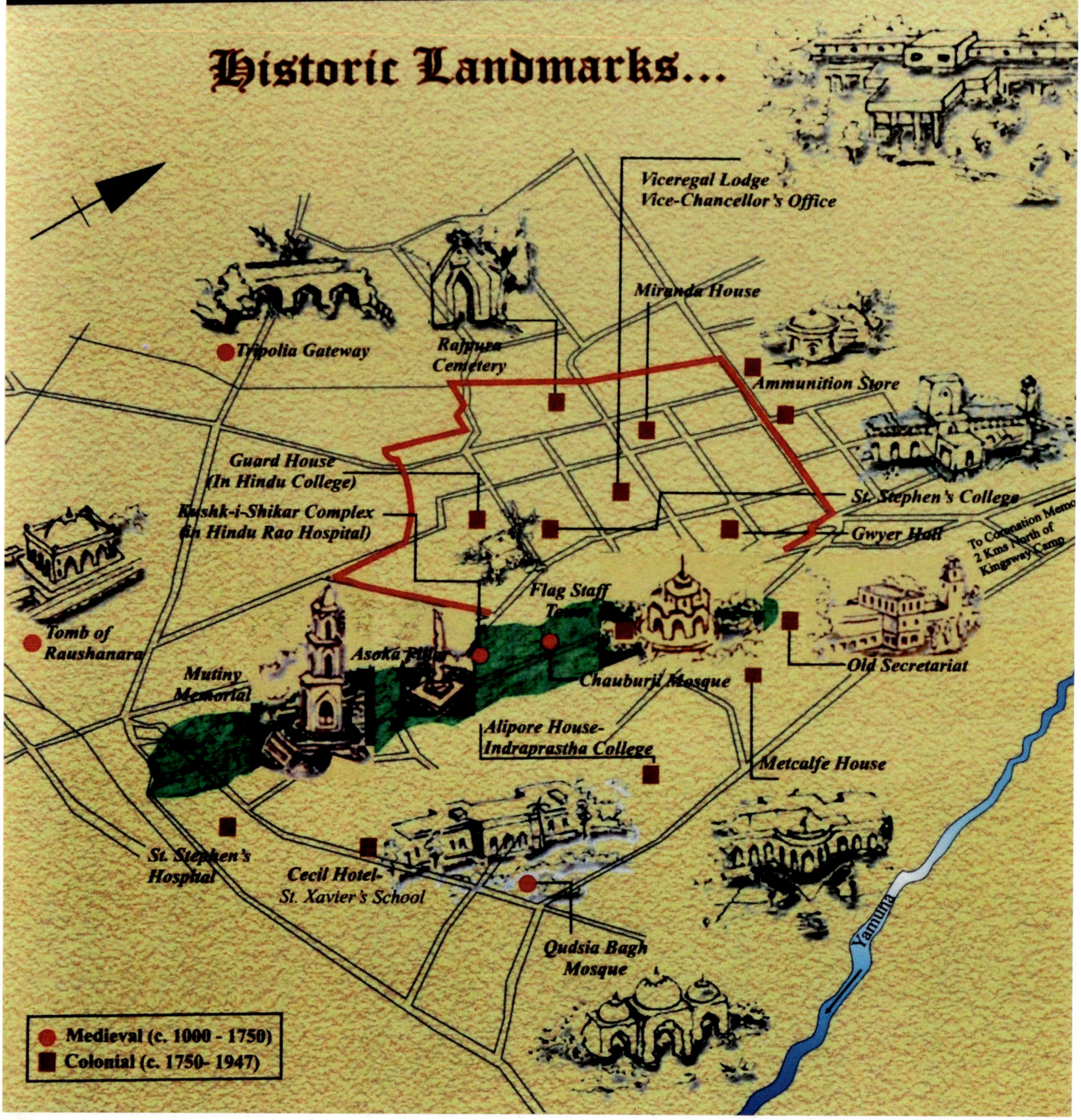

FOREWORD

Dr Kapila Vatsyayan

Needless to restate the obvious that 1857 brought about unprecedented changes, of course, at the political level as also socio-cultural. More specifically, in the educational field the Minute of Thomas Babington Macaulay (1835) had succeeded in laying the foundations of a new system of education which we recognise as the 'modern system of education'. It is also relevant to make a mention of the Dispatch of Charles Wood (1854) which stated 'by not giving recognition to the indigenous systems and institutions, we will succeed in shrivelling up the system and it will shed of its own accord without our being held responsible'. The indigenous systems of education and the institutions were certainly beginning to shrink and shrivel for lack of not only financial support but also diffidence in the efficacy of those systems. The establishment of the Presidency College in Kolkata (established as Hindu College in 1817 and renamed Presidency College in 1855), the Presidency College in Madras (established as Madras preparatory school in 1840, later upgraded as a college and affiliated to Madras University in 1857) and of the University of Bombay in 1857, was a consequence of the acceptance of an institutional system advocated by the 'Anglicans'.

Delhi was neither Calcutta nor Bombay nor Madras. Prima facie Delhi did not have a vibrant tradition of 'oriental' learning. Of course, there were centres of Sanskrit, Prakrit, Arabic and Persian learning. The initiative of establishing institutions in accordance with the new policy of education was with the missionaries. This is obvious from the founding of the St. Stephen's College in 1881. In contrast was the jerky and turbulent history of the Anglo-Arabic College established in 1792 (later known as Delhi College, taken over by the government, but closed down by the Punjab University in 1877). The history of the establishment of the Hindu College (1899) has to be situated against the backdrop of these developments.

The result of the tireless efforts of two alumni, Dr Kavita A. Sharma, the first woman principal of the Hindu College (1998–2008) and W.D. Mathur (Bobby), former bureau chief of *The Indian Express*, in tracing the history of the establishment of the Hindu College are as welcome as revealing. They have dug up material lying in a variety of sources—ranging from National Archives, Delhi Archives, Teen Murti House Library, Hardayal (Harding) Library,

Marwari Library and Delhi Public Library as also minutes of the Executive Council of the Delhi University from 1922 and other private sources. All this must have been a very difficult task demanding tenacity, conviction and dedication. Their findings uncover the urges and motivations of members of the civil society (even if they appeared to be 'loyalists') in establishing an educational institution which would be instilled with a commitment to nationalism and yet follow the systems of education that were now in place. Their effort is comparable to Sherlock Holmes in piecing together rare evidence to trace the journey of the college.

Their research identifies the commitment of a few residents in Old Delhi, such as late Lala Shri Krishna Dass Gurwala, Lala Sultan Singh and others to start an institution, find funds and a location. Their narration of housing the college in a small residence in Kinari Bazaar, Chandni Chowk, the inauguration ceremony performed by Pandit Madan Mohan Malaviya in a dharamshala in Chehlpuri on Basant Panchami, the financial support, the shifting of the college to Kashmere Gate in 1908, are as fascinating as educative. Among the first thirteen students was Sir Shri Ram, who was there for a brief of period of six months before he left to join his family business; he was later to become the chairman of the college Governing Body. His whole family has been dedicated to this college as is obvious from the fact that his son, Lala Bharat Ram, was also later to become chairman of its Governing Body.

The shifting of the college to Kashmere Gate was a milestone. Now, for decades the Hindu College has become a vibrant centre of learning, scholarship and more, with a distinct personality characterised by a commitment to nationalism. It provided a space for free and frank dialogues at many levels, between the faculty and the students and between and amongst students, of different disciplines. Just as important is the fact that the students of this college did not aspire for government service, although it is this college which produced a Khub Chand, one of the early members of the ICS. By and large the students explored many avenues, be it business, as in the case of a K.K. Birla, not to speak of a Sarup Singh, who rose to be a vice chancellor and governor, and of course the educationist B.M. Bhatia. The Hindu College nurtured diverse faculties of this young generation of the 1930s and 1940s. It resulted, in part and whole, for the flowering of those who have played an important role in shaping modern India. Just a few names may be mentioned from amongst the faculty as also the students: Dr Inder Sen, Professor of Philosophy (who later left to join the Aurobindo Ashram in Pondicherry), Dr S.K. Saxena (who was later a distinguished professor in University of Hawaii), Daya Krishna, Raj Krishna, Giri Lal Jain and L.C. Jain. The training ground was the parliament of the Hindu College, where, beyond the conventional curricula, there was opportunity for debating and being nurtured to perhaps a life in the larger sphere of nation-building. The authors mention these and also give a very vivid account of the contribution of successive principals, particularly N.V. Thadani.

Those of us who have also been students of the Hindu College will read this book with a sense of nostalgia and pride and others, especially the younger generation, it is my hope, will read it as revealing the initiatives and an unflinching commitment of the members of the civil society, long before the term NGO was coined.

PREFACE

From adventure to endless amazing revelations! From sheer exasperation to elation! It was a long journey leading us to the culmination of this book, *Hindu College Delhi: A People's Movement*; but only the first step has been taken. We realised that there was no book on Hindu College and that the circumstances of its establishment and evolution would gradually fade away from most people's minds, both students and teachers.

It was always intriguing what led so many rich and powerful businessmen who were Rai Bahadurs and Rai Sahibs to establish a nationalist college in 1899 when on the face of it, it would have been hazardous for them to do so; and what made so many influential people from all over the country come together and join the enterprise.

An RTI response revealed that the college started as a Joint Stock Company and the records of the Registrar's office provided the names of the Board of Trustees over the years together with the earliest Memorandum of Association that was filed. *Punjab Gazetteers* Vol. V A published at the beginning of 1910 observed, 'This college was established in May 1899 for the purpose of giving cheap but efficient secular education with sound religious instruction, according to the principle of Sanatana Dharm. ... In addition to the subjects prescribed by the University, all Hindu students are required to attend a religious class once a day.' The college was affiliated to the Punjab University.

A society by the name of Hindu College Delhi was registered to establish the college in 1899 with the objective of giving sound education in English up to the highest university standards. In the case of Hindus, the aim was also to combine secular education with thorough religious instruction according to the teachings of the *santana* dharma, on non-sectarian principles. Muslims were not prevented from joining and those who did, were not compelled to study the Hindu texts. Thus, religious instruction was a part of the agenda; the vision, however, was neither bigoted nor parochial and narrow-minded. Secularism and voluntary religious instruction were not seen as incompatible. Of course with the coming of Independence, the idea of what was secularism changed and so the clauses pertaining to religious instruction in the Memorandum of Association had to be modified.

As we got into this project, we realised that the information was coming; even though at a snail's pace. And then we hit the jackpot. We discovered that the college magazine *The Indraprastha*, the issues of which were there in the library right from 1930s, were a wealth of information, providing not only the missing links but also confirmation of certain events that were restricted to hearsay. These magazines also gave us a glimpse of the character of the institution, the commitment of teachers and the maturity and devotion of the students. But what was it that gave the college a nationalist character and a patriotic fervour? What was the root? The sad part is that the magazine during the decade of 1940s, the crucial time of the Quit India Movement, was missing. We do not know whether they had been published or had just got lost.

Serious apprehensions were being raised by the proselytising activities of the missionaries, especially in the mid-1860s when the city was wracked by a series of famines rendering the poor backward families vulnerable to conversions in lieu of material help from the missionaries. The fear was that the missionary educational institutions would be used for indoctrination.

The only existing college—the Anglo-Arabic College (later Delhi College) established in 1792, was taken over by the government in 1824. This only added to these apprehensions and created a vacuum of indigenous higher education in Delhi. The aim of the takeover was to transform it into a British institution of education and to make it a centre of new ideas. Following public outrage, attempts were made to revive it between 1871 and 1879 but in vain. The Punjab government closed it down because of poor enrolment depriving the city of the only Indian institution. The establishment of the Mission College (St. Stephen's) in 1881 was resented because it placed higher education solely in the hands of Christian missionaries.

When Hindu College was founded, this clearly formed the backdrop of the circumstances and little wonder that it was the breeding ground for anti-British feelings manifest in subsequent years. Coming up from the humblest beginnings, continuously facing financial constraints and resistance from the pre-Independence administrators, this college rose to become a giant, providing a forum and a base for our national leaders to address the youth of the country during the freedom struggle. Their visits were a great inspiration for the staff and the students. It was natural for them to get involved in the freedom movement. The college was born as a part of the nationalist impulse.

Several visits to the National Archives and the Delhi Archives provided us invaluable documents—police records of the Quit India period and the participation of Hindu College students. Visits to Delhi University led to the perusal of the Executive Council Minutes from 1922 (the year of the establishment of Delhi University) to the present. These gave an understanding of the role played by the three constituent colleges—Hindu, Ramjas and Stephen's—to ensure that the university stabilised and grew. Also they reflected the travails of growth especially of Hindu College which had a commitment to not turn any student from its doors in spite of its meagre resources.

Apart from the college magazine *The Indraprastha*, we mined material from the yearly directory of Hinduites brought out by Raj Kumar Oberoi which contained invaluable articles written by Hinduites; the little booklet brought out at the Diamond Jubilee celebrations; *In Retrospect*, a book of reminiscences of Hinduites published during the Centenary celebrations, together with the articles in the souvenir published on that occasion. There were oral histories we conducted and made innumerable telephone calls and trips to libraries—Teen Murti House, Hardayal (Harding) Library, Marwari Library, Delhi Public Library and Central Secretariat Library. The access to them and work there was facilitated by Dr Majumdar, Chief Librarian, India International Centre. Then there were visits to people's homes, pursuing them to part with photographs and any material that they might have.

Incidentally this fulfils the ambition of our former chairman of the Governing Body, Dr Bharat Ram, whose long association with the college as chairman, for four decades, can easily explain his great love for the college. While speaking at the College Founder's Day function way back in 1974, he said, 'I would like to suggest to Dr Bhatia (Principal) that he should commission some knowledgeable person to write the history of the college which is seventy-five years old.' While we could not say anything about this knowledgeable person, it took almost four decades before we could gather the courage to take up this stupendous work. There were times when we reached a dead end either because of non-availability of century-old records or complete ignorance or lack of interest on the part of the people who belonged to the families of those who had given the nation this great institution. We started talking about the futility of taking up this work of digging into the history of this college right from its inception. Yet we kept encouraging each other and managed to convince ourselves that there was a chance and there was no need to lose hope.

We know that a lot more could be written and discovered about this great institution and we leave it to the future generations and interested historians to fill in the gaps and come out with more revelations.

Kavita A. Sharma
W.D. Mathur (Bobby)

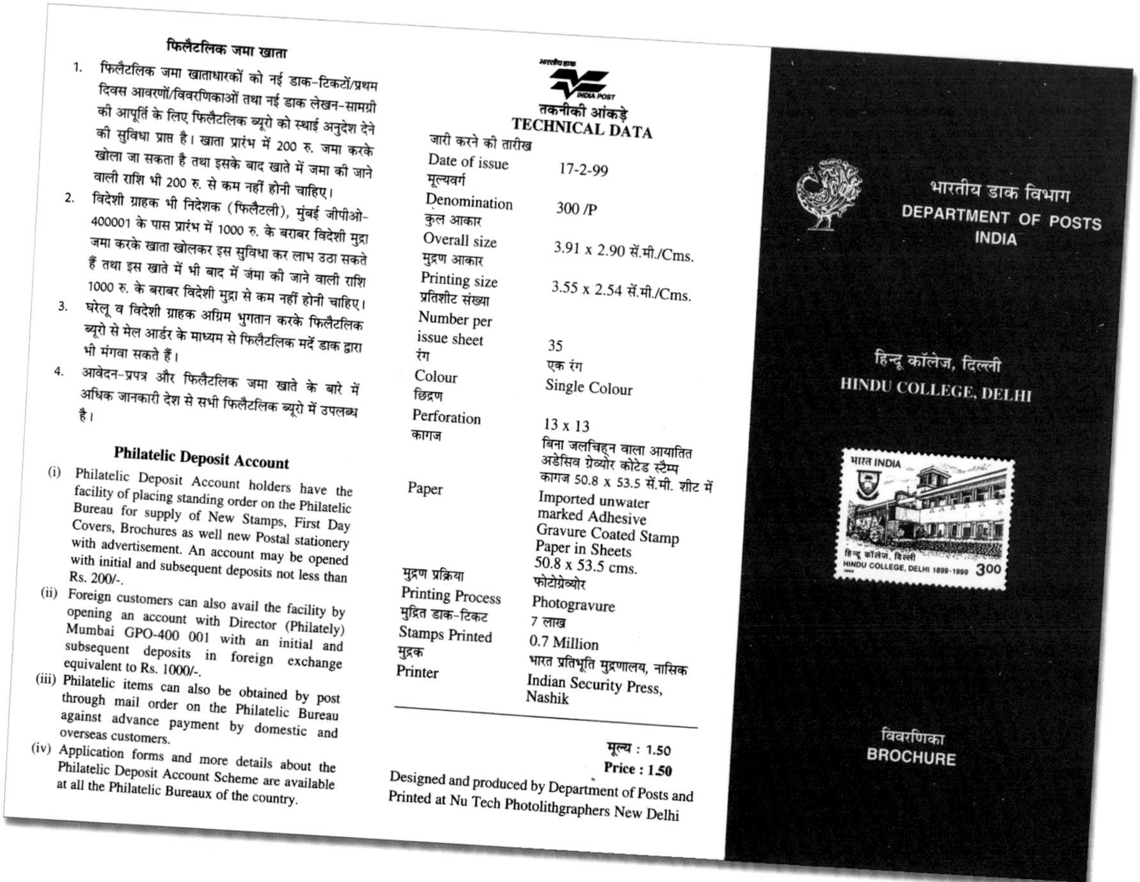

फिलैटलिक जमा खाता

1. फिलैटलिक जमा खाताधारकों को नई डाक-टिकटों/प्रथम दिवस आवरणों/विवरणिकाओं तथा नई डाक लेखन-सामग्री की आपूर्ति के लिए फिलैटलिक ब्यूरो को स्थाई अनुदेश देने की सुविधा प्राप्त है। खाता प्रारंभ में 200 रु. जमा करके खोला जा सकता है तथा इसके बाद खाते में जमा की जाने वाली राशि भी 200 रु. से कम नहीं होनी चाहिए।
2. विदेशी ग्राहक भी निदेशक (फिलैटली), मुंबई जीपीओ-400001 के पास प्रारंभ में 1000 रु. के बराबर विदेशी मुद्रा जमा करके खाता खोलकर इस सुविधा कर लाभ उठा सकते हैं तथा इस खाते में भी बाद में जंमा की जाने वाली राशि 1000 रु. के बराबर विदेशी मुद्रा से कम नहीं होनी चाहिए।
3. घरेलू व विदेशी ग्राहक अग्रिम भुगतान करके फिलैटलिक ब्यूरो से मेल आर्डर के माध्यम से फिलैटलिक मदें डाक द्वारा भी मंगवा सकते हैं।
4. आवेदन-प्रपत्र और फिलैटलिक जमा खाते के बारे में अधिक जानकारी देश से सभी फिलैटलिक ब्यूरो में उपलब्ध है।

Philatelic Deposit Account

(i) Philatelic Deposit Account holders have the facility of placing standing order on the Philatelic Bureau for supply of New Stamps, First Day Covers, Brochures as well new Postal stationery with advertisement. An account may be opened with initial and subsequent deposits not less than Rs. 200/-.

(ii) Foreign customers can also avail the facility by opening an account with Director (Philately) Mumbai GPO-400 001 with an initial and subsequent deposits in foreign exchange equivalent to Rs. 1000/-.

(iii) Philatelic items can also be obtained by post through mail order on the Philatelic Bureau against advance payment by domestic and overseas customers.

(iv) Application forms and more details about the Philatelic Deposit Account Scheme are available at all the Philatelic Bureaux of the country.

तकनीकी आंकड़े
TECHNICAL DATA

जारी करने की तारीख Date of issue	17-2-99
मूल्यवर्ग Denomination	300 /P
कुल आकार Overall size	3.91 x 2.90 सें.मी./Cms.
मुद्रण आकार Printing size	3.55 x 2.54 सें.मी./Cms.
प्रतिशीट संख्या Number per issue sheet	35
रंग Colour	एक रंग Single Colour
छिद्रण Perforation	13 x 13
कागज Paper	बिना जलचिह्न वाला आयातित अडेसिव ग्रेव्यॉर कोटेड स्टैम्प कागज 50.8 x 53.5 सें.मी. शीट में Imported unwater marked Adhesive Gravure Coated Stamp Paper in Sheets 50.8 x 53.5 cms.
मुद्रण प्रक्रिया Printing Process	फोटोग्रेव्यॉर Photogravure
मुद्रित डाक-टिकट Stamps Printed	7 लाख 0.7 Million
मुद्रक Printer	भारत प्रतिभूति मुद्रणालय, नासिक Indian Security Press, Nashik

मूल्य : 1.50
Price : 1.50

Designed and produced by Department of Posts and Printed at Nu Tech Photolithgraphers New Delhi

भारतीय डाक विभाग
DEPARTMENT OF POSTS
INDIA

हिन्दू कॉलेज, दिल्ली
HINDU COLLEGE, DELHI

विवरणिका
BROCHURE

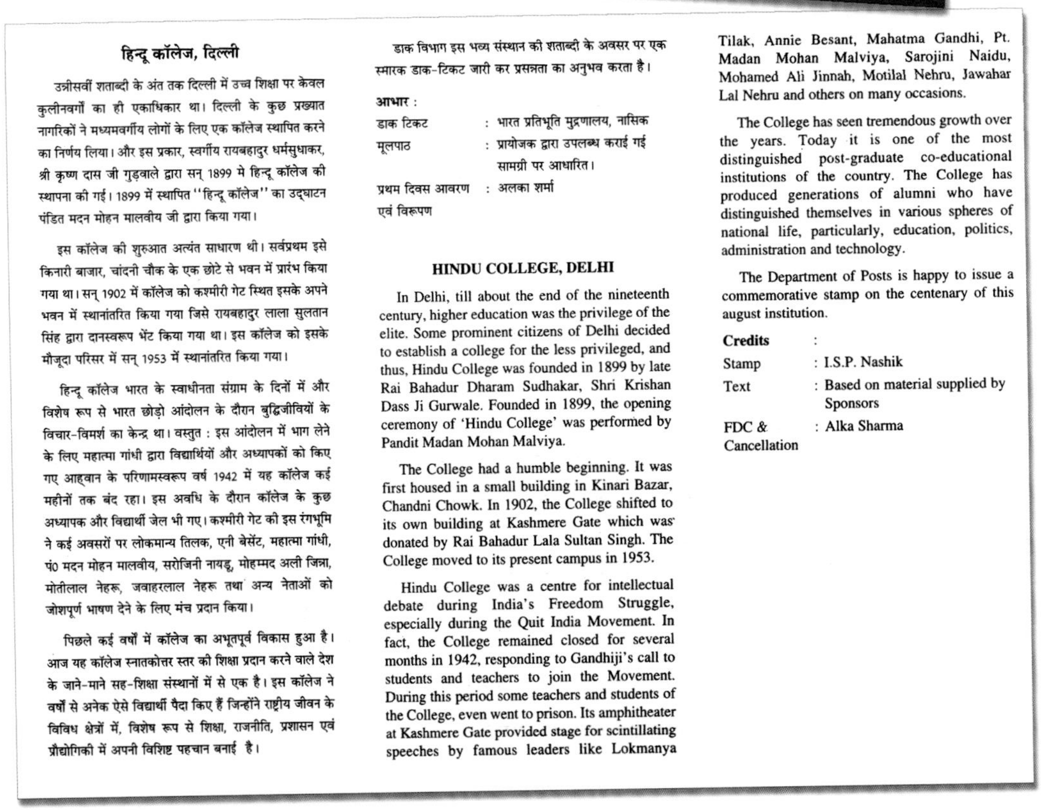

हिन्दू कॉलेज, दिल्ली

उन्नीसवीं शताब्दी के अंत तक दिल्ली में उच्च शिक्षा पर केवल कुलीनवर्गों का ही एकाधिकार था। दिल्ली के कुछ प्रख्यात नागरिकों ने मध्यमवर्गीय लोगों के लिए एक कॉलेज स्थापित करने का निर्णय लिया। और इस प्रकार, स्वर्गीय रायबहादुर धर्मसुधाकर, श्री कृष्ण दास जी गुड़वाले द्वारा सन् 1899 मे हिन्दू कॉलेज की स्थापना की गई। 1899 में स्थापित "हिन्दू कॉलेज" का उद्‌घाटन पंडित मदन मोहन मालवीय जी द्वारा किया गया।

इस कॉलेज की शुरुआत अत्यंत साधारण थी। सर्वप्रथम इसे किनारी बाजार, चांदनी चौक के एक छोटे से भवन में प्रारंभ किया गया था। सन् 1902 में कॉलेज को कश्मीरी गेट स्थित इसके अपने भवन में स्थानांतरित किया गया जिसे रायबहादुर लाला सुलतान सिंह द्वारा दानस्वरूप भेंट किया गया था। इस कॉलेज को इसके मौजूदा परिसर में सन् 1953 में स्थानांतरित किया गया।

हिन्दू कॉलेज भारत के स्वाधीनता संग्राम के दिनों में और विशेष रूप से भारत छोड़ो आंदोलन के दौरान बुद्धिजीवियों के विचार-विमर्श का केन्द्र था। वस्तुत : इस आंदोलन में भाग लेने के लिए महात्मा गांधी द्वारा विद्यार्थियों और अध्यापकों को किए गए आह्वान के परिणामस्वरूप वर्ष 1942 में यह कॉलेज कई महीनों तक बंद रहा। इस अवधि के दौरान कॉलेज के कुछ अध्यापक और विद्यार्थी जेल भी गए। कश्मीरी गेट की इस रंगभूमि ने कई अवसरों पर लोकमान्य तिलक, एनी बेसेंट, महात्मा गांधी, पं० मदन मोहन मालवीय, सरोजिनी नायडू, मोहम्मद अली जिन्ना, मोतीलाल नेहरू, जवाहरलाल नेहरू तथा अन्य नेताओं को जोशपूर्ण भाषण देने के लिए मंच प्रदान किया।

पिछले कई वर्षों में कॉलेज का अभूतपूर्व विकास हुआ है। आज यह कॉलेज स्नातकोत्तर स्तर की शिक्षा प्रदान करने वाले देश के जाने-माने सह-शिक्षा संस्थानों में से एक है। इस कॉलेज ने वर्षों से अनेक ऐसे विद्यार्थी पैदा किए हैं जिन्होंने राष्ट्रीय जीवन के विविध क्षेत्रों में, विशेष रूप से शिक्षा, राजनीति, प्रशासन एवं प्रौद्योगिकी में अपनी विशिष्ट पहचान बनाई है।

डाक विभाग इस भव्य संस्थान की शताब्दी के अवसर पर एक स्मारक डाक-टिकट जारी कर प्रसन्नता का अनुभव करता है।

आभार :

डाक टिकट	: भारत प्रतिभूति मुद्रणालय, नासिक
मूलपाठ	: प्रायोजक द्वारा उपलब्ध कराई गई सामग्री पर आधारित।
प्रथम दिवस आवरण एवं विरूपण	: अलका शर्मा

HINDU COLLEGE, DELHI

In Delhi, till about the end of the nineteenth century, higher education was the privilege of the elite. Some prominent citizens of Delhi decided to establish a college for the less privileged, and thus, Hindu College was founded in 1899 by late Rai Bahadur Dharam Sudhakar, Shri Krishan Dass Ji Gurwale. Founded in 1899, the opening ceremony of 'Hindu College' was performed by Pandit Madan Mohan Malviya.

The College had a humble beginning. It was first housed in a small building in Kinari Bazar, Chandni Chowk. In 1902, the College shifted to its own building at Kashmere Gate which was donated by Rai Bahadur Lala Sultan Singh. The College moved to its present campus in 1953.

Hindu College was a centre for intellectual debate during India's Freedom Struggle, especially during the Quit India Movement. In fact, the College remained closed for several months in 1942, responding to Gandhiji's call to students and teachers to join the Movement. During this period some teachers and students of the College, even went to prison. Its amphitheater at Kashmere Gate provided stage for scintillating speeches by famous leaders like Lokmanya Tilak, Annie Besant, Mahatma Gandhi, Pt. Madan Mohan Malviya, Sarojini Naidu, Mohamed Ali Jinnah, Motilal Nehru, Jawahar Lal Nehru and others on many occasions.

The College has seen tremendous growth over the years. Today it is one of the most distinguished post-graduate co-educational institutions of the country. The College has produced generations of alumni who have distinguished themselves in various spheres of national life, particularly, education, politics, administration and technology.

The Department of Posts is happy to issue a commemorative stamp on the centenary of this august institution.

Credits	:
Stamp	: I.S.P. Nashik
Text	: Based on material supplied by Sponsors
FDC & Cancellation	: Alka Sharma

Brochure inside the First Day Cover released on the occasion of Hindu College's Centenary celebrations, 1999

Page 6: *Historic Landmarks of Delhi University*

Roots of Nationalism

Hindu College was founded in 1899 by Lala Shri Krishna Dass Gurwala, as a part of the nationalist sentiment of providing affordable modern education to students from middle-class and less well off families. This was to be an education that would enable them to take part in the polity of the nation and become capable of impacting policy and decision-making and at the same time, remaining rooted in their own cultural and civilisational values. This was necessary because of nationalist sentiments and the freedom movement set in motion in India eventually led to her Independence. The Indian National Congress had been founded a few years earlier in 1885 so when Hindu College came into existence the city had already witnessed events that had a direct bearing on its formation. The genesis of the nationalist spirit in the college turning into participation in the freedom struggle can be traced to a number of factors.

Previous page: *Lala Shri Krishna Dass Gurwala*

Seth Ramji Dass, grandfather of Lala Shri Krishna Dass Gurwala

Historical Background

After the Revolt of 1857, Seth Ramji Dass, grandfather of Lala Shri Krishna Dass Gurwala who was regarded as the 'Rothschild' of northern India, was brutally killed by British rulers in the middle of Chandni Chowk because he refusesd to provide them finances. His death was also a punishment for helping Bahadur Shah Zafar, the last Mughal king, in reorganising his army, by providing Rs 3 crore and fourteen boats loaded with foodgrains. When the British asked for similar help, Seth Ramji Dass refused. His house was ransacked and his property confiscated by the infuriated British.

In his book, *Ek Shatabdi* ('A Century'), Colonel Brij Behari Sharan, who was also related to the Gurwala family, recalls how Ramji Dass, an affluent dealer in foodgrains and also a moneylender, supplied provisions to Bahadur Shah Zafar's army. According to him, Ramji Dass was a very close friend of the king and in 1857 he offered him his entire wealth. This help came at an opportune time as the king's coffers were almost empty.[1]

There was another reason for Ramji Dass helping the king as he too was annoyed with the 'black deeds' of the East India Company. Ramji Dass got busy in organising the army and a secret intelligence department for the king. British army commanders were surprised at his organising abilities. Unfortunately, many of the king's own close subjects, the *darbaris*, were disloyal, spying against him and they revealed all the secrets to the British.

Ramji Dass sent a message of freedom to Indian soldiers in the British army, promising to help them at an appropriate time. Infuriated by his actions, British army officers let loose hounds on Ramji Dass. Finally, they hanged him in Chandni Chowk in front of the *kotwali*.

Historians have analysed the various forces that were at work at that time. One was religious tension between Hindus and Muslims, who were almost in equal numbers following the resettlement of Delhi at the beginning in October 1857. Post-1857, the city was, in the words of Delhi's Commissioner, J.P. Saunders, 'deserted by all living beings except a few stray dogs'. Delhi was a victim of the vengeance unleashed by victorious soldiers and for another five months the people continued to be subjected to indiscriminate hangings and systematic looting. The Indian defeat in the 1857

1 Brij Behari Sharan, *Ek Shatabdi* (New Delhi, 2003), pp. 66-67.

uprising too left its mark. Tensions between Hindus and Muslims aggravated and led to rioting during 1884–87 because the festivals of Dussehra and Muharram fell within a few days of each other. This had not been a matter of contention earlier. Issues like cow slaughter cropped up and communal riots took place in the mid-1880s. This acrimony generated a large amount of polemical literature as Christian, Hindu and Muslim groups and organisations tried to attack each other. The Delhi administration was busy trying to sort out the problems and yet remain unbiased.

For three consecutive years, 1866–68, Delhi faced a great famine. Subsequent years saw an increase in taxes bringing greater misery to the already 'impoverished' citizens. Economic discontent and abject poverty made certain communities extremely vulnerable to the lure of assured education and better living conditions held out by the missionaries. This also resulted in political awakening, freely attributed to the spread of Western education.

Moreover at this time Delhi was becoming a centre for Hindu resurgence. It led to unease not only between Hindus and Muslims but also within various Hindu groups—among the orthodox Hindus, Arya Samajists and Jains. Nonetheless, there was a strong desire to defend and strengthen Hinduism, especially among educated Hindus. Many organisations

The kotwali *in Chandni Chowk near which Ramji Dass was hanged*

sprang up and by 1890 organisations such as the Arya Samaj and the Theosophical Society had heightened their activities. A national conference was held in 1900 in Delhi under the presidency of the Maharaja of Darbhanga with the aim of uniting the various Hindu organisations. The Bharata Dharma Mahamandala was formed in 1902 with Pandit Din Dayal Sharma as its secretary. He was also one of the first trustees of the Hindu College Education Society.

Education was one of the important objectives of the Bharata Dharma Mahamandala because of serious apprehensions raised by the proselytising activities of the missionaries. The new system of education also affected the monopoly of the pandits and maulvis in the sphere of education. The stated objectives of the Mahamandala were to:

- Promote Hindu religious education in accordance with the *sanatana* dharma, to spread the knowledge of the Vedas, *Smritis*, Puranas and other Hindu *shastras* and to introduce, in the light of such knowledge, useful reforms in Hindu life and society.
- Promote and enrich Sanskrit and Hindi literature in all its branches.
- Introduce such useful reforms as may be warranted by the *shastras* in the management of Hindu charitable and religious institutions and *tirthas* (sacred places).
- Establish, affiliate and control branch *sabhas* in different parts of India.
- Support existing Hindu colleges, schools, libraries and publishing establishments and find new ones in consonance with the objectives of the association.

There were several contentious issues between the various religious groups. Conversions caused the most heartburn as they essentially created strife between Christians and Hindus when Christian missionaries tried to re-establish themselves and convert people to Christianity. This heightened in the mid-1860s when the city was wracked by a series of famines that resulted in large-scale conversions largely among the community of shoemakers. Economic deprivation and the tyranny and discrimination of upper caste Hindus pushed these Hindus to the new fold. The missionaries started schools and arranged to indoctrinate these people. They were even taken away from their habitations and a *basti* was set up for them just outside Daryaganj. The missionaries did this to ensure that their conversions were permanent and the converts would not retract when their economic and social conditions improved. On the whole, the missionaries were not very successful but when upper caste Hindus converted it caused concern among both Hindus and Muslims.

British contempt for Indians, their religion and culture did not help matters. Apart from missionary propaganda, many civil and military officers behaved like evangelists. For example, Rev. M. Edmond issued a circular from Calcutta in which he stated:

> The time appears to have come when earnest consideration should be given to the subject, whether or not all men should embrace the same religion. Railways, steam

> vessels and the electric telegraph, are rapidly uniting all the people of the earth. ... Christian religion is the only religion which claims to have come from God by way of direct revelation. This is the only religion which can confer happiness in this world and in the other world whose conditions are revealed by it. ... It is our wish to see the churches filled with Indians, where not only foreigners but the people of the country also will proclaim regularly the good news of the Christian gospel, and where men and women will be required to seek repentance from their sins and to prepare themselves for meeting God; and where children will be taught morality and truth.[2]

While the 1857 uprising may have been seen as a 'mutiny' by the British Parliament and English writers, Disraeli, speaking in the House of Commons on 27 July 1857, was clear that it 'was a national revolt and not a military mutiny,'[3] recalls Tara Chand in *History of the Freedom Movement in India*. He also points out that Justin McCarthy said:

> The fact was that throughout the greater part of the north and north-west of the great Indian Peninsula there was a rebellion of the native races against English power. It was not by any means a merely military mutiny. It was a combination of military grievances, national hatred and religious fanaticism against the English occupation of India. The native princes and native soldiers were in it. The Mohammedan and the Hindoo forgot their old religious antipathies to join against the Christian.[4]

So the roots of nationalism were planted at that time itself.

Tara Chand further observes, 'The fifty years of direct rule by the British Crown from 1858 to 1905 were marked by the extension of the means of communication and transport, large increase in India's foreign trade and modernization of India's economy ...'[5] But amidst this progress, the country went through several calamities and millions died for want of food. There was heavier taxation, a decline in Indian handicrafts and lack of employment opportunities. Thus, the dominance of Europeans in civil and military services caused[6] great discontent and was a major cause of the opposition to British rule.

---

2 Cited by Tara Chand, in *History of the Freedom Movement in India*, Vol. II (Delhi: Publications Division, Ministry of Information and Broadcasting, 1967, rpt 1974), p. 66.

3 Ibid., p. 40.

4 Ibid., p. 41.

5 Ibid., p. 347.

6 Ibid., p. 347.

Tara Chand concludes:

> The analysis of the economy of India leads inevitably to the conclusion that basically the poverty of India was the consequence of foreign rule—the system of administration introduced by the British in India. It followed that no improvement in the economic conditions of the people could be expected without a radical change in the character of the Government. It was necessary, therefore, to agitate for a change in government, for the introduction of a representative and democratic system, for the transfer of political power from the British to Indian hands. Important and urgent as the economic questions were, their solution depended upon the attainment of self-rule by India.[7]

The Beginnings of Industrialisation

Japan's victory over Russia in 1905, in a rivalry that arose out of the imperial ambitions of the two nations over Manchuria and Korea had very important consequences in India. It gave emotional direction to the nationalist movement and its political demands. The Japanese had succeeded because of their economic power and their high degree of scientific and technical ability. This gave birth to economic nationalism and strengthened the Swadeshi movement in India which was originally initiated by the boycott campaign in Bengal. It not only became a political weapon but also led to the development of small-scale industries. Under this economic nationalism large sums were raised for sending students abroad for technical education. The trading classes began to align themselves with the political class. World War I opened further opportunities for industrial development in India and by the end of the War, the government had to appoint an Industrial Commission to recommend how Indian industries could be best financed and developed. The steel industry came into being at this time and a substantial portion of the capital for the jute manufacturing industry passed into the hands of Indian trading classes.

Under the British Crown

After 1858, when India came under the direct rule of the British crown, means of communication and transportation expanded, India's foreign trade increased and the modernisation of the Indian economy began. Three ingredients became important for the merchant class: wealth based on land holdings and commerce; influence wielded in local society as an entrepreneur and public figure; and close ties maintained with British authorities. All three came together in the urban *rais*. Urban *rais*, as defined by C.A. Bayly, was an agent of informal political authority who exercised his patronage and control through a network of 'cross-caste and cross-community connections' and was sought by the British for his function as the local intermediary. What gave him influence was his affluence and standing in society. *Rais* was neither caste nor class but 'a category of

7 Ibid., p. 348.

political power whose main characteristics were ability to mediate with higher authority and to control the web of patronage beneath.'[8] From among the *rais* the British recognised some with the titles of Rai Bahadur and Rai Sahib.

Many leading Indian trading and business families began adopting British modes of commerce and exploiting the new opportunities. These became especially important for the aspiring new class of government officials, urban professionals, businessmen and publicists. The most efficient was philanthropy and patronage of charitable, educational and religious institutions. The founders and trustees of Hindu College were mainly from the mercantile class and from among rising urban professionals. Most of them were influential *rai bahadurs* and *rais'*, who straddled both the worlds of the rulers and the ruled. They were given important civic responsibilities like those of municipal commissioners, honorary magistrates, inspectors of schools and others. But at the same time they were also nationalists who established a college in which the nationalist urge was obvious. It was this nationalist urge which led Hindu College to actively participate in the struggle for Independence.

In post-1857 urban society, the Indian municipal commissioner was typically a commercial or professional man of substance who maintained a relationship of mutual interest with the government and also frequently used his office to consolidate his local influence. This class contributed to medical and educational philanthropy and supported public libraries, the latter being a new addition to the colonial state's educational agenda. The Indian intelligentsia adopted the project of public libraries and although these were generally supported by government grants, they depended heavily on Indian sponsorship for their upkeep and supply of books.

In a period of rapid modernisation when religious identity was in the process of being negotiated, reformulated and asserted, the institution of caste was rediscovered. The latter half of the nineteenth century saw the formation of formal caste associations, another powerful association web. Susan Bayly has argued that Indian thinkers and social reformers came to view caste as a tool in the social and cultural regeneration of India, investing it with the new meaning of 'a bond of moral community at the national level'. Underlying this 'idealised corporation view' was the notion that caste was vested with moral messages.[9] The newly emerging caste associations emphasised social service and reformist activities. Agendas for uplifting community members had a clearly patriotic thrust and were seen as a means of uplifting the Indian nation at large. The culture of forming associations also saw a proliferation of debating clubs, scientific institutes and literary or reformist societies. With its focus on education, literature and social

8 C.A. Bayly, 'Local Control in Indian Towns—the Case of Allahabad 1880–1920', *Modern Asian Studies*, Vol. 5 No. 4 (1971), pp. 292-293.

9 Susan Bayly, *Caste, Society and Politics in India from the Eighteenth Century to the Modern Age*, in *The New Cambridge History of India*, IV.3 (Cambridge: Cambridge University Press, 1999), pp. 97–232.

reforms, this new form of organised indigenous agency grew out of, and catered to, the needs of the educated Indian elite to debate the implications of colonial rule and to participate in the process of India's modernisation.

The new voluntary associations fulfilled various functions. They allowed for participation in the East-West encounter at the cultural, literary and scientific levels and provided a forum in which to debate public affairs while becoming actively engaged in 'modern' forms of philanthropy. In the process, the nucleus of future political representation as an institutional framework that enabled the urban elite to become self-styled spokesmen of indigenous society and act as intermediaries between the colonial state and the Indian masses came into existence. Associations, in Anil Seal's pointed formulation, brought nineteenth-century India to the threshold of modern politics. The intelligentsia also attempted to use the associations to make its own claims of leadership and dominance.[10]

C.A. Bayly points out in 'Local Control in Indian Towns—the Case of Allahabad 1880–1920' that the commercial and banking element had always been powerful, although not always dominant in most Indian cities, particularly in towns like Allahabad that had flourished as riverine trading centres before 1850:

> ... the first circle of connection also included a *rais'* legal adviser or *vakil* and his publicist, often the same man, who ran small newspapers propagating his interest, circulated ethnologies, family histories and religious tracts, or drew up petitions to the local authorities for him. Now it is obviously true that even in the 1880s in Allahabad, some professional men associated with the High Court and a few leading members of the district court bar were local notables in their own right. The majority, however, were clients or dependents of the *rais'* as far as local society was concerned. They could act as ambassador (a word whose force is conveyed by *vakil*) between patronage systems, or between patronage systems and government and the courts. But professional men were rarely able to attain the status of *rais* in the eyes of the populace or to stand out as obvious intermediaries with a substantial section of the population as far as government was concerned. In Allahabad before 1900, professional men were also denied the status of major patrons for other reasons. Most were much more recent immigrants into the city than the commercial families; many were socially unorthodox or even outcaste. Generally speaking, they were less active as philanthropists or religious patrons, which reflects both the unsure financial circumstances of the bar and their isolation by an Indo-Persian cultural background from some aspects of Hindu cultural activity. Above all, their control over the urban labour market was more limited. They could control only direct patronage within

10 Anil Seal, *The Emergence of Indian Nationalism: Competition and Collaboration in the Later Nineteenth Century* (Cambridge: Cambridge University Press, 1968), p. 194.

> the bar, among lawyers' clerks, agents, etc., whereas bankers and moneylenders could enmesh any class from Muslim artisans to subordinate government servants in debt-bondage.[11]

There were intersections of both synergy and conflict between various sections of people whether they were upcoming professionals, small-scale house owners, old service communities, religious groupings, merchants or others. Each of them attempted to establish local areas of influence. The whole structure of local-level politics in the middle of the nineteenth century turned on a balance between the various connections based on credit control in cities, on land control in rural areas and on the interface between the two. The grip of the old *rais* families over the social life of the city gradually weakened and in many senses professional men and publicists came to replace them as intermediaries with local authorities.

Influence of Local Politics

Local politics began with a change at the municipal level. The control of nominations by *rais'* became less frequent. Municipal elections were harder fought. House-to-house canvassing was used and considerable publicity was given to campaigns in the local press. This becomes evident if the situation between 1908 and 1915 in Allahabad as analysed by Bayly is compared. In 1908, municipal politics and the committees of municipal boards were controlled by connections based on two mercantile kin groups of Ram Charan Das and Jagat Narayan. By 1915, as professionals became increasingly important, a powerful group of professional men, including two members of the Malaviya and Nehru families, became a part of a progressive faction led by Dr D.R. Ranjit Singh. The collectorate-supported faction too was a mixture of professions comprising of Muslim district Bar lawyers, some representatives of the old *rais* families and a Jain banker, Sheo Charan Lal, who had a degree and was a qualified lawyer. In the decade of 1900–1910, fifteen mercantile and house-owning magnates sat on the board as against five professional men who were mostly local *vakils*. But between 1912 and 1917 there were thirteen individuals with professional backgrounds as compared to ten *rais'*.

An outbreak of 'communal' tension between 1909 and 1917 provides an insight into the shifts in local influence and power. While members of the old *rais* families and some powerful new traders continued to play an important role in maintaining peace, professional men and publicists were active whether in compromising, or aggravating, tensions. During the outbreaks of 1917 and after, active lawyer-politicians like Purushottam Das Tandon, Madan Mohan Malaviya and Shaikh Zahur Ahmed consulted with the authorities and arranged bodies for conciliation. Although the old *rais'* were still significant, there were many more actors in the urban political arena and this weakened the whole structure of local control as far as the *rais'* were concerned.

Madan Mohan Malaviya

11 C.A. Bayly, op.cit., p. 298.

In caste bodies too, professional men increasingly challenged the authority of the rich mercantile or house-owning patrons. Caste *sabhas* or associations challenged traditional authority, even in ritual matters. In the early years of the twentieth century a number of organisations felt the need to reorganise 'castes' over a much wider area. They tried to coerce parochial brotherhoods to adopt measures of 'westernisation' and began to patronise marriage funds and educational charities. They used their literacy and province-wide professional contacts to play a more significant role to free caste patronage from the hands of the local *rais*' and their dependants.[12]

This shift in attitude was also seen in the tradition of giving gifts which acquired a nationalistic flavour. As Haynes points out, while South Asian businessmen became the main participants in philanthropic activities during the late nineteenth century, many of them were also behind the scenes in the agitations of the late colonial period.[13] By donating to charitable institutions, they were actually making 'statements' about how they saw themselves and about the causes important to them. In pre-colonial times, wealthy Hindu and Jain merchants had engaged in acts of great munificence such as building wells, temples and rest houses. These were essentially propitiation or service to their deities and deeds by which they could acquire merit. But by the beginning of the nineteenth century, several merchants were contributing money to schools, colleges and other public works and such causes. British civil servants saw this as a sign of 'progress' and came to regard the contributors as agents of 'progress', people who could help them transform a backward society into a more 'modern' one. But these conservative merchants, averse to bold actions yet standing on the door of westernisation, seemed contradictory to C.A. Bayly.[14] On the other hand, Haynes argued that involvement in philanthropy was in fact consistent with the cautious, risk-averse character of the merchant mentality.[15] They were building a large 'portfolio' of symbolic investments to develop stable social relationships both with members of their community and with their rulers. It was their way of adjusting to the changed socio-political world around them.

Joining the Freedom Movement

The increasing industrial and commercial activity led to widening of disparities. It caused economic discontent and distress in people that got translated into opposition to British rule. India became a colonial economy that served British interests but created mass poverty in the process. At the same time, greater awareness came with the spread of Western education,

---

12 Ibid., pp. 306-307.

13 Douglas E. Haynes, 'From Tribute to Philanthropy: The Politics of Gift Giving in a Western Indian City', *The Journal of Asian Studies*, Vol. 46 No. 2 (May 1987), pp. 339–360.

14 C.A.Bayly, *Rulers, Townsmen and Bazaars: North Indian Society in the Age of British Expansion 1770–1870* (Cambridge: Cambridge University Press, 1983), pp. 369–472.

15 Haynes, op. cit., pp. 339–360.

which introduced new political thought and modern ideas about science and technology. With increased trade and commerce, the middle class expanded and became better educated. It realised that mass poverty was a consequence of the burden of taxation, wasteful expenditure and drain of wealth because of colonisation. It concluded that India's poverty was because of foreign rule and that the situation would not improve as long as foreign rule remained. The ground was thus ready for a political revolution as the realisation that if her problems had to be solved it was necessary for India to be a free and sovereign state turned into conviction.

The influential mercantile and professional classes responded to Gandhi's Non-Cooperation Movement. A new nationalist force emerged in India. However, this force neither abandoned its religious endowments nor its long-term philanthropic commitments that it was already engaged in. These people continued to spend conspicuously on wedding feasts and religious festivals, on building temples and rest houses, but contributed as well to building schools, colleges, libraries, dispensaries and hospitals. The Congress appealed to them in the familiar idiom of mercantile status and a devotional religion. Thus, giving to the Congress became incorporated in the portfolios of gifting.[16]

Missionary Education

Missionary education was looked upon with suspicion. When Delhi College (then Anglo-Arabic College), established in 1792, was taken over by the government in 1824, it added to these apprehensions and created a vacuum in higher education. The aim of the takeover was to transform it into a British institution of education and to make it a centre of new ideas. This did not succeed, and after 1857 vain efforts were made to revive it. Between 1871 and 1879, the college managed to admit only fifty-six students. This poor performance gave rise to serious discussions on closing it down. Delhi's citizens bitterly objected, but eventually the Punjab government closed the college on 1 April 1877. This deprived the city of the only Indian institution of higher education. St. Stephen's College was established in Delhi in 1881. This move was resented because it placed higher education solely in the hands of Christian missionaries.

Missionary education was supported by administrators like Sir Charles Trevelyan, Herbert Edwards and the Lawrences who were not alarmed by what could be the fallout of a good modern education.[17] They believed that the old religious and social conventions were a menace for a good government. In 1857 the educated class had stood by the government to restore stability during and after the uprising. British administrators, missionaries and English-educated professionals like teachers, doctors and subordinate officials had sustained the

16 C.A. Bayly, *The Local Roots of Indian Politics: Allahabad 1880–1920* (London: Oxford University Press, 1975), pp. 122–176; 271–283.

17 *Report of the Commission on Christian Higher Education in India: An Enquiry into the Place of the Christian College in Modern India* (London: Oxford University Press, 1931), p. 33. **Henceforth the Report is referred to as** *Christian Higher Education in India.*

government. However, in spite of this realisation, security became a prime concern of state policy and political liberalism took a back seat. At the same time, the administration and the missionaries realised that the best way to commend themselves was through welfare service. Missionary bodies carried on their humanitarian schemes of education, medical relief and other such activities 'apart from their evangelical task', not only under government patronage but also with the aid of government grants.

Those missionary institutions of higher education were thought to have had a proselytising or at least evangelising agenda. This was not far off the mark as is evident from the *Report of the Commission on Christian Higher Education in India and Burma*. The commission was constituted by the International Missionary Council at its meeting in Williamstown, Massachusetts in July 1929. Christian colleges had to play their part in the higher education system in India but they also had to serve their missionary purpose. If this was thought to be conversion or baptism, the commission found that hardly any were taking place. But that could also be because life had become too engrossed in the external world to pay much heed to the claims of religion. However, the influence of Christian colleges was significant because Indian public opinion valued them for their character and the atmosphere and the spirit that their missionary purpose gave them. Hence, it was important for them to maintain their high standards of education rather than follow a low educational standard just to serve the missionary purpose.

The report was a remarkable document that analysed the social forces at work and recommended how to position Christian education. It stated that these institutions had to be so excellently staffed and so well equipped that even if they became a minority amid the number of colleges in India, their alumni would furnish the best leaders of Indian thought and life. The institutions had to serve the Indian church not only by providing first-rate educational facilities, but by leading the way in scholarly research and keen reflection that would be needed as Hindu thought began to earnestly grapple with its Christian rival.

The commission pointed out that in the past the stability of Indian society had depended on three factors: village communities that ensured adequate exploitation of land; the caste system that divided society into units with specific and complementary functions organised on a cooperative basis; and beliefs that embodied sociological, transcendental values that gave meaning and direction to an individual's life in relation to society and the universe. As long as these factors remained intact, India remained unchanged and could face the challenges posed by Buddhism and Islam. Even Christianity had not been able to make much headway. The economic foundations on which Indian society was built had been modified in the nineteenth century and this had led to fundamental and substantial changes. One of these was science and technology, the symbol of which was the steel bridge linking the two banks of the Ganges in Varanasi. Alien forces, of which the railways were a symbol, were disintegrating the material foundations of a village society of which Hinduism was the religion. But, said the commission:

> ... the devoted and untiring efforts of Pandit Madan Mohan Malaviya have created a modern Hindu University, whose purpose among others is to stimulate studies in Hindu literature and culture, religion and philosophy. But what has it actually accomplished? The recognised and apparently outstanding achievement of the Hindu University has been the creation of an efficient department of engineering. Hinduism and the railway bridge are coming to terms.[18]

One of the significant layers when it comes to analysing the social stratification of a village society was members of hereditary professions like village priests, accountants and merchants. Theoretically, they did not possess any rights to land but their material and professional services were rated so high that they held honourable and even influential positions in the village community. They possessed some common traditions of learning with varying degrees of accomplishments and provided officials for the civil administration irrespective of whether the ruling dynasties were Hindu or Muslim. This group had also benefited the most thanks to English education and provided the bulk of the officers in the government administration. Within the group, however, a further distinction was pointed out between the trading and professional classes. The report's findings were:

> The professional castes were the first to accept European education, and were the first to enter the services to which Indians were admitted first by the East India Company and later more extensively under the Crown. The trading castes, on the other hand, were not pressed by circumstances to avail themselves of the new educational advantages. The internal trade of the country offered the fullest opportunities for careers to young men, irrespective of whether they bore the hall-mark of the new schools that the foreign government had established or not.[19]

The old professional classes provided the foundations of the new political and intellectual classes while economic development was based on the willing agency of the trading classes under the direction of the East India Company's mercantile administration.

Discontent stirred when political liberalism of the educated class met the increasing political conservatism of the government and was stimulated into political radicalism. The contact between India and Western education, government, commerce and religion reinvigorated Hinduism, opening up the traditions of both service and aggressive nationalism. It also created many contradictions. On the one hand, religion that had always been central to India was used to revive practices like Ganapati Puja and Saraswati Puja, the rallying points for nationalism. On the other hand, these also created religious conflicts between Hindus and

18 *Christian Higher Education in India*, p. 31.

19 Ibid., p. 32.

Muslims. Paradoxically, the ensuing strife led to educated people turning against religion and leaning towards secularism. This was also aided by the popularity of science.

At least one response among the Hindus was to re-energise Hinduism to take its place in the modern world of activity and competition. Attempts were made to direct Hinduism's energies towards service to humanity and to show that it had moral aims that could be served through social service. When social service and vigorous action came together, it led to the call for a Hindu Mahasabha for military training; the centrality of the Bhagavad Gita that advocated action; the influence of Bal Gangadhar Tilak's *Gita Rahasya*; Aurobindo Ghose; the Brahmo Samaj and Arya Samaj movements; the Servants of the People Society by Lala Lajpat Rai; and the Radha Swami sect with its emphasis on educational and industrial enterprises.

The undercurrent of suspicion about the Cambridge Mission's activities and subsequently of the British government, prompted social reformers and prominent citizens to establish an educational institution to counter this influence and provide an alternative to the young generation going in for higher education—an institution rooted in the passion to protect Hindu religion. Like-minded influential people of Delhi wanted to provide education on the lines of *sanatana* dharma and at the same time reach out to those students who could not afford the elitist St. Stephen's College run by the Cambridge Mission. Thus, was born Hindu College. Its founding fathers were prominent citizens from different walks of life, who were not only influential but also well-educated. They ensured a secular system where students from the Muslim community and other religions could study. The Gurwala family had suffered directly in 1857 and could not have accepted the growing influence of British missionaries. They were the first to grab the initiative to set up the Hindu College even if it had a very humble beginning in a small house in the narrow lanes of Chandni Chowk.

Revolutionaries and Martyrs

The period between the 1857 Revolt and the Quit India Movement was dominated by revolutionaries fighting the British. Although the Congress was founded in 1885, Gandhi took over the reins of the party in 1919. This was also the beginning of the Non-Cooperation and Non-Violent movements. However, before this happened, India had witnessed a number of revolutionaries with a burning desire to see the British out of this country.

There were great martyrs who dared the British, ready to lay their lives for their country. Balshastri Hardas in *Armed Struggle for Freedom*, observes about the situation in the aftermath of 1857:

> The British administration had swept clean the whole country of all turbulent elements. The public had been terrified by the excessive punishments meted out to the fighters of freedom. With leaders behind prison bars, common workers without plans and programmes and the masses cowed down by the cruel hand of the merciless administration, there seemed to descend on India a thick shadow of despair and

Facing page: *Master Amir Chand*

resignation of fate. It must not be supposed however that the will to be free had died down ...[20]

As the struggle for freedom spread outside India from Shanghai to San Francisco, 'the torch of revolution was lighted in the South where the arrest of Chidambaram Pilley along with another associate of his, Subrahmanya Shiva, on March 12, 1910', resulted in a violent outburst of public frenzy. Hardas says, 'All the government offices were mobbed and set on fire.'[21] This fire spread to Punjab and Delhi.

Lala Hardayal, the Indian nationalist revolutionary who founded the Ghadar Party, had returned to England but had entrusted the work to his comrades Lala Hanumant Sahay and Master Amir Chand. Ganeshilal and Avadh Behari joined them. A small group of young revolutionaries was growing, occasionally directed by Lala Hardayal, but a new leader emerged in Ras Behari Bose. Says Hardas, 'In a very short time, as a result of Ras Behari's guidance and the endeavours of his associates like Sachindra Nath Sanyal, Bhai Bal Mukand, Basant Kumar Biswas and Hanumant Sahay, the whole atmosphere in the Punjab was surcharged with smouldering discontent likely to erupt in serious violence.'[22] The government was conscious of this and had warned Michael O'Dwyer when he was appointed the Governor of Punjab. As soon as he took over, there was the most daring bomb attack on Viceroy Lord Hardinge on 22 December 1912. Known as the Delhi Conspiracy case, thirteen persons were arrested—four were hanged, two were sentenced to seven years imprisonment and two turned approvers.

A lot was happening in the country even before the Delhi Conspiracy case. There were meetings, some open and some secret, especially in Punjab, Bengal and in the southern states. The director of the Criminal Intelligence Department (CID) and other secret agencies were monitoring all meetings and exchanging notes. Yet, the officers were wary of taking direct action. This is evident from the weekly reports of the director of Criminal Intelligence conveyed to senior officers during 1907, 1909, 1910 and 1912.

The director of Criminal Intelligence was trying to follow every attempt by individuals to dissuade government servants to work for the British or attempts by religious organisations like the Arya Samaj to convince people to respect Hindu religious teachings and counter attempts by the missionaries or Muslim leaders to convert people.

20 Balshastri Hardas, *Armed Struggle for Freedom: Ninety Years War of Indian Independence—1857 to Subhash*, trans. by S.S. Apte (Poona: Kal Prakashan, 1958), p. 225.

21 Ibid., p. 226.

22 Ibid., p. 229.

Facing page:
Chandrashekhar Azad hid in the Hindu College hostel premises and hoodwinked the British

The director of Criminal Intelligence and other secret agencies of the British government closely followed Arya Samaj meetings held in different parts of India and the North-West Frontier Province, reporting these to the chief commissioner's office. Such meetings also pointed out the need for Hindu-Muslim unity, which caused a lot of discomfort to British administrators.

Prominent leaders like Bal Gangadhar Tilak, Gopal Krishna Gokhale and Lala Lajpat Rai were actively involved in garnering support from Hindus and Muslims. Rulers of the states of Bharatpur, Indore, Faridkot and Chamba were named by informers as being behind a conspiracy against the British; a conspiracy claimed to have been going on for almost ten years. This is mentioned in a weekly report of 9 September 1907 of the director of Criminal Intelligence.

While organisational efforts by the Arya Samaj continued, other groups also started their activities against the government. By 1919 things had started heating up even more. Martial law in Punjab during April and July 1919 resulted in the arrest of more than 700 persons, most of them implicated for causing disturbances or joining unlawful assemblies. The arrested persons included railway employees, shopkeepers, lawyers, cultivators and even labourers.

In the introduction to his book, *History of the Indian Revolutionary Movement*, Manmath Nath Gupta[23] says that Bal Gangadhar Tilak and Aurobindo Ghose began as revolutionaries but strayed from this path because of the hardships that they faced; these hardships were also faced by leaders like Bipan Chandra Pal, Surendranath Banerjee and Lala Lajpat Rai. He points out that the revolutionary movement, even before 1919, had produced a number of martyrs like Shyamji Krishna Verma, V.D. Savarkar, the Chapekar brothers, Hardayal and Ras Behari Bose.

Gupta observes:

> After 1919 when Gandhi captured the Congress and converted it into a mass organization, the revolutionaries, in deference, postponed their movement till Chauri-Chaura, where a number of policemen were burnt to death. Then onwards the Gandhian movement and the revolutionary struggle ran on parallel lines, sometimes coming closer when Lala Lajpat Rai died after a lathi-charge and it was avenged by Bhagat Singh. Even the non-cooperation movement was triggered off by the Rowlatt Bill, an offspring of the Rowlatt Committee, also known as the Sedition Committee, appointed to suggest ways and means to suppress the revolutionary movement.[24]

Non-Cooperation in Educational Institutions

In 1921 the government noticed a Non-Cooperation Movement in educational institutions. Starting with Bengal, student strikes spread all over the country. In a confidential letter to all local governments and administrations, the secretary to the Government of India, Henry

23 Manmath Nath Gupta, *History of the Indian Revolutionary Movement* (Bombay, New Delhi: Somaiya Publications Pvt. Ltd., 1972).

24 Ibid., p. ix.

Sharp, said, '... every means should be taken to induce the cooperation of moderate opinion in combating this pernicious movement'.[25]

Sharp notes that news about the disturbances was available largely from press telegrams and reports in newspapers. He observed that the Government of India did not have, 'the advantage of receiving special reports from the local governments upon the apparent recrudescence of this movement in the last few weeks'. The government believed that the trouble was partly instigated by students in Bengal but to a greater extent by the renewed efforts of the agitators throughout India, 'who desire that the Royal visit should be accompanied by a demonstration of this nature on as large a scale as possible'.

If students' involvement continued, he suggested that each province should summon meetings with educational experts and public men interested in educational institutions with a view to diagnosing the situation and suggesting remedies. He took a cautious view when he suggested that parents of students should be involved as he felt that they were opposed to the Non-Cooperation Movement in educational institutions.[26]

While the movement against the British had spread to various cities, the revolutionaries were organising themselves in groups and identifying places where they could stay incognito and strike at will. Chandrashekhar Azad, called Panditji by his associates, found such a haven in the Hindu College hostel. However, the atmosphere that prevailed at the time was such that one could be betrayed by one's own comrades who acted as informers.

Professor N.K. Nigam, a freedom fighter, who after completing his MA from the college had joined it as a lecturer, was the hostel warden. Nigam provided shelter to Azad and his associates. They successfully hoodwinked the British intelligence for a long time. According to Professor Nigam, the college was unaware of his activities and the fact that Chandrashekhar and some of his associates were hiding in the hostel till such time when Nigam was arrested on 4 December 1930.

In an interview recorded at the Nehru Memorial Museum and Library on 1 March 1968, Professor Nigam recalled how, as secretary of the Literary Union in 1928, he had wanted to invite Subhash Chandra Bose, who was then considered a leftist leader, to the college, but did

25 Confidential Letter No. 263 dated 19 February 1921, Department of Education (New Delhi: National Archives of India, Government of India).

26 Ibid.

not fearing action against the college.[27] He then invited famous journalist, G. Harniman who proved to be a greater firebrand than Subhash Chandra Bose. Principal S.K. Sen told him later that had he known Harniman was being invited, he would have allowed Subhash Chandra Bose to be invited instead.

Nigam recalled that the revolutionary group was betrayed by Kailashpati, a close associate of Chandrashekhar, who also stayed in the hostel for quite some time.

'Lord Irwin was visiting Delhi to have talks with Gandhiji on the morning of December 23, 1929. On December 22, a meeting was held in Hindu College hostel in which Chandrashekhar, Virbhadra Tiwari, Bhagwati Charan Vohra, Yashpal and Kailashpati were present.

'Chandrashekhar did not want the action since the Viceroy was coming to meet Gandhiji and a settlement could be there. But there were two different views. After heated arguments Bhagwati Charan Vohra and Yashpal left saying they would carry out the action. Bhagwati Charan went to Lahore but Yashpal put on a military suit and went to Old Fort behind which they had kept the bomb in hiding,' recalled Nigam adding that, 'it was Yashpal who pressed the button and the bomb exploded.'

Professor Nigam said that there were two main cases in what could be termed as the Second Conspiracy case. One was the bomb attack on the viceroy's train and the other the Gadodia dacoity case. There were thirteen accused, four absconders and four approvers. The defence consisted of Asaf Ali, Sardar Raghubir Singh and B. Banerjee. Later Asaf Ali left and Saifuddin Kitchlew became the chief defence counsel. For lack of evidence, Nigam was sentenced to two years imprisonment under the Arms Act. This can be described as the first involvement of a Hinduite in the freedom struggle.

The Second Conspiracy case was withdrawn in 1933, 'in view of the unsatisfactory progress of the trial before the Tribunal constituted for the purpose'.[28] A letter from the government's Home Department in February was sent to the deputy commissioner's office in Delhi listing fourteen persons: Dhanwantri, Baishampayan, Potdar, Watsyana, B.P. Jain, Babu Ram Gupta, Kapur Chand, N.K. Nigam, Vidya Bhushan, Kheali Ram Gupta, Rudra Dutt Misra, Harkesh, Bhagirath Lal and Hardwari Lal Gupta.

Professor N.K. Nigam

This letter from the Home Department further noted that the first eight accused, 'are alleged to have committed serious overt acts and the Government of India have decided that they should be placed on their trial under the provisions of the ordinary law in respect of the specific offences alleged against them.' It also noted that accused Vidya Bhushan and Kheali (Khyali) Ram 'though not charged with any specific offences, cannot, in the public interest, be set at liberty', and should be detained under the regulation specifically on the grounds

27 Oral interview given on 1 March 1968, Oral History Transcript No. 70 (New Delhi: Nehru Memorial Museum and Library).

28 Letter No. D813/33, Pol. dated 3 February 1933 from the Government of India, Home Department to the Chief Commissioner, Delhi.

of their 'connection with terrorist activities, the facts will be submitted for the opinion of two judges'.[29]

Mahatma Gandhi's visit to Hindu College on 25 January 1930 generated immense enthusiasm. It was a great moment in the life of the college. The students collected Rs 500 and presented the purse to Gandhi. The college magazine, *The Indraprastha*, chronicled the occasion and Gandhi's evening meeting with students and teachers

College students' full-fledged involvement started with strikes and non-cooperation. Khub Chand, a Hinduite and the first Indian to top the Indian Civil Service examination, recalls that in the early 1930s the students marched in Chandni Chowk against the visit of the Simon Commission, shouting 'Simon, go back!'[30]

Even as discontent against British Raj was simmering, national leaders had been visiting the college parliament or its Literary Union to address the students. This picked up in the mid-1930s, and more so with the Quit India Movement on 9 August 1939. The years between 1939 and 1942 were the most active and volatile as far as the students of Delhi University, particularly Hindu College, Ramjas College and Indraprastha College for Women, were concerned. It is ironical that while on the one hand, the students were studying under the British system within the college precincts they were fighting to remove the British as rulers of India in their quest for Independence. Both were done with equal passion and zeal without any sense of dichotomy between the two.

As the British government kept a close watch, the students surreptitiously engaged in anti-government activities. The local administration in Delhi was angry at educational institutions. It even threatened to stop financial help that was being given to these institutions.

Preet Chablani, a student of Hindu College from 1938 to 1941, and daughter of legendary Principal N.V. Thadani, a staunch nationalist, recalls how the Independence movement had become a part of her life. An article in the *In Retrospect* published on the occasion of the college's Centenary says:

> While the authorities kept a close watch on its growing tentacles, they wanted to closely monitor the educational system and keep it under control. The Principal realized that unless the meaning of Education and Independence were clearly understood and the two kept apart, the authorities would throttle their growth. This would stunt the national interest. There had been various instances where an attempt by the students to raise the national flag had led to a forcible hoisting of the Union Jack. It was only when this aspect of the movement was explained to the students and understood by

Khub Chand

29 Ibid.

30 *In Retrospect*, published on the occasion of college Centenary celebrations, edited by Kapila Vatsyayan, Kavita A. Sharma, Suroopa Mukherjee, Tapan Basu and Sunil Dua (New Delhi: Har-Anand Publications, 2000), p.30.

them that, without any direct confrontation with the authorities, the College was able to conduct its free and liberal policies.[31]

Around this time, Professor N.K. Nigam had started working for the Congress Party. 'In 1942, since the British were expected to leave India and the Japanese were coming, Maulana Azad asked me to join Congress and fight for the freedom of the country,' he recalled, adding, 'Communists, after the attack on Russia by Germany, became supporters of the British Government and the Students Federation of India was in their control. They gave me a challenge that they would hold a meeting on August 6, 1942 and see that students supported the British Government. I accepted the challenge. The meeting was held in the Students Park (Tikona Park) just opposite the Hindu College Building in Kashmere Gate. I made them commit that whatever the decision at the meeting, they would abide by it. There were 900 students and 960 voted against the resolution to support British Government after I had spoken for about an hour and they agreed that they would participate in the movement. On August 9, 1942, when arrests started taking place, students came to me for instructions and it was Sunday and all colleges were closed. I asked them to go to the hostels and bring out the students and take the procession to the Gandhi Grounds. I was the first man to be arrested.'[32]

Right and below: *Tikona Park and the signboard outside the park*

The Quit India Movement started on 9 August 1942 and continued for several days. Delhi witnessed students joining the demonstrations and destroying government installations at various places in protest against British rule. P.C. Sood of the English department recalls how Hindu College was the hub of fierce activity, a veritable storm centre of anger and agitation. The Kashmere Gate Square swarmed with students raising clenched fists and shouting themselves hoarse. A contingent of *lathi*-wielding policemen reinforced by armed guards stationed themselves at a corner ready to swing into action. Crowds swelled

31 Ibid., p. 59.

32 Oral interview of Professor N.K. Nigam at the Nehru Memorial Museum and Library. There is a discrepancy in figures, probably because there were others present at the meeting besides students. It appears that, out of 960 who voted against the resolution, 900 were students.

as people from the locality joined the agitation. What followed is anybody's guess as the police suddenly charged at the crowd. After a while the crowd came under control and dispersed. A batch of students retreated to the College grounds for safety.[33]

Principal Thadani, sensing trouble, stood at the gate and watched the developments for some time. As the students scampered in he closed the gates behind them to prevent the policemen who were charging them to enter the gates; he also asked them to leave his students alone. That seemed to calm the police down. That day, Principal Thadani proved his mettle for a worthy cause. In contrast, Principal S.N. Mukarji of St. Stephen's College, across the street, though an able administrator himself, suffered by comparison and was run down for a long time thereafter, more so when his students had merely fluttered about in the corridors at a time when destiny was being shaped outside on the streets. Hindu College, of course, had risen to great heights![34]

The Delhi administration was alarmed when cases of arson were reported. In a note sent by the Senior Superintendent of Police, H. Kilburn, to the Chief Commissioner of Delhi, A.V. Askwith, he suggested stern action against the students of Ramjas College situated on Rohtak Road. He asked the principals of Ramjas and Hindu colleges to restrain their students or else the government grant would be suspended.

Although there was no concrete evidence that students of Hindu College had participated in arson and sabotage, they had apparently staged minor demonstrations in the Kashmere Gate area. The principal was formally warned that he was responsible for controlling his students and if he failed to do so action would be taken. Students of Hindu and Ramjas colleges were not isolated. The fire had touched Indraprastha College for Women where the students, in their own way, had started agitating by picketing the houses of members of the Viceroy's Executive Council.

In view of these disturbances, many schools sought permission to close down till the situation improved. The first to do so were the Convent of Jesus & Mary and Harcourt Butler.

Principal N.V. Thadani

33 Article from the college magazine *The Indraprastha*, 1983 issue, reproduced in the *Centenary Souvenir* of the college in 1999, p. 10.

34 Ibid.

Others that sought closure for a few days included the Government Industrial School and Jain Mahabir School, Egerton Road (now Nai Sarak).

The administration was worried by this growing influence on schools which forced their closure. In an attempt to prevent schoolboys from joining the agitation, the administrators wanted schools and colleges to function normally and maintain discipline, promising protection if required. The officers were in a quandary about how to deal with the situation as students kept up the tempo in disrupting the administration.

Chief Commissioner, A.V. Askwith wrote to Vice Chancellor, Sir Maurice Gwyer, 'I am not greatly interested in punitive action against the colleges, merely for the sake of punitive action, but am anxious that everything possible should be done to make the Governing Bodies and the Principals of the colleges to realize their responsibility and take effective action to control their students. Threats (a) to exclude from University examinations those students who misbehave or absent themselves from college on *hartal* days and (b) to stop Government grants to the colleges would possibly have some effect.'[35]

He hinted that the first course of action to be taken was a matter for the university while the second could be left to the government. The vice chancellor had his reservations. Much to the annoyance of the administration, Gwyer wrote to Askwith:[36]

> The problem of controlling University students is really an all-India one, and, so far as I am aware, no University in the whole of India has found a satisfactory solution for it. ... I cannot help thinking that the conduct of students at St. Stephen's College, though not wholly beyond criticism, is to be attributed to the greater influence

Right: *Young age photo of A.V. Askwith (standing 3rd from right) in a Rugby team group photo, 1911*

Vice Chancellor, Sir Maurice Gwyer

35 The letters following from this note have been taken from file number D.C. No. F-123/42.6 of the Confidential Branch, Chief Commissioner's office. Letter to Vice Chancellor, p. 5 of 14 August 1942, Delhi Archives.

36 Ibid.

> which the teachers of that College are able to exercise over them, owing to the existence of a sound tradition and high standards dating from the earliest days of the College. I would not however lay too great stress on this, because I cannot doubt that the fact that many of the students are sons of persons in the employment of the Government of India has not been without effect.[37]

He did not agree that the threat to exclude students from university examinations would produce any effect, except for further strikes. He felt that this approach would also penalise many innocent young men as it would be impossible for them to stand up against threats coming from hundreds, or even thousands who took a contrary view.

The vice chancellor also felt that stopping government grants might have some effect but 'unfortunately it would penalise the wrong people' as the sufferers would be teachers. He wrote, 'I expect you will find after the subject has been thoroughly examined from every angle that so long as students are told or believe, rightly or wrongly, that they live in an unfree country which is being governed against its will, so long will it seem natural for them to go out in the streets on occasion by way of protest against governmental action. This may be regrettable, but I fear it is true,' adding that he himself did not condone this action by the students and regretted that he could not offer a remedy.

While the officers felt that Sir Maurice Gwyer's reply was not very helpful, they dilly-dallied on restricting or stopping grants to colleges. The chief commissioner wrote to J.D. Tyson, Secretary, Education, Government of India, that he had asked the superintendent of Education to warn the governing bodies of Hindu and Ramjas colleges that unless they took effective action to restore discipline, maintenance grants from central revenues would not be given to them.

He said, 'In the case of Hindu College and Ramjas College, not only is there ample evidence that students have participated in rioting, picketing and unlawful processions but there is more than a suspicion that some of the professors have encouraged the students in these courses. For the best part of the month no serious work has been done in either college, and unless this state of affairs is quickly terminated, it would be preposterous to pay grants this year from government revenues.'[38]

While conveying his decision of issuing a warning and threatening suspension of grants to these two colleges, Chief Commissioner, Askwith wrote to the vice chancellor, observing:

> I realize that this action may not prove effective in checking students, and that as you suggest in your letter, it will hit the teaching staff more than anyone else; but in the case of these two colleges there is more than a suspicion that some of the

37 Ibid., p. 12.

38 Ibid., Confidential D.O. No. F 123/42-c dated 9 September 1942.

> professors are in sympathy with riotous behaviour of the students. In any case it seems to me that to go on paying grants from Government revenues to educational institutions which have practically ceased to function as such, and the pupils in which are manifestly engaged in anti-Government activities, would be demoralizing to all concerned.[39]

Asserting that similar action against Indraprastha College too would be justifiable, he felt that it was better to confine this action against only Hindu and Ramjas, the two men's colleges. He also hinted that Indraprastha College would suffer a blow as Alipur House, which housed the college, would be reacquired for government purposes.

The vice chancellor wanted to put the onus on the principals of the colleges. According to him, no university ordinance gave the power to the university to prevent any students from appearing in the examination except under conditions like not fulfilling a certain percentage of attendance in classes and not producing good character certificates. He felt that no principal would refuse to give a character certificate for participating in unlawful activities.

Regarding Indraprastha College, the vice chancellor felt that the conduct of the students was deplorable, 'But there are two considerations which oppress me a good deal, first, that the college is the only women's college in the whole of Delhi; and, second, that the taking over of the College may be thought to be an act of reprisal by the Government, though I do not for a moment suppose that it is.'[40]

Professor A. Bhattacharya

Following a letter from the superintendent of Education asking college authorities to explain the conduct of the students after the incident on 9 August 1942, the Hindu College Managing Committee deputed Professor A. Bhattacharya to meet Askwith with a response. A large crowd collected outside the only gate of the college on 9 August and on the following few days for picketing; the principal arrived on the scene and asked for the pickets to be withdrawn and advised the students to disperse and go home; they did. Earlier experiences had shown that things would quieten down and students would return to normal life in a few days. The college staff also had the same opinion. However, this time the conditions continued to remain disturbed for a longer period.

Professor A. Bhattacharya of Hindu College delivered a letter on behalf of the college management to the superintendent of Education, Delhi in which it was pointed out that the presence of a large police force could either have excited or scared the students and requested the magistrate to withdraw the police assuring him that with the help of college staff, he would ensure good conduct of the students and normal attendance in the college. After the withdrawal of the police force things went back to normal. The letter accepted that there were some cases of

39 Ibid., Letter to the Vice Chancellor dated 9 September 1942.

40 Ibid., Vice Chancellor's secret letter to the Chief Commissioner dated 13 September 1942 from Hindu Rao Hospital, Delhi.

indiscipline, which were dealt with by expelling three students. It was hoped that within a few days there would be full attendance.

'In conclusion I would add that the Principal and all members of the Staff have done their best, individually and collectively, to control an admittedly difficult situation; and I and my Committee have no doubt they would succeed in their efforts before long. They are of the opinion that in dealing with students it is necessary to combine strictness with patience and tact; and the measure of success they have achieved during the last 12 days warrants the hope that the situation would be under their complete control in the next few days,' the Secretary of the Managing Committee said in his reply to Askwith.[41]

Meanwhile, the administration had prepared a list of students who had participated in the Civil Disobedience Movement and proceeded with action against them, including arrests and convictions. The chief commissioner asked for the list to ensure that the students who were convicted were not readmitted.

Forwarding a list to J.D. Tyson, Secretary, Government of India, the chief commissioner felt that in most cases only a comparatively short sentence of imprisonment, or none at all, was imposed and wanted to know the future course of action regarding the readmission of these students and their appearing in the examination. Tyson said:

> My view is not merely that a college Principal who gave a certificate of good character to a student who had been convicted in the Congress movement would show himself unfit for his position, but that any student who had been so convicted ought not to be allowed to return to his college and should be permanently rusticated. I propose to have this conveyed to the Principals and the governing bodies of all the colleges concerned and inform them if students convicted in the movement are permitted to continue their studies, the usual maintenance grant will not be paid.
>
> I would qualify this by saying that if in any particular case the Principal of a college, having regard to facts of the particular case thinks that the strict enforcement of this principle would be unduly harsh to the students concerned and the student gives an unqualified expression of regret, with satisfactory assurances for his future good behaviour, it will be open to him to refer the case through the Superintendent of Education for my orders.[42]

Since it was a policy decision and the proposed course could give rise to comments in the press or the legislature, he referred it to the government for a decision. The submitted

41 Ibid., p. 25. Letter No. 1752 dated 17 September 1942 from the Honorary Secretary, Committee of Management, Hindu College, Delhi to the superintendent of Education was personally handed by Professor A. Bhattacharya.

42 Ibid., D.O. Letter No. F-123/42C, 17 November 1942.

list of twenty-four students had sixteen from Hindu College, two from Ramjas, five from Indraprastha and one from Commercial College (now known as Shri Ram College of Commerce—SRCC).

According to the list prepared by the police, five students from Hindu College, 'Siri Niwas, Siri Kishan Kapur, A.N. Shashadri, A.S. Krishna Swami and Krishan Kumar' were arrested on 29 August 1942. The charge against them was that they had formed a procession of about 100 to 150 persons behind Jama Masjid and shouted anti-government slogans. All of them except these five had dispersed when the police arrived. They were convicted and sentenced, 'to produce security with bond of Rs 300 each under section 562 Cr.P.C. for a period of six months'.

On 2 October 1942, a big procession formed in Chandni Chowk. According to the First Information Report (FIR), those who gathered threw stones at the police party when they were asked to disperse. Some of the constables were injured. At this point the magistrate ordered the police to open fire to disperse the crowd and stop them from throwing stones. Among the twenty-two arrested were Kanilay Singh of Ramjas College and Diwan Chand from Commercial College. When the list was prepared, the case was still pending in the court while many others had been convicted.

Onkar Nath was found throwing some envelopes into letterboxes on 4 October 1942. One envelope exploded in his pocket. He was arrested on the spot. His brother Rameshwar Nath had been arrested earlier on 9 September 1942. According to the FIR, he was participating in a procession of about 250 to 300 persons coming from Tis Hazari Hospital shouting anti-government slogans. When the police officer asked the people to disperse, Rameshwar Nath, along with two others, did not move and were arrested. He was convicted and sentenced to pay a fine of Rs 200 or undergo rigorous imprisonment for six months.[43]

Six students of Hindu College along with a student from Ramjas College were arrested for picketing outside St. Stephen's College in a group of about fifty persons. They were Mohammad Hanif Hashmi, Brij Mohan Lal, Bishan Sarup, Krishan Kumar Vaidi, his brother Raj Kumar Vaidi and Giri Lal. The student from Ramjas was Kesho Bhargau (Bhargava) of India Coffee House. All of them were convicted and sentenced to pay a fine of Rs 200 each or undergo two months of rigorous imprisonment if they defaulted.

Not to be outdone by boys, three girl students, one from Hindu College and two from Indraprastha College were also arrested on 8 September 1942 for picketing the house of J.P. Srivastava, a member of the Viceroy's Executive Council; they did not allow anyone to enter. Snehlata was from Hindu College while Pushpa and Lajiawati (Lajyawati) were from Indraprastha College.

Three other girls from Indraprastha College, Lilawati, Vije Kumari (Vijay Kumari) and Roop Khanna and two boys from Hindu College, Ravinder Kumar and Santosh Kumar Anand,

43 Ibid., pp. 36–39. List of cases registered in connection with recent disturbances in which college students were arrested.

were arrested for picketing the house of another member of the Viceroy's Executive Council, Sir Homy Modi. The police report said all the accused, except Santosh Kumar, were fined Rs 200 each or in default undergo two months simple imprisonment. Santosh Kumar was asked to produce a security bond of Rs 300.[44]

L.C. Jain, freedom fighter and a doyen of the Non-Cooperation Movement, who left Hindu College for a year during the Quit India Movement, recalled how the:

> Relatively quiet political activism burst into an explosion from the day the Quit India Movement was launched. Interestingly, many of those who were active participants in the College Parliament, persons like Giri Lal Jain (later editor, *Times of India*) who was one time Prime Minister of College, came to the fore to rally students and faculty members. During the Quit India days, a number of them were jailed, a number of them went underground and still others continued to distribute the leaflets and reading material circulated by the underground activists of the Quit India Movement. The students had built up an alert and effective communication system across colleges in the Delhi University and I had some hand in building up this communication network which could within a space of few hours organize strikes and protest rallies with lightning speed.[45]

A number of chemistry students from Hindu College had formed a bomb squad for disruptions in public places by underground activists. 'Life in the college was also tense because a number of military officers used to come and prompt the students to enroll in the British Indian Army. They were always confronted with some harassment. Often, the tyres of their vehicles were deflated or some sand put into the petrol tank,' L.C. Jain recalled.[46]

Dr Kapila Vatsyayan, an old student of the college, recalls the charged atmosphere that prevailed in the college after Gandhi's visit and the onset of the Quit India Movement. 'On August 9, we heard the clarion call of Quit India and "Do or Die". Spontaneously we marched from Kashmere Gate to St. Stephen's College to have it closed. A procession was formed. Lakshmi Jain (L.C. Jain) was in the forefront, accompanied by Kusum (now Mrs Keyt) and Shakti Dutta. The vanguard was arrested while those in the rearguard like me dispersed and others absconded. Lakshmi, Kusum and Shakti were sentenced.'[47]

Professor J.N. Kapur, also an old student of Hindu College, recalls an incident concerning the Quit India Movement:

L.C. Jain as a student

44 Ibid.

45 *In Retrospect*, p. 66.

46 Ibid., p. 67.

47 Ibid., p. 72.

List of cases registered in connection with recent disturbances in which college students were arrested.

Serial No.	F.I.R.No. etc.	Name of accused with name of college	Precis of the case	Remarks
1.	381 dated 29.8.42 u/s. 88 I.P.C. Kotwali, P.S.	Siri Niwas s/o. Om Swami, Brahman of Jahangir Road, New Delhi, student 2nd year Hindu College, Delhi.	On 29.8.42 at about 11 a.m. the accused formed a procession consisting of about 100/150 persons behind Jama Masjid. They shouted anti-government slogans seeing the police party, all other members of the procession except the accused dispersed. They were arrested on the spot.	The accused were convicted and sentenced to produce security with bond of Rs 300 each u/s 562 Cr. P.C. for a period of 6 months by Chaudhri Mushtaq Ahmad, Magistrate 1st class, on 5.9.42.
2.	"	Siri Kishan Kapur s/o. Moti Lal Kapur Khatri of Connaught Place, New Delhi, student 2nd year Hindu College, Delhi.		
3.	"	A.N. Shashdri s/o. A.V. Rai Narain, Brahman of 19/B Irwin Road, New Delhi, student 2 year, Hindu College, Delhi.		
4.	"	A.S. Krishna Swami s/o. A.S. Iyango Brahmin of Narindra Place No.4, Parliamentary Street, New Delhi. Student IV year class, Hindu College, Delhi.		
5.	"	Krishan Kumar s/o. Pankath Nath, Khatri, of Bagh Karol, plot No.15 Block No.6, Hindu College, Delhi.		
6.	450 dated 2.10.42 u/s. 307/147/188 I.P.C. Kotwali P.S.	Kanilay Singh s/o. Gurdit Singh, Khatri of Gandhi Gali, Kotwali, Delhi, student 2nd year, Ramjas College, Daryaganj, Delhi.	On 2.10.42 at about 5.30 p.m. a big procession was formed in the Chandni Chowk, the members threw stones at the police party when ordered to disperse by a magistrate. Some of the constables received injuries. At this the magistrate ordered the police party to open fire in order to disperse the processionists and to stop them from throwing stones. 22 persons including the accused were arrested on the spot.	Case still pending in court.
7.	"	Diwan Chand s/o. Chandu Lal of Pahari Dhiraj, Sadar Bazar, Delhi. Student, Commercial College, Daryaganj, Delhi		
8.	287 dated 4.10.42 u/s.34/38 Defence of India Rules, Faiz Bazar P.S.	Onkar Nath s/o. Sri Ram, Vaish of Maliwara, Kotwali P.S. Delhi. Student 2nd year, Hindu College, Delhi.	On 4.10.42 the accused was found throwing some envelopes into letter boxes. One envelope exploded in his pocket. He was arrested on the spot by F.C. Roshan Lal.	The case is still under investigation.
9.	235 dated 9.9.42 u/s.188 I.P.C. Sabzimandi P.S.	Rameshwar Nath s/o. Sri Ram, Vaish of Maliwara, Kotwali P.S. Delhi, student 2nd year, Hindu College, Delhi.	On 9.9.42 at about 2.30 p.m. a procession of 250/300 persons was seen coming from the direction of Tis Hazari Hospital, shouting anti-Government slogans. H.C. Bashir Ahmad who was on duty with a police party ordered the processionists to disperse. Rameshwar Nath mentioned along with two others did not disperse and was therefore arrested.	The accused was convicted and sentenced to pay a fine of Rs 200 in default to undergo R.I. for a period of 6 months by Chaudhri Mushtaq Ahmad, Magistrate 1st class, on 29.9.42.
10.	115 dated 31.8.42 u/s 188 I.P.C. Civil Lines P.S.	Kesho Bhargau s/o. Roop Singh, Mahajan of India Coffee House, New Delhi, student Ramjas College, Delhi.	On 31.8.42 the A.D.M. having received information that 40/50 students had collected in front of St. Stephen's College for picketing, reached the spot along with a police party and found many students collected on the road outside the main gate of St. Stephen's College. Seeing the police arrive the gathering dispersed except the 7 accused who were arrested.	All the accused were convicted and sentenced to pay a fine of Rs 200 each, in default to undergo R.I. for a period of 2 months by K.B. Mahmud Husain Zaidi Magistrate 1st class on 12.9.42.

11.	"	Mohamad Hanif Hashmi s/o. Mohd. Adris Hashmi of Verma Hashmi & Co., Kashmere Gate, Delhi. Student Hindu College, Delhi.		
12.	"	Brij Mohan Lal s/o. Panna Lal of Mohalla Dassan, Ballimaran, Delhi, student, Hindu College, Delhi.		
13.	"	Bishan Sarup s/o. Kalyan Singh, student Hindu College, Delhi.		
14.	"	Krishan Kumar Vaidi s/o. Ved Viyas, near Imperial Bank, Delhi. Student Hindu College, Delhi.		
15.	"	Raj Kumar Vaidi s/o. Ved Viyas, near Imperial Bank, Delhi, Student, Hindu College, Delhi		
16.	"	Giri Lal s/o. Shahzad Rai of Pipalkhera, Ganaur, P.S. Rohtak District. Student Hindu College, Delhi		
17.	558 dated 8.9.42 u/s. 7 Criminal Law Amendment Act. P.S. New Delhi	Pushpa d/o. Des Raj, Khatri of Kunjah, Gujrat District at present Fatehpuri. Student 2nd year, Indraprastha Girls College, Delhi.	On 8.9.42 the accused picketed the house of J.P. Srivastawa, Esquire, Member of the Viceroy's Executive Council, and did not allow anybody to enter the house.	The accused were convicted and sentenced to pay a fine of Rs. 200 each in default to undergo S.I. for a period of 2 months by K.B. Mahmud Husain Zaidi, Magistrate 1st class, Delhi, on 14.9.42.
18.	"	Snehlata d/o. Sohan Lal, Brahman of No.3 Mangal Building, Chandni Chowk, Delhi. Student 1st year, Hindu College, Delhi.		
19.	"	Lajiawati d/o. Hakam Rai, Khatri of No.3 Daryaganj, Delhi. Student 2nd year Indraprastha Girls College, Delhi.		
20.	559 dated 3.10.42 u/s. 188 I.P.C. New Delhi P.S.	Lilawati d/o. Harchan Singh, Khatri of Katra Nil, Delhi. Student 2nd year, Indraprastha Girls College, Delhi.	On 8.9.42 at about 11 a.m. the accused picketed the house of Sir Homy Modi, Member of the Viceroy's Executive Council, New Delhi.	Accused were convicted and sentenced on 14.9.42 by K.B. Mahmud Husain Zaidi, Magistrate 1st class as follows:- All accused except Santosh Kumar were ordered to pay a fine of Rs.200 each, in default to undergo S.I. for a period of 2 months Santosh Kumar was ordered to produce security with bond of Rs.300/- each u/s. 562 Cr. P.C. for a period of three months.
21.	"	Vije Kumari d/o. Ram Narain, Tandon, Khatri of Mahabir Bazar, Cloth Market, Delhi. Student 2nd year, Indraprastha Girls College, Delhi.		
22.	"	Roop Chand Khanna d/o. Jagan Nath, Khatri of No.13 Sri Ram Road, Delhi. Student 3rd year, Indraprastha Girls College, Delhi.		
23.	"	Ravinder Kumar Sohni s/o. Balbir Singh Sohni, Khatri of Gurdaspur, now New Delhi. Student 2 year, Hindu College, Delhi.		
24.	"	Santosh Kumar Anand s/o. Barkat Ram Anand, Khatri of Gokal Niwas, New Delhi, Student 1st year, Hindu College, Delhi.		

> The British Government had arrested all top leaders. The student community of Delhi automatically marched towards Hindu College, since the students of the college were the natural leaders of the students' movement in Delhi. Within an hour 10,000 students had collected in and around the small park in Kashmere Gate, opposite Hindu College (Tikona Park). A huge procession was formed and moved via Hamilton Road and Chandni Chowk. We moved for four hours and decided to meet again the next day. We continued this for three days. On the third day, the police lost patience and fired at the students near Gurdwara Shishganj. The police and the British soldiers became quite panicky and intense patrolling in armoured jeeps was undertaken, especially near Hindu College. On the next day I went to the college and was standing at the main gate entrance, when a jeep with six British soldiers with all their guns pointing at me, approached the gate and asked me what I was doing there. I remember the fearlessness in those days. I told them quietly, 'I am in my college and you cannot enter here without the principal's permission. Better leave immediately.' They looked at one another and quietly went away.[48]

It was after 1942 that serious talks between Indian leaders and the British government began regarding the handing over of power to Indian leaders. The role of the students had ended on a fruitful note. Many of them went on to take up national duties in various capacities.

In spite of the intense political activity in the freedom movement of the country, it is remarkable that Principal N.V. Thadani's educational vision was very clear. This is seen in

48 Ibid.

Kapila Vatsyayan at Amitabh Sengupta's painting exhibition in 1965, AIFACS, New Delhi

the significant exchange between him and Mahatma Gandhi when the latter proposed to start a college in Benaras and invited him to head it. One of the issues in the letter was whether an educational institution should consciously plunge itself into political activity. Principal Thadani showed the letter to the honorary secretary of the college who requested that Gandhi should, 'consider whether the aim of education would not be satisfied if the students were given all freedoms consistent with national ideals and the College were run unobstructed by any considerations of Government Grant-in-aid or University affiliation.' He felt that, 'it was for the students finally to decide whether or not they would read for a University degree and it was for the Government to withdraw their Grant-in-aid. In case the students desired to give up their University degree, he for his part would do his best to help them and expected the Board of Trustees to agree; and in case the Government withdrew the grant it was open to them to do so.' While Thadani recognised the force of Mahatma Gandhi's arguments, he personally regarded 'the "Non-Cooperation" movement as more or less negative in character.'

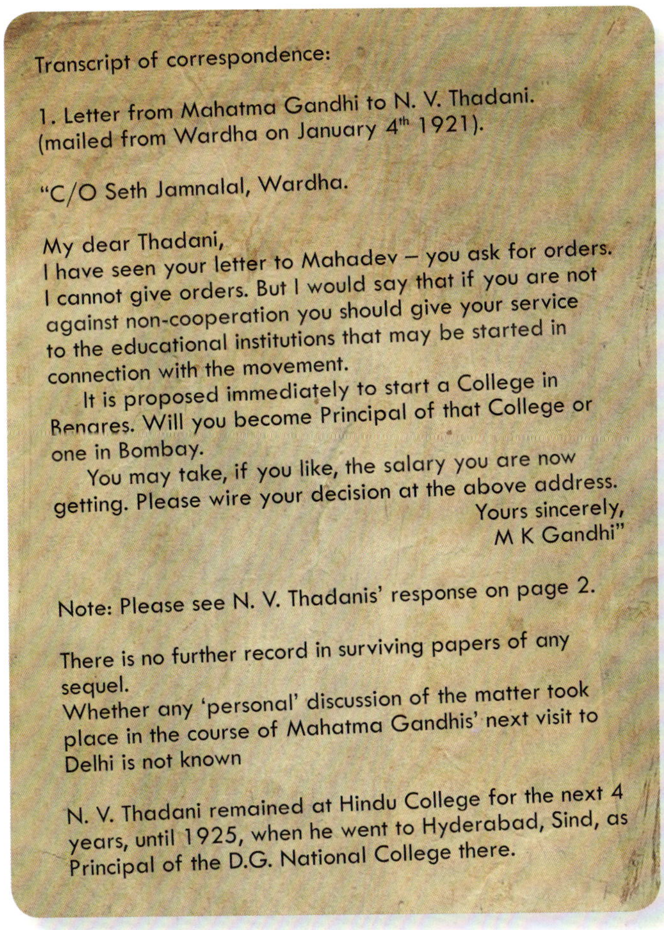

Transcript of correspondence:

1. Letter from Mahatma Gandhi to N. V. Thadani.
(mailed from Wardha on January 4th 1921).

"C/O Seth Jamnalal, Wardha.

My dear Thadani,
I have seen your letter to Mahadev – you ask for orders. I cannot give orders. But I would say that if you are not against non-cooperation you should give your service to the educational institutions that may be started in connection with the movement.
It is proposed immediately to start a College in Benares. Will you become Principal of that College or one in Bombay.
You may take, if you like, the salary you are now getting. Please wire your decision at the above address.
Yours sincerely,
M K Gandhi"

Note: Please see N. V. Thadanis' response on page 2.

There is no further record in surviving papers of any sequel.
Whether any 'personal' discussion of the matter took place in the course of Mahatma Gandhis' next visit to Delhi is not known

N. V. Thadani remained at Hindu College for the next 4 years, until 1925, when he went to Hyderabad, Sind, as Principal of the D.G. National College there.

Letter of M.K. Gandhi to Principal Thadani on 4 January 1921

Principal Thadani's reply to M.K. Gandhi on 7 January 1921

Letter from N V Thadani,
"Hindu College, Delhi
7th January 1921.

My dear Sir,
I am much obliged by your letter of the 4th inst.

I showed it to the Honorary Secretary of the College and he asked me to request you to consider whether the aim of education would not be satisfied if the students were given all freedoms consistent with national ideals and the College were run unobstructed by any considerations of Government Grant-in-aid or University affiliation. He repeated that a full scope would be given to me in the matter – if you allowed me to remain in the College. He said that it was for the students finally to decide whether or not they would read for a University degree and it was for the Government to withdraw their Grant-in-aid. In case the students desired to give up their University degree, he for his part would do his best to help them and expected the Board of Trustees to agree; and in case the Government withdrew the grant it was open to them to do so. He further informed me that you were expected here in a few days when matters could be discussed and decided personally.

Under the circumstances I find myself in a difficult situation.

I could not wire my decision to you as it was so difficult to decide.

I see that the students are not prepared and it is they with whom the teacher is principally concerned; and I feel that the attitude of the Management is honourable to them. I am bound to the latter by more than ordinary ties. I came here at their cordial invitation and there are few young men who have been more fully trusted in the management of a College.

On the other hand I recognize the force of the argument on your side and though I regards the "Non-Co-operation" movement as more or less negative in character, it rests on certain fundamental principles of life without which no nation can exist. On its educational side it stands for something equally significant and, though the problem is by no means new, the question of "national" education would perhaps be more easily solved now than at any other time, with the force of the Nation behind it.

And then there is your Call.

To my mind there seems no inconsistency in working for an affiliated institution under altered conditions; the forces of "non-co-operation" are so working in different parts of the country that it would perhaps be difficult for sometime to distinguish education from politics in the present conditions. You would, however, come to Delhi in a few days when the matter could personally be settled. In any case the College Management would like to have some time; and so far as I am concerned Bombay or Benares would be all the same to me.

I am grateful for the offer of my present salary; but I do not think I could accept it. One half or perhaps less would suffice.

Yours sincerely,
N.V. Thadani."

On the other hand it rested, 'on certain fundamental principles of life without which no nation can exist. On its educational side', it stood, 'for something equally significant and, though the problem' was 'by no means new, the question would perhaps be more easily solved now than at any other time, with the force of the Nation behind it.' As far as Gandhi's call for non-cooperation was concerned, the forces of non-cooperation were so 'working in different parts of the country that it would perhaps be difficult for sometime to distinguish education from politics in the present conditions.' What really emerges is that at least Thadani realised the need for a nationalist education but was wary of what politicisation, needed at that time, could lead to.[49]

49 Correspondence between Dr N.V. Thadani and Mahatma Gandhi made available by Shri Jivat Thadani.

The Establishment and Growth of Hindu College

Hindu College, now a flourishing institution which is over 100 years old with over 3,000 students, began as a small people's movement for higher education within the framework established by the government, but free of religious, missionary or elitist biases. To use the words of N.K. Nigam who joined the college as a lecturer in 1923, it was a 'janta' college, as opposed to the only other institution of higher education that existed at that time, the elite Christian missionary-run St. Stephen's College. Unlike St. Stephen's College, Hindu College was born as a part of the nationalist impulse and actively took part in the struggle for Independence. Its ethos and efforts to survive and grow stem from its origins and roots. The essential difference between the two institutions cannot be better explained than in the words of Professor Prem Chand, who had studied mainly at St. Stephen's College, taken a break and then finished the final year of his Masters from Hindu College. He went on

Previous page: *Professor Prem Chand*

to become a much loved teacher at the college and one of the most inspiring speakers of its parliament, an institution unique to Hindu College:

> I noticed two big differences in the atmosphere of the two colleges: (i) In St. Stephen's College, the concept of 'freedom from national bondage' had only a cognitive meaning for us: there was neither passion in it nor action. For one thing, most of us belonged to that section of society, which was a part of the ruling system of the country. For another, the 'negative' force of Nationalism was missing in us. How could it have been otherwise, when we came into contact with some very fine Englishmen, full of Christian love and service, who were on the teaching staff of the College. In Hindu College, the picture was entirely different—nearly everyone was a fierce nationalist, with love in his heart for the great nationalist leaders, and hatred in his heart for Englishmen and British Imperialism; politics was a passion, with them. (ii) In St. Stephen's, the most admired students were those who were good both in studies and in sports. To be admired, you had to achieve this rare combination. Strange though it may sound, the combination in my days was not rare either. In Hindu, the most admired students belonged to an entirely different category: these were the persons who were known as good public speakers.[1]

Punjab District Gazetteers, Vol. V A on the Delhi District published at the beginning of 1910, observed, 'This college was established in May 1899 for the purpose of giving cheap but efficient secular education with sound religious instruction, according to the principle of Sanatana Dharm. It is managed by a Board of Trustees, registered under the Joint Stock Companies Act. It teaches upto the B.A. standard of the Punjab University to which it is affiliated, its students (as in the case of St. Stephen's College) being prepared for the examinations of the Punjab University. In addition to the subjects prescribed by the University, all Hindu students are required to attend a religious class once a day. It is maintained by subscriptions from the Hindu public and endowments. The staff consists of six professors, and as the number on the roll at the end of 1909 was only 18, the institution does not seem to be thriving. The college has a building of its own opposite that of St. Stephen's Mission College, Delhi.'[2]

A society by the name of Hindu College Delhi was registered to establish the college in 1899. The objective was to give sound education in English up to the highest university standards. In the case of Hindus, the aim was also to combine secular education with thorough religious instruction according to the teachings of the *sanatana* dharma, on non-sectarian

1 Raj K. Oberoi (ed.), *The Hinduites, Biographical Directory* (Delhi: Old Students' Association, Hindu College, February 1979), p. 23.

2 *Punjab District Gazetteers*, Vol. V A (Delhi District), p. 212. See also University of Delhi Calendar, 1922-23, pp. 213–216.

principles. Subject to the availability of funds, the society was also to:

- ◇ Establish or facilitate establishing similar educational institutions elsewhere.
- ◇ Promote similar religious instruction in colleges and schools in which such instruction might not be given.
- ◇ Prepare students for the degree examinations of the Punjab University in the Oriental Faculty and the Oriental Titles examination as also for similar Oriental Examination held in other provinces.
- ◇ Found fellowships for encouraging learning and research.
- ◇ Establish or facilitate establishing libraries in approved places for the dissemination of a taste for learning.
- ◇ Encourage the preparation, translation and publication of scientific and other works in and from Sanskrit into the vernacular.
- ◇ Establish or facilitate establishing technical institutions and industrial schools in the country.
- ◇ Establish or facilitate establishing boarding houses for Hindus in connection with the educational institutions maintained by the Society.[3]

First Memorandum of Association of the Hindu College

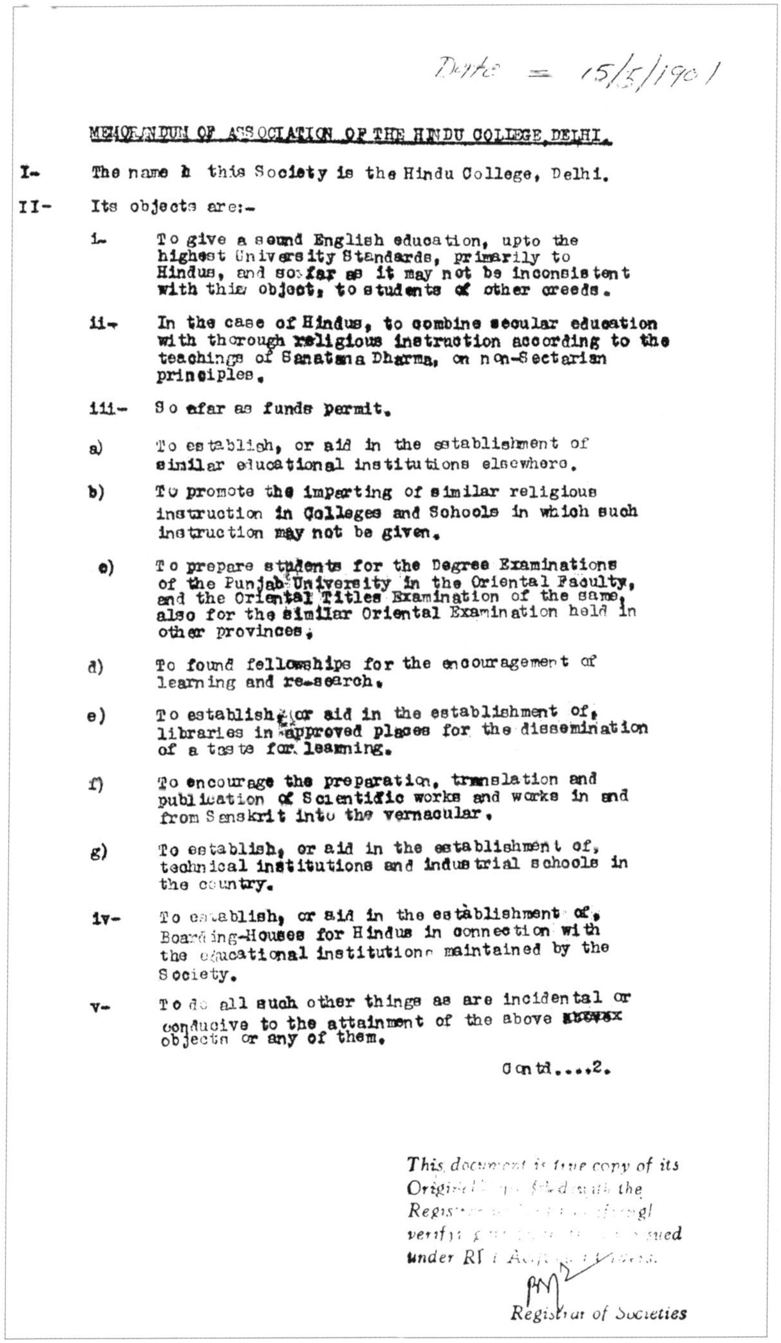

Date = 15/5/1901

MEMORANDUM OF ASSOCIATION OF THE HINDU COLLEGE, DELHI.

I- The name of this Society is the Hindu College, Delhi.

II- Its objects are:-

i- To give a sound English education, upto the highest University Standards, primarily to Hindus, and so far as it may not be inconsistent with this object, to students of other creeds.

ii- In the case of Hindus, to combine secular education with thorough religious instruction according to the teachings of Sanatana Dharma, on non-Sectarian principles.

iii- So far as funds permit.

a) To establish, or aid in the establishment of similar educational institutions elsewhere.

b) To promote the imparting of similar religious instruction in Colleges and Schools in which such instruction may not be given.

c) To prepare students for the Degree Examinations of the Punjab University in the Oriental Faculty, and the Oriental Titles Examination of the same, also for the similar Oriental Examination held in other provinces.

d) To found fellowships for the encouragement of learning and re-search.

e) To establish, or aid in the establishment of, libraries in approved places for the dissemination of a taste for learning.

f) To encourage the preparation, translation and publication of Scientific works and works in and from Sanskrit into the vernacular.

g) To establish, or aid in the establishment of, technical institutions and industrial schools in the country.

iv- To establish, or aid in the establishment of, Boarding-Houses for Hindus in connection with the educational institutions maintained by the Society.

v- To do all such other things as are incidental or conducive to the attainment of the above objects or any of them.

Contd....2.

This document is true copy of its Original [illegible] filed with the Registrar [illegible] verify [illegible] issued under RTI [illegible]

Registrar of Societies

Although this memorandum may sound chauvinistic in today's ethos in its mention of Hinduism, the institution that was established was essentially secular. Muslims were not prevented from joining and those who did, were not compelled to study Hinduism. Thus, religious instruction was a part of the agenda; the vision, however, was neither bigoted, parochial nor narrow-minded. Secularism and voluntary religious instruction were not seen as incompatible.

Essentially, the desire was to encourage Hindu teachings but not force them. This could be seen in a few of the scholarships that were instituted. In 1918 Pandit Sukhdeo Singh proposed to donate Rs 2,000 in cash for

3 Memorandum of Association of the Hindu College, Delhi, 15 May 1901.

Mention of Hindu College in Bashiruddin Ahmad's book Waqiat-I Dar al-Hukumat-i-Dilli *(in 3 Vols) describing events from 1337–1919*

احاطے میں ایک بیس ددہ کا نہایت نفیس بورڈنگ ہوس بنا ہوا ہے جس میں چار بڑے بڑے کشادہ کمرے ہیں جن میں بورڈر رہتے ہیں۔ اس کے رو کار پر یہ کتبہ ہے:۔

Sri Ram Ashram. Built by the sons of the late Diwan of Alwar 1917

ترجمہ سری رام آشرم (جس کو) متوفی دیوان الور کے صاحب زادوں نے سنہ ۱۹۱۷ء میں بنوایا۔

جس کا ستر روپیہ ماہانہ کرایہ دیا جاتا ہے۔

ہندو کالج
۱۸۹۹ء

سینٹ اسٹیفنز کالج کے محاذ میں ایک وسیع کوٹھی میں یہ کالج ہے جو ہندو صاحبوں کی عالی ہمتی کی زندہ یادگار ہے۔ کوٹھی کے دروازے پر

Hindu College Established 1899.

لکھا ہوا ہے (ہندو کالج جس کی بنا سنہ ۱۸۹۹ء میں پڑی) یہ مکان کالج کے واسطے بنایا نہیں گیا بلکہ یہ کوٹھی در اصل کرنل سکنر صاحب کی تھی ان سے لالہ سلطان سنگھ صاحب نے خرید کر کالج کے ہاتھ فروخت کر دی۔ اس کے

Right: *Hindu College was registered under the Joint Stock Companies Act, 6 June 1901*

Below: *List of office occupations and addresses of the members of the Board of Trustees of Hindu College at the end of 1901*

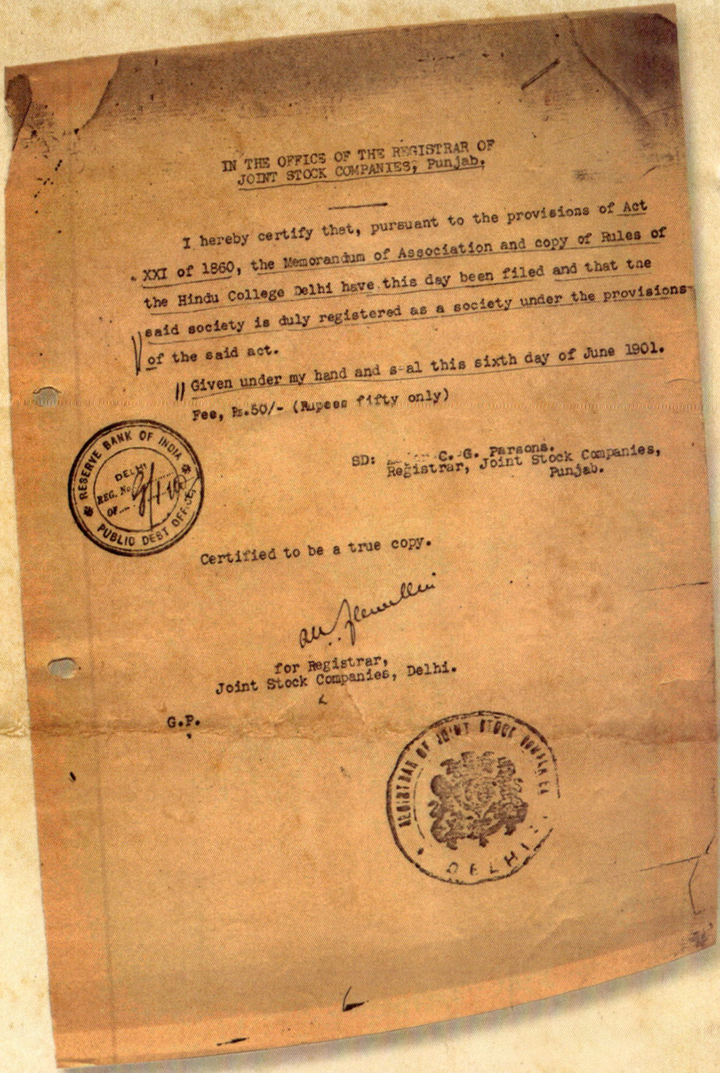

IN THE OFFICE OF THE REGISTRAR OF
JOINT STOCK COMPANIES, Punjab.

I hereby certify that, pursuant to the provisions of Act XXI of 1860, the Memorandum of Association and copy of Rules of the Hindu College Delhi have this day been filed and that the said society is duly registered as a society under the provisions of the said act.

Given under my hand and seal this sixth day of June 1901.

Fee, Rs.50/- (Rupees fifty only)

SD: C. G. Parsons.
Registrar, Joint Stock Companies,
Punjab.

Certified to be a true copy.

for Registrar,
Joint Stock Companies, Delhi.

G.P.

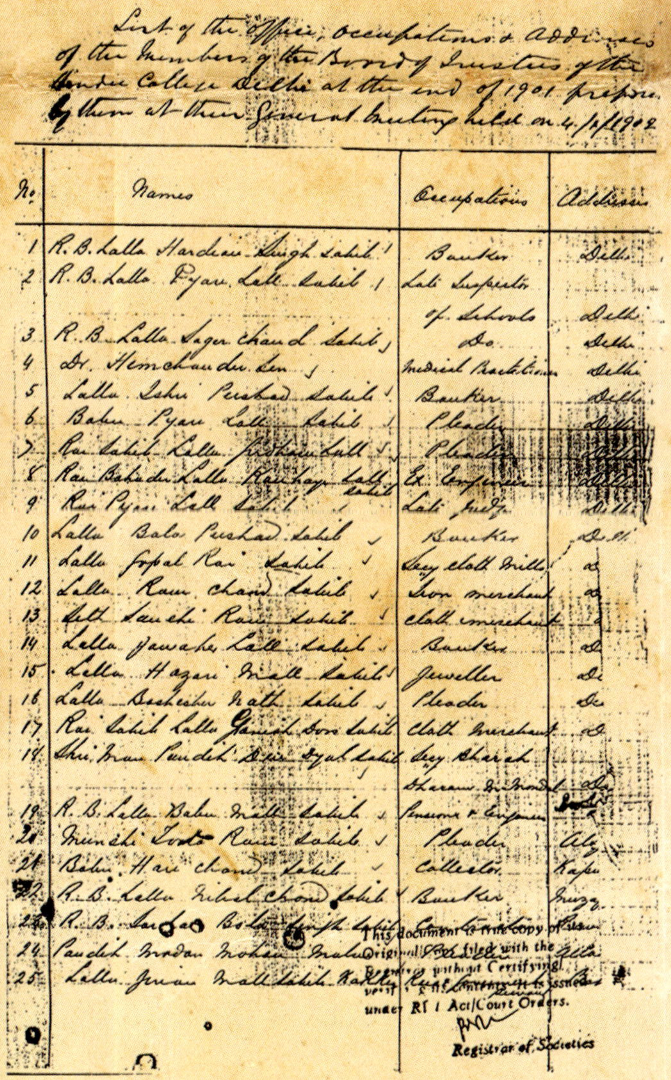

List of the office, occupations & addresses of the Members of the Board of Trustees of the Hindu College Delhi at the end of 1901 prepared by them at their General Meeting held on 4/1/1902

No.	Names	Occupations	Addresses
1	R. B. Lalla Hardeo Singh Sahib	Banker	Delhi
2	R. B. Lalla Pyare Lall Sahib	Late Inspector of Schools	Delhi
3	R. B. Lalla Sagar Chand Sahib	Do.	Delhi
4	Dr. Hemchander Sen	Medical Practitioner	Delhi
5	Lalla Ishri Pershad Sahib	Banker	Delhi
6	Babu Pyare Lall Sahib	Pleader	Delhi
7	Rai Sahib Lalla Kishan Lall	Pleader	Delhi
8	Rai Bahadur Lalla Kanhaya Lall Sahib	Ex Engineer	Delhi
9	Rai Pyare Lall Sahib	Late Judge	Delhi
10	Lalla Bala Pershad Sahib	Banker	Delhi
11	Lalla Gopal Rai Sahib	Secy Cloth Mills	Do
12	Lalla Ram Chand Sahib	Iron merchant	Do
13	Seth Sanchi Ram Sahib	Cloth merchant	Do
14	Lalla Jawahar Lall Sahib	Banker	Do
15	Lalla Hazari Mall Sahib	Jeweller	Do
16	Lalla Bisheshar Nath Sahib	Pleader	Do
17	Rai Sahib Lalla Ganesh Dass Sahib	Cloth Merchant	Do
18	Shri Man Pandit Din Dyal Sahib	Secy Bharat Dharam Mandal	Do
19	R. B. Lalla Babu Mall Sahib	Pensioner & Engineer	[illegible]
20	Munshi Tota Ram Sahib	Pleader	Aligarh
21	Babu Hari Chand Sahib	Collector	Kapurthala
22	R. B. Lalla Nihal Chand Sahib	Banker	Muzaffarnagar
23	R. B. Sardar Bishan Singh Sahib	[illegible]	[illegible]
24	Pandit Madan Mohan Malaviya	Pleader	Allahabad
25	Lalla Jiwan Mall Sahib Kakkar	[illegible]	[illegible]

This document is true copy of its Original filed with the Registrar without Certifying its contents. It is issued under RTI Act/Court Orders.

Registrar of Societies

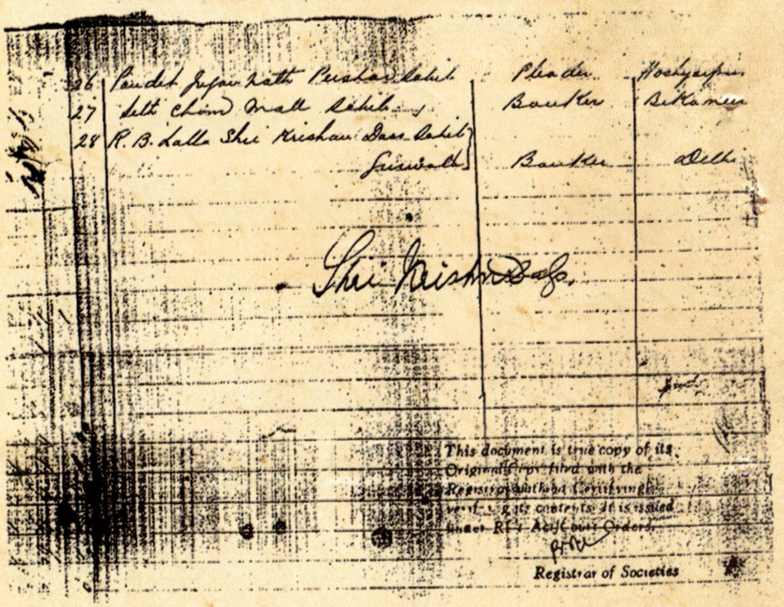

No.	Names	Occupations	Addresses
26	Pandit Jugal Kishore Pershad Sahib	Pleader	Hoshiarpur
27	Seth Chand Mall Sahib	Banker	Bikaner
28	R. B. Lalla Shri Kishan Dass Sahib Gurwala	Banker	Delhi

Shri Kishan Das

This document is true copy of its Original filed with the Registrar without Certifying its contents. It is issued under RTI Act/Court Orders.

Registrar of Societies

two scholarships, the Shrimati Kirpa Devi Gita scholarships, of Rs 5 each to selected first year students for the first and second years, out of the interest accruing on the donated amount. To be eligible, students had to privately study one or two prescribed *adhyayas* (sections) from Lokmanya Bal Gangadhar Tilak's *Gita Rahasya* in Hindi. By the end of the first term, the principal and the college professor of Sanskrit together with the donor or his successor or successors as nominated by him would hold a written examination to test the candidates and select the best for the award of the scholarship. The selected candidate had to master the first half of *Gita Rahasya* and he would be tested in it by the end of the first year. Only on being found up to the mark, was the scholarship continued in the second year, at the end of which the whole of *Gita Rahasya* had to be studied. The successful candidate was also given a certificate.[4]

In April 1941 two scholarships—the Rai Achhni Ram scholarships—of Rs 12 each for MA students were instituted by Shri Ram Narayan, Judge, Small Causes Court, Delhi from an endowment of Rs 7,200. These were primarily for Jains securing the maximum marks and at least a second division in the university BA examination and joining MA classes in Hindu College. In the absence of a Jain student, the scholarship could go to an Agarwal student. In the absence of both, it could go to a Hindu student with the same terms and conditions.[5]

Shri Basheshar Nath Goela instituted three gold medals of Rs 100 each at the newly established Delhi University: the annual M. Makhan Lal medal for the best Hindu lady candidate in the university; the M. Bhole Nath medal to be awarded to the best Hindu candidate in the BA examination, provided he knew Sanskrit; and the annual L. Jageshar Nath Goela medal for the best candidate in Technical Education.[6]

These scholarships were open to both boys and girls, something remarkably progressive for those times.

The First Premises

Hindu College was first housed in a small residence in Kinari Bazaar, Chandni Chowk with limited rooms that could be used as classrooms. The college started functioning with thirteen boys. One of them was Sir Shri Ram who was there for a brief period of six months before he left to join his family business. He later became the chairman of the college Governing Body, and one of its biggest builders. The inauguration ceremony was performed in a dharamshala in Chehlpuri on Basant Panchmi by Pandit Madan Mohan Malaviya, who also remained on the

Facing page:
A small section of this old map of Delhi and its environs shows the location of Skinner's house and garden (above, highlighted); Letter of invitation to the inaugural ceremony of Hindu College by the founder Shri Krishna Dass Gurwala (below)

4 Proceedings of the adjourned meeting of the Board of Trustees, Hindu College held on Tuesday, 19 February 1918 at 5 pm in the college premises.

5 Proceedings of a meeting of the Board of Trustees, Hindu College, Delhi held on Thursday, 10 April 1941 at 4:30 pm in the college.

6 Minutes of the meeting of the Provisional Executive Council of Delhi University held on Thursday, 8 June 1922 at 5 pm.

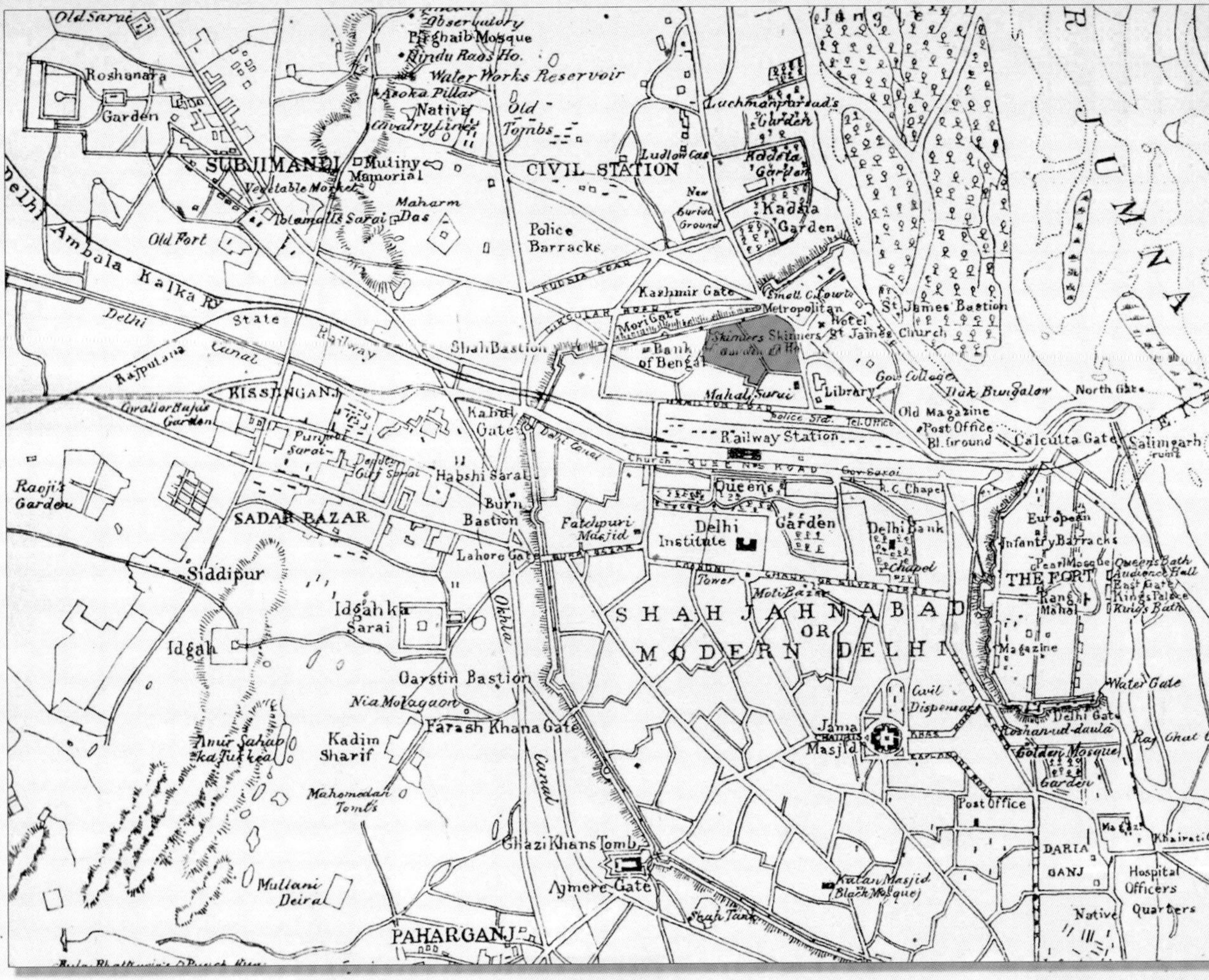

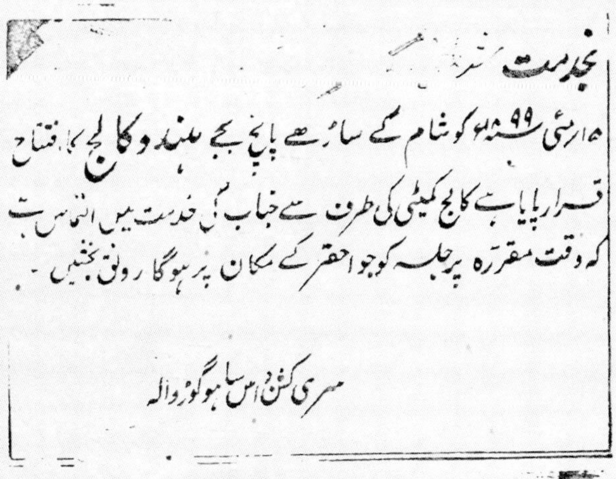
بخدمت شریف

۱۵ مئی ۹۹ سنہ کو شام کے ساڑھے پانچ بجے ہندو کالج کا افتتاح قرار پایا ہے کالج کمیٹی کی طرف سے جناب کی خدمت میں التماس ہے کہ وقت مقررہ پر جلسہ کو جو احقر کے مکان پر ہوگا رونق بخشیں۔

سری کشن داس ساہو گوڑ والہ

ENGLISH TRANSLATION

At your service,

The inauguration of Hindu College has been fixed for May 15, 1899 at 5:30 PM. On behalf of the College Committee, you are requested to grace the function which will be held at the house of this humble servant, at the fixed time.

Shri Krishna Dass Sahu Gurwala

Hindu College was first housed in Kinari Bazaar, Chandni Chowk

college's Board of Trustees for the first ten years. Additionally, the college had the blessings of Mrs Annie Besant, Lokmanya Tilak and other freedom fighters.

The facilities then were very poor even for the small number of students who were on the rolls. There were no proper library arrangements, no playgrounds and no common room. Professor Phani Bhushan Adhikari, who joined as Professor of Philosophy in 1900, and who later became its principal (1903–05) describes the early years thus:

> I could not even believe that it was really a College, situated as it was inside a narrow lane off the Bara Dariba. The building was a private house, not a large one consisting more of open *dalans* than of rooms on the ground and in upper flats. The classes had to be held in the *dalans* or in the few available rooms each open on two sides and which could by no means be closed.[7]

He wondered how teaching could be done in such a place, even for the small number of students. There were only two Intermediate classes, first and second year, as they were called. The BA class or third year had just opened with only a few students. Books of reference were needed but there were no library facilities. Only the textbooks used by teachers and students

7 An article published in *The Indraprastha*, 1951-52.

were available. The first book accessioned to the library on 13 June 1908, was *The Century Dictionary: An Encyclopaedia Lexicon of the English Language*, a set of ten volumes donated by Lala Chiranji Lal, a banker in Hissar. The laboratory was poorly equipped for the needs of Physics and Chemistry, the two science subjects taught in the first and second years of Intermediate Science.

The teaching staff consisted of a professor for both Science and Mathematics; a teacher for Sanskrit and one for Persian, that is, a Pandit and a Maulvi respectively. There was no teacher for English or History and there was no principal. The first principal, Professor B.B. Mookerji, who taught both Logic and English had left and no replacement had been found. Phani Bhushan Adhikari had been appointed to teach Logic and Psychology to the Intermediate classes and Philosophy to the BA class that had just been introduced. The students were helpless; Adhikari decided to teach all the subjects for which no teacher was available and also administer the college.

In July 1899, Rs 94 was collected as fees and Rs 10 as admission fees; thus the total was Rs 104. The monthly salary bill was Rs 254.50. This meant a deficit of Rs 150, which had to be made up from donations and voluntary contributions. A salary statement for December 1899 reads:

Principal B.B. Mookerji	Rs 100.00
Babu N.N. Roy, Vice Principal	Rs 80.00
Pt. Harnarayan Shastri	Rs 25.00
Moulvi Mir Hufza	Rs 25.00
Mr Pearey Lal, Clerk	Rs 12.00
Mr Mangal Sain, Clerk	Rs 7.00
Lachman Chaprasi	Rs 5.00
Sweeper	Rs 0.50
Total	Rs 254.40[8]

Boarding House

Attached to the Hindu College was a boarding house for the few students coming from outside Delhi. There was no one in charge of this, so the students lived in very poor conditions. This was a matter of continuous concern for the college's management. Adhikari, moved by the plight of the students, took charge of the boarding house as well. He realised that in spite of the poor conditions in which it was functioning, the college fulfilled the requirement of many and somehow had to survive. He was, therefore, willing to work towards achieving this.

8 Raj K. Oberoi, 'College through the years 1899–1978', *The Indraprastha*, July 1978.

Even when the college moved to a better building, the boarders had to continue living in their unhealthy quarters in a narrow lane. There was no playground, nor any open space where the residents could spend their leisure hours.

The construction of a boarding house was apparently contemplated in January 1920 and a committee was formed six years later to find a suitable place for it. Eventually, the boarding house was situated at 4, Ramchandra Lane in Civil Lines. Whatever the living conditions, it was a site of intense revolutionary activity. N.K. Nigam, a revolutionary himself, reminisced of his days at Hindu College as a lecturer and as the superintendent of the hostel where several revolutionaries found refuge. Notable among them was Chandrashekhar Azad who died fighting the British rulers on 27 February 1931 in Allahabad. Azad had stayed in the boarding house with Nigam. Nigam was offered a reward of Rs 2 lakh by the British to betray Azad when they arrested him on 4 December 1930. Although Nigam knew Azad's whereabouts, he feigned ignorance. Yashpal, Bhagwati Charan Vohra, Dhanwantri, Surya Sen and Anant Singh of the Chittagong Armoury Raid fame and a host of other revolutionaries also came to the hostel.[9]

Facing Page: *Pandit Harnarayan Shastri (above); R.B. Lala Sultan Singh (below)*

Challenges of Survival and Growth

In the early years, the college continuously faced financial difficulties. The Board of Trustees tried to raise resources both for the college and the hostel. There was the recurrent question of repair and maintenance of the shops owned by the Trust because the rent from them was used for running the college. Non-recovery of rent worsened the financial situation and hence this became a constant preoccupation. There were no government grants up to 1904. Each time the need arose, Lala Shri Krishna Dass bailed out the college till the amount reached Rs 30,000. He ultimately wrote off this sum and treated it as his donation to the college. In all, he donated Rs 45,000.

Lala Shri Krishna Dass Gurwala also managed to collect funds with the unwavering support of staff members, who went door-to-door asking for donations. Under the inspiring leadership of Pandit Harnarayan Shastri, Professor of Sanskrit, the entire staff offered not to draw their salaries until the finances of the college improved. The business community of Delhi also rose to the occasion. Wholesale cloth merchants, as a body, decided to collect two pice per bale of cloth by way of contribution to the college. This continued to bring in substantial money for quite a few years.

It was the government that seemed reluctant to support Hindu College. For example, in March 1912 the Board of Trustees requested the Municipal Committee to reconsider giving the college a grant of Rs 100 per month as recommended by Mr Hemphrays, President of the Committee in 1908. But to no avail.[10]

---

9 Dhanwantri was one of the Founder members of Naujawan Bharat Sabha with Bhagat Singh. He masterminded the viceregal train case (Delhi Conspiracy case) and was given life imprisonment. He remained in Andaman jail.

10 Proceedings of a meeting of the Board of Trustees, Hindu College, Delhi held on 24 March 1912 at 5 pm in the college.

However, despite the college's poor financial condition there was also concern about improving education standards. To this end, Adhikari was asked to present a scheme to the secretary of the Managing Committee, Shri Krishna Dass. Dass not only approved the scheme but also agreed to shoulder the financial responsibilities of implementing it for the time being. The most immediate need was for an experienced principal and competent professors for subjects that lacked proper teaching provisions although students in the college had to take the Intermediate and BA examinations from Lahore University. Advertisements were placed in important newspapers in Bengal and Punjab for the positions. Mr Prasanna Kumar Basu, an MA from Calcutta, who had just then retired as principal of Bhawalpur College (Punjab) was appointed as the principal of Hindu College; he also had to teach English and History. He was given two assistants to teach these subjects to the Intermediate classes. A full-time Mathematics professor was appointed so that the Science professor could concentrate on teaching Physics and Chemistry.

The functioning of the college became smoother; the results improved remarkably, and a larger number of students joined in the following session. Many had to be turned away as there was no space in the building to accommodate them. This matter was brought to the notice of the college Committee and despite its vague and inadequate response, the college did manage to find a vacant three-storeyed house on the main road which had more space. It had enough classrooms and rooms for the library and laboratory but none for boarders. This was a handicap and the search continued for even better accommodation. Eventually, after two years, a place was found near Ajmere Gate. Meanwhile Principal P.K. Basu left for Bengal and Professor Phani Bhushan Adhikari was made the college's permanent principal. He once again took charge of the college while carrying on with full-time teaching.

A sketch of Skinner's bungalow which formed the premises of Hindu College in Kashmere Gate

On 14 October 1908, R.B. Lala Sultan Singh was persuaded to sell part of his historic property in the Kashmere Gate area, which had originally belonged to Colonel James Skinner, for Rs 87,000. There was only Rs 56,559.50 in the college bank account. From it an amount of Rs 40,500 was paid to Lala Sultan Singh with the promise that the balance amount would be paid in two years. At the new location in Kashmere Gate, on the right was a mosque and just opposite was the Mission College or St. Stephen's College. This location was appropriate because despite the goal of giving religious instructions to Hindus, Hindu College had secular education as one of its aims. While Pandit Harnarayan Shastri taught Sanskrit, Maulvi Mohd. Hufza taught Persian and Arabic. Both were given the same salary of Rs 25 per month; later both were given Rs 50 per month.

This indicates that the college had no permanent building till it moved to Kashmere Gate. While the initial ceremony for the establishment of the college may have been done in a dharamshala in Chehlpuri, the college was housed in at least two buildings—one a two-storeyed private house off Bara Dariba and the other a three-storeyed building on the main road before moving to Kundewalan near Ajmere Gate.

Despite the initial years of struggle, the determination and perseverance of its founders and their successors kept the college on the path of growth and did not allow their progressive vision and goals to be diluted. For example, in spite of financial difficulties they acknowledged the need for a bus for girl students as their numbers had increased considerably.

The college was threatened with disaffiliation by Punjab University a few times because of lack of resources and infrastructure. A letter dated 18 February 1910, from the registrar pointed out that apart from lack of proper infrastructure, the college also depended on support from only one individual for its existence while the public seemed to have no interest in the institution. From 1 April 1910 the Board of Trustees ceased to draw upon Lala Shri Krishna Dass Gurwala's firm and instead depended on Lala Bakshi Ram Mohan Lal to make up the deficiency. As on 31 March 1910, Rs 32,000 was owed to the firm represented by Rai Bahadur Lala Shri Krishna Dass and Rs 47,313 and 12 annas was due to Lala Sultan Singh, being the balance price of the building that the college had bought. Of these, it was felt that the second liability had to be met urgently and funds for the future maintenance of the college had to be found.

Fresh attempts were made for donations from chiefs and nobles in the country for which the lieutenant governor's support was solicited. It was further resolved that in case these efforts failed, the college building would be sold. It was likely to fetch about Rs 1 lakh, which would meet both the liabilities of Lala Sultan Singh and of Lala Shri Krishna Dass. In the appeal it was distinctly stated that the funds would not be used to pay the debt of Lala Shri Krishna Dass Gurwala but would in fact be returned with interest to the donors in case the college had to be abolished in the following five years. Following this, a Hindu College *Bhikshuk Mandali* was formed. It was authorised to collect funds and popularise the cause of the college among the people. The *mandali* had to draw up its rules and regulations and submit accounts to the Board. The Board had to be kept informed about the *mandali's* work and kept in the picture if there were any changes in the composition of its membership.

Rai Kedar Nath Sahib

But despite these efforts, the question of funds continued to haunt the college. A meeting of the Trust on 28 August 1914, records a letter received from the registrar of Punjab University, Lahore, laying down the condition that the third year class could not be started unless Rs 50,000 in cash was collected before 31 August. Due to the shortness of time, it was not possible to collect subscriptions and hence efforts had to be made to find ten gentlemen who could contribute or collect Rs 5,000 each. Four persons immediately volunteered:

1. Rai Bahadur Lala Kanahiya Lal Sahib
2. Rai Kedar Nath Sahib

3. Rai Kedar Nath Sahib on behalf of L. Raghu Mal
4. Rai Kedar Nath Sahib on behalf of L. Devki Nandan

Again, in 1924, a resolution was passed to form a committee to raise funds for the college. It was also resolved to invite respectable Hindu citizens to consider steps to save the college from its precarious financial situation. The college already had a debt of Rs 29,000 as advanced by Rai Bahadur Lala Kanahiya Lal, Seth Sanchi Ram, R.B. Lala Sultan Singh, R.B. Lala Pearey Lal and Lala Shiv Narain. This had to be repaid at the earliest.

Even in the 1930s, lack of adequate finances kept cropping up with regularity indicating that the college had never really got on to a sound financial footing.

The Succession of Principals

Along with the quick succession of the chairman of the Board of Trustees in the early years till Sir Shri Ram took over, there was also a rapid succession of principals. Up to 1917, the principalship of the college changed hands with alarming regularity: Shri B.B. Mookerji (1899–1906), Shri N.N. Roy (1906–1911), Shri Phani Bhushan Adhikari (1911–1915), Shri S. Sen (1915–1917). Shri N.V. Thadani joined in 1917; he played a pivotal role in building the college and brought stability to it. He had two tenures and was the principal of the college for about twenty-six years. At the time of joining, Thadani was a young lecturer from Dayal Singh College, Lahore. He raised the prestige of Hindu College to it being regarded as one of the premier institutions in North India.

Sir Shri Ram

When Professor Thadani left Hindu College in 1928 to take up the principalship of a new National College in Sind he was succeeded by Professor S.K. Sen, an Oxford graduate in History and a reputed teacher. Unfortunately he died tragically of a heart attack in the college hall while addressing the students on 1 October 1934. After an interregnum of one year, Thadani returned to serve the college as principal till 1950. After him, Shri Bhattacharya, head of the Department of English became the principal (1950–1958); he made a significant contribution in shifting the college to the university campus. Undaunted by the shortage of funds, Professor Bhattacharya took keen interest in the construction of the new building. It was a great achievement for him when the E-shaped building was ready in October 1953 and the college shifted to its new location in 1953-54. Bad health forced Professor Bhattacharya to resign in March 1958. In July 1958, Shri Raj Narain Mathur became the first old student to become the principal of the college. Next was Dr B.M. Bhatia from 1964 till 1980 with a break between 1971–1973. Subsequently, Mr P.C. Verma was appointed principal in 1980; he retired in 1995. Dr S.N. Maheshwari from the neighbouring Shri Ram College of Commerce succeeded him. However, his stint was short as he left in 1997. Dr Kavita A. Sharma then became the first lady principal of a co-educational college in the University of Delhi thus bringing to a culmination the progressive vision of its founding fathers which had never wavered in keeping Hindu College co-educational in its 100-year history. After her departure in August 2008, Professor Vinay Srivastava, from the

Department of Anthropology at Delhi University, became the principal in 2010. In between there were two officiating principals, Dr D.N. Gupta and Dr S. Choudhary. Two years later, Dr Srivastava too left to rejoin his parent department and since then Dr Pradumn Kumar has been officiating as the principal of the college.

Left: *Professor S.K. Sen*

Right: *Lala Pearey Lal*

Inception of Delhi University

Hindu College, together with St. Stephen's, Ramjas and Lady Hardinge Medical College, played a significant role in setting up Delhi University. The idea first took shape in 1911, when Emperor King George V, addressing a magnificent *durbar* in Delhi, announced that the capital of India would be transferred from Calcutta to Delhi. Professor Aparna Basu has given a succinct history of the birth and growth of the university. To begin with, the government thought of a government college and not a university, but this idea had to be shelved because of the outbreak of World War I in 1914. When the War ended in 1918, the proposal was revived and a committee consisting of principals S.K. Rudra of St. Stephen's College; N.V. Thadani of Hindu College; A.T. Gidwani of Ramjas; and Wali Mohammed submitted a report on the constitution of such a university. In the meantime, the report of the Calcutta University Commission set up under the chairmanship of Sir Michael Sadler, was published. It recommended that henceforth universities should be unitary, teaching and residential. Following this, Punjab University decided to reshape its constitution and concentrate all MA and BA (Honours) teaching in Lahore. This made it necessary to have a university in Delhi.[11]

In December 1919, the chief commissioner of Delhi presided over a meeting attended by representatives of the three colleges and the chief engineer. It was unanimously resolved that a

11 Aparna Basu (ed.), *University of Delhi 1922–1997, Platinum Jubilee* (Delhi: University of Delhi, 1998), p. 11.

unitary, teaching university should be established. The colleges that had at first enthusiastically welcomed the proposal, soon realised that they would lose their autonomy. Hence, at a meeting on 25 June 1921, N.V. Thadani, Lala Shiv Narain, Lala Pearey Lal and S.K. Sen from Hindu College, Lala Kedar Nath and N.D. Gidwani of Ramjas and F.F. Monk, S.N. Mukarji and C.H.C. Sharp of St. Stephen's College impressed upon the Education Secretary that it was necessary to consult the colleges before drafting the bill for the proposed university. They also demanded that at least two-thirds of the controlling body of the university should consist of representatives of the colleges. It should have the statutory powers to determine the date of the move to the new site and the time frame for separating Intermediate from BA classes. It was stipulated that all the three colleges had to agree on these issues.[12]

The bill was introduced in the Imperial Legislative Assembly on 16 January 1922 by the Education Secretary and was debated at length both in the Legislative Assembly and in the Council of States. Various amendments were introduced but all were defeated. The bill was finally passed by the Assembly on 22 February 1922 and the Council of States on 28 February 1922. The viceroy gave his assent on 5 March 1922. In the course of discussions in the Legislative Assembly, members, on behalf of the colleges, demanded assurances that the term 'unitary' be interpreted liberally and that colleges should be associated directly with university teaching. The colleges were apprehensive and wanted assurances that their identities would not be destroyed by the university. This issue together with others led to the bill being referred to a Joint Select Committee.

After some discussions with the principals, the Governor-General-in-Council directed that the Act should come into force on 1 May 1922 and a notification to this effect was issued on 6 April 1922. The Viceroy, Lord Reading, was the first chancellor of Delhi University and he appointed Sir Hari Singh Gour, a distinguished barrister-at-law from Nagpur, as its first vice chancellor. The first meeting of the Provisional Executive Council of the University of Delhi was held on 31 May 1922. Among its members were those associated with the three colleges. From Hindu College were Principal N.V. Thadani, Pandit Harnarayan Shastri, R.B. Lala Sultan Singh and R.B. Lala Amba Prasad. From St. Stephen's were Rev. P.N.F. Young and Mr Khub Ram. Principal N.V. Thadani was appointed proctor and Khan Bahadur Muhammad Husain was the first librarian. Principal N.V. Thadani was also a member of the Procedure Committee appointed by the Provisional Council to examine the draft statutes, ordinances, regulations and rules laid before the Provisional Council. The Council also formed a Finance Committee with N.V. Thadani and R.B. Lala Sultan Singh as its members.[13]

A Selection Committee was constituted to appoint a registrar for the university; Lala Sultan Singh was a member of the Selection Committee. On the eve of Principal Rudra's retirement from St. Stephen's College, Lala Sultan Singh moved a resolution in the second meeting of the

12 Ibid.

13 Ibid., pp. 11–15.

Provisional Council to place on record, the 'deep appreciation' of the Council, 'of his long and highly meritorious services in the cause of higher education'. Thadani served as the secretary of the Provisional Council for its second meeting. He was continuously active in the evolution of the university. Three members were added to the Provisional Council. Among them were Pearey Lal and Shiv Narain who were also on the Board of Hindu College. The three existing colleges were recognised as colleges of the university and their teaching staff was recognised as teachers of the university. Punjab University conducted the examination for Delhi University in 1923 but in April 1924, Delhi University conducted its own examination.[14]

At the time of recognition of colleges, it was stated that Hindu College was maintained by grants from the government, endowments and public subscriptions. It had its own building near Kashmere Gate and had provided residence to about 150 students in the college's main and attached hostels. They were supervised by a warden, a superintendent and two assistant superintendents. The college provided sports facilities for cricket, hockey, football and tennis and also had a small gymnasium. It had a well-equipped library and a reading room, which was kept open for students even outside college housing. The college had a rich co-curricular life through its literary and debating society, parliament, social union, dramatic society and a scientific union, all guided by staff members. Five scholarships of Rs 7 each were given to deserving Khatri students from an annual donation made by Sri Ram MA. The management of the college vested in the principal and a registered Board of Trust, ordinarily acting through a Managing Committee appointed by itself.

An interesting fallout of Hindu College becoming an integral part of the newly formed university was seen in a question that arose as to whether, because of its position in the university, it could admit students for the MA class, which it was not entitled to do earlier. According to the legal opinion given to the vice chancellor, the question depended on the construction of S.2 (a) of the University Act. A college meant an institution recognised by the university in which instruction was provided under conditions provided in the statutes. Hindu College was recognised as a college of the university by Statute No. 18 but no conditions were prescribed. Hence it became unconditionally entitled and justified to teach students up to and including MA classes.[15]

Soon after its foundation, the very existence of the university was threatened in September 1922. The government wanted to curtail expenses and drop the idea of the university. It was saved because of the firm stand taken by the Vice Chancellor, Hari Singh Gour, who together with Rector F.J. Western and the principals of the three colleges, F.F. Monk, N.V. Thadani and Kedar Nath, jointly submitted a memorandum in May 1923, pleading for the

Below: *Rai Sahib Sri Ram*

Pearey Lal, advocate, was a founding member of Board of Trustees and Managing Committee of Hindu College

14 Provisional Executive Council Meeting No. 2. Minutes of the meeting held on 3 June 1922 at 8 am, pp. 7–22.

15 Executive Council's first meeting of the permanent EC held on 23 March 1923 at 8:30 am, p. 75 (Vice Chancellor's legal opinion).

university's continued existence. They pointed out that Delhi University was established and was functional. Many consequent actions had already taken place. One of them was that the three arts colleges with 750 undergraduates were disaffiliated from the University of Punjab, and were the constituent colleges of Delhi University. The colleges had increased their staff strength and indented for apparatus to strengthen their physical and chemical laboratories. They had incurred expenditure that could not now be reduced. The colleges and the university were interdependent. Any reduction in the grant of one would prejudicially affect the other and the cause of education in Delhi would suffer as a whole. In any case, the university was being run on unprecedentedly economical lines, the colleges being private institutions. Their expenditure was minimal, commensurate with efficiency, and there could not be any further cutbacks without impairing their utility.[16]

The combined efforts of the university and its constituent colleges obviously succeeded as the first convocation was held in the Legislative Assembly hall on 26 March 1923. The ceremony was preceded by hectic meetings to complete all technicalities. The office staff was almost in a state of nervous breakdown while the principals of St. Stephen's and Hindu had to take leave after the event to recuperate.[17]

The university was allotted its site in 1933; the site already had a few government bungalows, possibly built for the viceroy's staff, horse stables and quarters for bandmasters and servants. According to one account, Probyn Road got its name from the stables there and the syces that lived here were *purabiyas* whom the British called by a name, which sounded like 'probyn'. However, this site was not given immediately because the court trying the Delhi Conspiracy case was housed there. There is widespread belief that the revolutionary Bhagat Singh was kept in the dark, dingy basement underneath the present Academic Council hall. When the trial was over, the university's registrar requested the chief commissioner to transfer the buildings to Delhi University, which was done in October 1933.[18]

Relocation of Hindu College

Shifting Hindu College to the new site was not without hiccups as perennial financial difficulties and discriminatory treatment came in the way. As is evident from the deliberations of the Managing Committee in December 1934, the college could not be shifted piecemeal to the new site, as it was neither financially nor academically feasible to do so. The college could not shift without a building grant of Rs 5 lakh from the government for constructing the college and hostel buildings; quarters for the teaching and clerical staff had to be provided as well. This position was reiterated in February 1935 when college authorities made a formal application

16 Aparna Basu, op. cit., p.14. See also University of Delhi Calendar for 1922-23, pp. 29–38.

17 Ibid., p. 15.

18 Ibid., pp. 18-19.

for the transfer of the site and buildings provisionally allocated to Hindu College on the site plan forwarded by the government to the university. They reiterated that the conditions had to be similar to those laid down for St. Stephen's College.[19]

Eventually, Shri R.N. Mathur was appointed the architect for the college building on a maximum remuneration of Rs 1,000 and Babu Pearey Lal and R.B. Suraj Narain were authorised to settle terms. The architect was to make a plan for 750 students that also included a plan for an additional 550 students and for a hostel or hostels with residential accommodation for 300 students. There were some existing buildings on the site and a decision had to be taken about these.[20]

In the mid-1930s amidst hectic activity the college was streamlined according to the requirements of the university. In December 1937, the Board of Trustees offered their cooperation to the modified scheme of a Federal University of Delhi and gratefully accepted the proposed offer of Rs 1 lakh for building a hostel to accommodate about 100 students and the offer of one of the houses on the estate as the residence of the principal. As funds were extremely limited, the Board requested that the college be excluded from contributing to the cost of construction of the proposed hostel since it was an institution of the government. Moreover, with due economy and strict supervision it was possible to construct the hostel in Rs 1 lakh provided it was not done through the Public Works Department.

Apart from the buildings on the twenty-five-acre site that was allotted to the college, it had also been promised space in the Old Viceregal Lodge till it could construct its own buildings for conducting tutorials and other academic activities required to supplement university classes. Since the teaching had to be done at different places, a government grant was needed for conveyance to and from the college and Old Viceregal Lodge.

Significantly, the college drew attention to the fact that its annual maintenance grant had been continuously reduced since 1928. However, the college had engaged highly qualified staff at high monthly salaries to ensure a good standard of teaching and discipline. Since the college imparted instruction to the largest number of students in the province, an adequate recurring maintenance grant, commensurate with its expenditure, status and work was essential. In any case, the grant could not be lower than that of St. Stephen's College. Further, as and when more buildings were required, the government would have to give an adequate building grant as also a recurring maintenance grant. The Board further stated that the college would cooperate in the scheme pertaining to BA (Honours), BSc and MA courses only if it was given an adequate building and maintenance grant and if all other colleges were also required to simultaneously participate in the university scheme.[21]

---

19 Proceedings of the meetings of the Board of Trustees held on 5 February 1935 and 12 February 1935 in the college.

20 Proceedings of the meetings of the Board of Trustees held on 28 June and 1 July 1935.

21 Proceedings of the meeting of the Board of Trustees held on 8 December 1937, p. 55.

The Board of Trustees was really trying to ensure that the financial machinery of the college did not break down and that its just and rightful claims were recognised and honoured. There was the perception that Hindu College was discriminated against because of its nationalist vision, its intense participation in the Independence struggle and because of its harbouring so many revolutionaries. While this was not necessarily true of Sir Maurice Gwyer's attitude, there had always been a difference in the treatment of St. Stephen's and Hindu College. The antagonism between Sir Maurice Gwyer and Sir Shri Ram did not help matters either. As Khushwant Singh and Arun Joshi have pointed out:

> The only serious clash that Shri Ram had was with the Vice Chancellor, Sir Maurice Gwyer. The two had long known each other and had once travelled on the same boat from England to India. They took an instant dislike to each other. The dislike erupted into their needling each other at meetings and exchanging acrimonious correspondence. Sir Maurice felt that Shri Ram threw his weight about; that he was eager to become a member or chairman of whatever committee he could; and being only semi-literate (in the estimation of Sir Maurice) had no business to have the dominant voice in educational matters. Most of their disagreements were aired over the affairs of Hindu College.[22]

The wrangle with the authorities continued well into the 1940s. In March 1940, the Board of Trustees again resolved to inform the vice chancellor that the college would move to the new university only when funds were available and necessary safeguards had been provided. The earlier estimates for the college buildings were Rs 12,51,770. A minimum of Rs 9 lakh was required to make the move worthwhile. The college had only Rs 1 lakh in the building fund and it could add Rs 50,000 in the following five years. The sale of its premises would yield Rs 2 lakh.

However, there were additional difficulties; the original estimate of Rs 1 lakh for the hostel had increased considerably because of the outbreak of World War II so a further grant of Rs 50,000 was needed. In actual fact, the cost had more than doubled and all the resources were exhausted. Moreover, the shoddily constructed building collapsed even before it was occupied. This caused a major disagreement between Vice Chancellor, Sir Maurice Gwyer and Sir Shri Ram, Chairman of the college Governing Body at that time. Sir Maurice Gwyer voiced his discontent about the Governing Body and Sir Shri Ram. He made no secret of his view that the affairs of all the four colleges of which Sir Shri Ram was the chairman—Hindu, Ramjas, Indraprastha and Commerce—were in a bad way because of him. Gwyer disbursed Rs 5.5 lakh of the university building fund given by the government for colleges singling out Hindu College as the sole recipient for 'nil'. Sir Shri Ram protested to Minister of Education, Maulana Abul Kalam Azad, on 3 March 1948:

22 Khushwant Singh and Arun Joshi, *Shri Ram: A Biography* (New York: Asia Publishing House, 1968), pp. 180-181.

I am writing this personal letter in connection with a matter relating to the Hindu College ... As you are no doubt aware I have been associated with a number of colleges in Delhi for some time, and know the difficulties they have had to experience in the University during recent years. The Hindu College ... received very little consideration at the hands of the former Government (British) ... Its difficulties have rather increased ... in connection with the hostel building we tried to put up some time in 1941. I enclose herewith a separate statement of the actual facts of the case. The Vice Chancellor has taken an adverse view of the whole affair ... but so far as I can see, our chief offence has been that we have fallen into line with the views of the government as well as the university a little too complacently and carried out all their directions, both in letter and in spirit. The collapse of the hostel building was due to two causes—bad design and bad workmanship—and the main responsibility in regard to both rests elsewhere than with the college ... whereas the Vice Chancellor would fasten it on to the college alone. We appointed the architects approved by the Government of India, we submitted the plans and estimates in detail to both the Government and the University. The C.P.W.D. made certain suggestions and we gave effect to them. But, if, at a later stage, the design of the columns was found to be defective, I am sure, you will agree that it is the architects and the C.P.W.D. that are to be held responsible and not the laymen who constitute the Governing Body of the college. With regard to bad workmanship, it was the college that complained and in spite of the architects certificate to the contrary ... it was the Vice Chancellor who insisted that a reference be made to the C.P.W.D. It was done and the latter issued clearance certificate to the contractor and so he had to be paid ... I acted on the certificate of the C.P.W.D. and allowed them to continue the work. The whole thing proved to be a disaster.... The Vice Chancellor, however, has taken the view that the whole responsibility rests with the college, and that the building must be dismantled and put up afresh at a cost of 4.5 lakhs at the entire charge of the college. I need hardly say how unjust the position is ... the Principal of the college has repeatedly suggested the Vice Chancellor to appoint an impartial committee to go into the matter, and allocate responsibility, but the Vice Chancellor has declined to entertain the suggestion ... the matter has come to a head, for the Vice Chancellor has intimated a few days ago that a sum of Rs 5.5 lakh had been provided by the Government of India for the purpose of collegiate buildings on the University site, and I understand that he had decided to distribute the amount among other colleges, leaving the Hindu College severely alone. I do not think I need to comment any further on the matter.

As certain adverse comments had been made on the college, we decided, some time ago, to institute legal proceedings against both the contractor and the architect and the matter is still before the Court. But I would beg that an impartial committee be

> appointed to go into the whole question and allocate responsibility, and I need hardly add that the college would be willing to abide by its decision....[23]

A year later new charges were brought against the college. Sir Shri Ram wrote to Dr Radhakrishnan, Chairman, University Grants Commission (UGC). Among other things he said:

> I understand that in the memorandum, which the University of Delhi has submitted to you, certain remarks have been made which reflect on the management of the four colleges with which I am connected. There is also an observation against my being the Chairman of the Governing Bodies of these colleges. I believe, the memorandum has been issued on the authority of the Vice Chancellor; and I am very sorry to find that he should have thought it fit to make these observations.
>
> I think I should tell you how I have come to be connected with these colleges.
>
> With regard to Hindu College, I was a member of the Managing Committee ... as there were a number of difficulties in connection with both the management and the staff, I was asked to become the Chairman of the Governing Body to see if things could be improved. I am glad to say that while there is still room for improvement a great deal has been achieved ... I would have succeeded completely but for the excessive interference on the part of those in authority in the University.[24]

Sir Shri Ram, charged the vice chancellor of high-handedness saying:

> ...all the colleges with which I am connected—the Hindu College, the Ramjas College and the College of Commerce are anxious to move to the new site in the University area, and have submitted their plans and estimates both to the Government and the University, but no reply has yet been received.... I think it necessary to observe that the difficulties of the colleges with which I have been associated are due largely to the attitude of the Vice Chancellor himself ... we have had to struggle against heavy odds, but have tried to carry on. If you believe that there is anything in which we have not acted properly or that my connection with the college to which the Vice Chancellor has referred, is or has been against their interest, I need hardly say how happy I should be to put things right, and get myself relieved.[25]

---

23 Arun Joshi, *Lala Shri Ram: A Study in Entreneurship and Industrial Management* (New Delhi: Orient Longman, 1975), pp. 392-393.

24 Ibid., p. 393.

25 Ibid., pp. 393-394.

The feud only ended with the departure of Sir Maurice Gwyer. In 1952 Sir Shri Ram was nominated member of the newly constituted Faculty of Technology as well as member of the Executive Council of Delhi University. During the same years, Dr V.K.R.V. Rao requested him to become a member of the Board of Governors of the Delhi School of Economics, which he had started. Sir Shri Ram maintained these university contacts to the very end when illness made it difficult for him to fulfill the obligations that they imposed.

Ongoing Struggle

Another issue that came up several times during the period of setting up the university and integrating its constituent colleges into its structure were the number of students that each college would accept. Hindu College was inclined to offer the opportunity of education to as many who came to its door. This led to congestion and inadequate facilities for the library, reading room, common room, staff room and others. In 1942, the university adopted the principle that a classroom should provide for 12 square feet of space per student and should not seat more than seventy-five students. By this time, the Anglo-Arabic College (Zakir Hussain College), Commercial College (Shri Ram College of Commerce), Ramjas Inter College and Indraprastha Girls' College (Indraprastha College for Women) had also become part of the university. While every other college fixed the maximum number of students between 300 and 500, Hindu College reduced its numbers to 800 from the 1,166 that it had reached in December 1941.[26]

In the university's inspection report of 1942, Hindu College was the most congested. It had 1,135 students on its rolls of which forty-four were women students. Only seventy-two lived in six scattered bungalows on the university estate. With roughly 7 square feet per student as against the required 10 square feet, it should not have had more than 793 students. The principal said that the best he could do was to try and provide 8 square feet, and for this two additional classrooms needed to be built. To do this he wanted an assurance from the university that the college would not be moved to the university site for the next five years. Alternatively, multiple sections would be needed for each year but that entailed additional staff.

The principal pointed out that the college had been given very small grants. Had the university laid the annual financial requirements of Hindu College before the Governor-in-Council, the grant would have been enhanced. The university did not agree and thought that if the Governing Body wanted to run such a big college, it should have some responsibility for its financial arrangements. The budget of the college needed to be re-scrutinised to see whether more teachers could be appointed. However, the principal refused to accept that lesser-paid

26 Board of Residence, Health and Discipline Report of Annual Inspection of the Constituent Colleges and University Departments, 1942 as presented to the Executive Council on 30 April 1942. See also Reorganisation of the Constituent Colleges of the Delhi University to Executive Council, 3 November 1942.

teachers could be employed who might prove to be equally efficient. In any case, money had to be found for increments.

The alternative of restricting admissions was equally unacceptable to the principal because he felt that, 'the college had a sort of tacit obligation to cater for the children and wards of the Delhi public who flocked to his college'. In that case, the university Inspection Board felt the Delhi public also had an obligation to help the college financially. Otherwise, there would be no alternative but to curtail admissions and reduce teaching staff. In any case, it was for the Governing Body to find funds because congestion was detrimental to efficiency. Apart from inadequate classroom accommodation, the Assembly hall was not big enough, there was no proper library; a number of small rooms were used for the purpose. The two reading rooms were also very small, measuring 14 feet by 10 feet each. Girl students did not have proper facilities.

While a new hostel was coming up, the residents lived in six bungalows on the university site allotted to the college. The Board could not approve of these arrangements. Kitchen facilities were inadequate. There were no proper dining rooms. Normally the students ate in the open when the weather permitted; otherwise in the small open verandahs. Although there were two wardens looking after three bungalows each, this was difficult for them. There were no amenities for outdoor or indoor games and the playing fields were 2 kilometres away as was the college itself. The college needed more facilities for outdoor sports. Proper medical facilities also needed to be put in place. No doctor was attached to the hostel although one lived near the bungalows and could be called upon in times of emergencies.

While Hindu College had the largest number of students and hence its challenges were bigger, the other colleges, with the exception of St. Stephen's were only marginally better off. As reorganisation of the constituent colleges of Delhi University took place in 1942, several conditions were laid down for receiving grants. One of them was that no college would have more than 600 students and even Hindu College would gradually reduce its numbers to reach the required figure by 1947-48. The teacher student ratio had to be at least 1:20. The number in the preparatory classes for Delhi University's degree courses during the transition stages would not be included in the college rolls.

The Governing Body of a college would not have more than fifteen members, of whom, not more than ten would be foundation or ordinary members. Not less than three, including the principal, were to be from the teaching staff of the college. At least two persons were to be appointed by the university. All of them, except the principal had a three-year term. The principal was the ex-officio member of the Governing Body. The powers and duties of the Governing Body were laid down and streamlined. This necessitated systematising procedures of appointing the principal and teachers, their required qualifications and terms and conditions of service. The reorganisation of the university necessitated corresponding changes in the Memorandum of Association of Hindu College. Grants from the University Grants Commission depended on these. The amendments were registered under the Societies Registration Act on 24 October 1945.

The college's move to the university campus in North Delhi in 1952 marked the end of an era. India had become an independent republic. The University of Delhi had got established not as a unitary university, an Oxbridge kind of an institution as envisaged by Sir Maurice Gwyer but as an affiliating university with its constituent colleges. A new phase began in the life of the college too as it established itself on the Delhi University campus.

In the earliest constituent colleges like Hindu College, there were deficits and these increased in subsequent years because the trusts running them did not make full payments. In the Executive Council meeting of 22 April 1967, the vice chancellor reported that he had written to the University Grants Commission taking up the question of raising the maintenance grant from 90 to 95 per cent and even to 100 per cent in the case of good colleges. This was being considered by the University Grants Commission and the grant was likely to be raised to 95 per cent. This would go a long way, he felt, in stabilising these colleges financially. It was also thought that endowment funds should be created in each of the colleges so that they did not face an uncertain financial future. The colleges, however, had not managed to create such funds although the matter had first been raised in 1958 when the provision for it had been incorporated in Statute XVIII of the Ordinance for a college seeking recognition as a constituent college by Delhi University. A constituent college was to have an endowment of Rs 5 lakh while an affiliated one that of Rs 3 lakh. In 1964 the position was reviewed as the colleges had not raised this money. Perhaps the sums envisaged were not realistic and needed to be scaled down. It was felt that the required endowment fund could be reduced to Rs 2 lakh but college trusts should guarantee to meet annual deficits. This matter continued to be discussed well up to the late 1960s.[27]

The University Grants Commission's response to the proposal that it consider giving 100 per cent grants to good colleges to prevent them from deteriorating was that in such a situation, the university could consider taking them over. However, it was reported in the Executive Council that the Delhi University Act did not provide for such a contingency. It was finally settled that constituent colleges like Hindu College should create an endowment fund of Rs 5 lakh of which Rs 3 lakh should be immediately available and the remaining could be deposited during the course of the following four years.

Library

One major struggle was to establish a proper library. Normally a library is the heart of an educational institution, but up to 1917 only 1,545 books were added to the library, averaging eighty-one volumes per year. By 1960 there were almost 29,000 books in the library but the first qualified librarian, C.P. Vashishth, was appointed only in the latter half of 1967 after Shri G.S. Nautiyal, the first librarian, retired.

The first sixty-eight years of the library were insignificant except that a separate library building was constructed after the college moved to North Campus. The library came into its

27 Minutes of the Executive Council meeting of Delhi University on 22 April 1967.

own with C.P. Vashishth who revolutionised it, literally unlocking its treasures for its readers. As one student exclaimed, 'The locks are gone. One gasps in wonder and amazement. No ... it cannot be.... A swift renaissance has triggered within the precincts of the Hindu College Library. To seek knowledge one does not have to fill in demand slips, one has just to open the (unlocked) cupboard to carry away armful of books.... Reference books too are easily accessible now.' The 'open access system' was introduced in 1967. The students were excited and eager to touch the books and make their notes in an environment where books were readily available.[28] What a change from today when photocopies and Internet rule the day.

In the 1960 issue of *The Indraprastha*, the Hindi Editor, Satyavir Tyagi, a senior journalist now, talked about Hargovind, a library attendant or Babuji as he was popularly known. Tyagi described Babuji as a lively man, getting livelier with age: 'Time has washed his hair clean white always covered by a black cap.'

Below: *Lala Bharat Ram*

C.P. Vashishth was the first qualified librarian of Hindu College

Short-statured Babuji wearing a long coat and a dhoti, invoked an instant smile with his talk and mannerism: 'With his red lips due to paan chewing and a bag containing his lunch, he will enter the college through the rear wicket gate opening towards Bungalow Road, as he lives in Kamla Nagar, and one can correct his watch, exact 10 am', because of his strict punctuality.

He was equally strict in the matter of books returned by the students. He would not relent even if a student was late only by a day. Yet some students found a way to manage a concession by tickling his funny bone. They would say, 'Babuji is angry. Give him a rasgulla.' It is not clear whether they really offered him the sweet, but it was enough to bring a smile on his face. This masterstroke worked and gave Babuji the nickname, Rasgulla.

A strict disciplinarian, he ensured no disturbance or noise in the library. He would shout, full-throated, 'Aye Mister, don't disturb here.' Everybody loved him.

Sir Shri Ram passed away in 1963 and his son Dr Bharat Ram became the chairman of the Governing Body. After his passing away, there was a quick succession of two chairmen, Lala Satya Narain Gupta and Shri S.N.P. Punj. Several issues, however, remained unresolved and their echoes can be heard even today. One of them is the question of the financial share to be paid by trust colleges for their maintenance and functioning; the genesis of this lies in the roots of the formation of Delhi University, the relationship of the university and its constituent colleges and the degree of control that the university can exercise on them. While Hindu College's endowment fund was eventually created with the help of a fund-raising show, the issues of finances and the Governing Body still have not been resolved. These issues pertain to most of the trust colleges and on their resolution depends what will be the shape of their governance in the future. Considering that the first three constituent colleges preceded the university and helped to set it up, they find the degree of administrative and financial control over them oppressive.

28 J.K. Anand, 'The Story of a Century Old College Library', *Centenary Souvenir*, Hindu College, University of Delhi, pp. 24–26.

The People

As we turn the leaves of time, it is only natural to look back and see the human emotions, passions, values and ideals that went into making Hindu College a leading institution. People have come and gone but all of them have left a mark, contributed to the collective pool and given it a part of their lives, hopes, dreams, aspirations, fears and apprehensions.

The journey of the institution has been a human journey. It had few material resources but plenty of grit and determination and a fervour for nation building. That is why all who participated and all those who are a part of it today and will be in the future will always be bound by unimaginably strong primordial ties.

The First Board

People from different walks of life came together to form the first Board of Hindu College.

***The first Managing Committee*:**

Rai Bahadur Lala Shri Krishna Dass	Banker
Rai Bahadur Lala Hardhian Singh	Banker
Rai Sahib Lala Girdhari Lal	Hony Magistrate, Pleader
Rai Bahadur Lala Piyare Lal	Pensioner, Hony Magistrate
Dr Hem Chandra Sen	Medical Practitioner
Rai Bahadur Lala Sagar Chand	Inspector of Schools
Pandit Din Dayal Sharma	Religious Preacher—Sec. Bharata Dharma Mahamandala
Lala Hazari Mal	Jeweller
Lala Ram Chand	Iron Merchant
Lala Bala Parshad	Banker
Lala Jawahar Lal	Banker

***Other members on the Board of Trustees*:**

Lala Ishri Parshad	Banker, Delhi
Babu Pearey Lal	Pleader, Delhi
Rai Bahadur Lala Kanahiya Lal	Ex. Engineer, Delhi
Lala Gopal Rai	Secretary Cloth Mills
Lala Sanchi Ram	Cloth Merchant, Delhi
Lala Basheshar Nath Goela	Pleader
Rai Sahib Lala Ganesh Das	Cloth Merchant
Rai Bahadur Lala Babu Mal	Pensioner and Engineer
Munshi Tota Ram	Pleader, Aligarh
Babu Hari Chand	Collector, Kapurthala
Rai Bahadur Lala Nihal Chand	Banker, Muzaffarnagar
Rai Bahadur Sardar Boota Singh	Contractor
Pandit Madan Mohan Malaviya	Pleader, Allahabad
Lala Jivan Mal	*Rais*
Seth Chand Mal	Banker, Bikaner
Pandit Jagan Nath Parshad	Pleader, Hoshiarpur

Previous page: *A commemorative stamp of Pandit Madan Mohan Malaviya released on his 150th Birth Anniversary in 2011. He was on Hindu College's Board of Trustees for the first ten years*

Since Krishna Dass Gurwala was the leading figure in establishing both Hindu College and the Delhi Cloth and General Mills, it is natural that many of those associated with the Delhi Cloth and General Mills were also part of establishing Hindu College; they continued to be associated with both the college and the mill with one generation succeeding the previous one. Many significant and wealthy people from trades and industries such as banking, iron, flour and jewellery joined the Board of the college. As a part of the awakening of nationalist consciousness, the heightened religious consciousness also brought men like Pandit Din Dayal Sharma of the

Bharata Dharma Mahamandala to the institution. Men from the legal profession, Pandit Madan Mohan Malaviya and later Barrister Raj Narain, and his businessman son, Shivraj Bahadur from Old Delhi; engineers, R.B. Lala Kanahiya Lal and R.B. Babu Mal; medical practitioner, Dr H.C. Sen; and teachers, Master Amir Chand and Pandit Raghubar Dayal Shastri, were all on the Board of the Hindu College Trust in the early years. There were also the *rais* (the wealthy and the powerful), such as Babu Hari Chand, Collector of Kapurthala.

Although from diverse backgrounds, they shared a common vision of nationalist education. While many came from Delhi, there were also others who came from far-off places. Munshi Tota Ram was from Aligarh; Babu Hari Chand from Kapurthala; Seth Chand Mal from Bikaner; Pandit Jagan Nath Parshad from Hoshiarpur; Lala Nihal Chand from Muzzafarnagar; Sardar Boota Singh from Rawalpindi; Lala Jivan Mal Kakkar from Peshawar; and Pandit Madan Mohan Malaviya from Allahabad. This tradition continued for a few years after the first Board. Around 1903, Seth Ram Rikh Das came from Calcutta, Raja Gokul Dass from Jabalpur and Rai Bahadur Shyam Sunder Lal from Kishangarh, being also its *diwan*. Around the 1910s, Harkishan Lal, Bar-at-Law from Lahore, Lala Sukhbir Singh, a banker from Muzaffarnagar and Thakur Dutta Dharan, a retired district judge from Gujranwala joined the Trust. The Trust gradually became more centred round Delhi from the second decade of the 1900s.

Some of the descendants of the first or early Board members continued on the Hindu College Trust through third or fourth generations. Many of them have been forgotten in the womb of time. Some are remembered by the roads, buildings and institutions named after them, some of which still survive.

Rai Bahadur Lala Sagar Chand: He came from an illustrious family of *diwans* of the erstwhile Gwalior state. His uncle, Bidhi Chand was shot dead in the struggle for liberation in 1857. Sagar Chand was an inspector of schools who opened the Sunder Nanhi Girls School in 1906 to commemorate the memory of his daughters Sunder Devi and Nanhi Devi. The only son of Seth Manak Chand, Sagar Chand also established a banking concern in Agra. A scholar in English, he served as lecturer in government colleges in Punjab. He expired in 1912. The school was later looked after by his son, Rai Sahib Moti Sagar.

Left: *Present-day photo of Sunder Nanhi Girls School*

Outside view of the Sunder Nanhi Dariba leading to the school

***Rai Sahib Moti Sagar*:** An illustrious lawyer, he joined the Bar around 1899 and very quickly gained prominence in his profession. He got the building of the Sunder Nanhi Girls School erected with the help of philanthropists. He joined the Board of Hindu College around 1912. Although he shifted to Lahore in 1914 where he became the Justice of Punjab High Court, he continued to be on Hindu College's Board. After a short period he returned to his legal practice and was made Rai Bahadur in 1923. He became the vice chancellor of Delhi University (1925–30) and was knighted in June 1930 before his premature death in Lahore in the same year.

***H.C. Sen*:** H.C. Sen Marg in the Fountain area in Old Delhi is named after him. Dr H.C. Sen was a freemason who ran his medical practice from his clinic in the area after a stint in the railways. It later became a pharmacy shop.

***Rai Bahadur Pearey Lal*:** Of Pearey Lal Motors, Janpath, New Delhi.

***Rai Bahadur Girdhari Lal*:** A pleader after whom is named L.N. Girdhari Lal School.

***Lala Ram Roop*:** A *rais* of Delhi who joined the Board of Hindu College in the 1940s. The Clock Tower in Sabzi Mandi was named after him. The school, Ram Roop Vidya Mandir, was also named after him. After him his son Lala Jagannath was on the Board of Hindu College.

Facing page: *Lala Jagannath (above); Lala Shri Krishna Dass Gurwala (below)*

Left to Right: *Dr H.C. Sen (2nd); Lala Ram Roop (3rd); Rai Bahadur Girdhari Lal (extreme right)*

Rai Sahib Moti Sagar

Lala Jagannath: An entire market in Sabzi Mandi is named after him as also a dharamshala, a school and a road in this area as he was involved in philanthropy and social activities. Deeply involved in education, Lala Jagannath was not only connected with Hindu College but also Ramjas and Indraprastha colleges.

Among the others: Adishwar Lal Jain's grandson, Shri Sheel Chandra converted his ancestral property into a multi-storeyed building on Ferozeshah Road right next to the Diwanchand Trust and Diwanshri Apartments.

Sardar Bahadur Ranjit Singh was the owner of Meridian Hotel. Later his son Charanjit Singh donated money to Hindu College for the construction of the sports complex. Ganesh Flour reminds us of Lala Maha Narain and his son Lala Kirpa Narain after whom too there is a road in Civil Lines. Raj Kumar Gupta, Lala Jagannath's son, is still a trustee.

Lala Shri Krishna Dass Gurwala and his Family History

But who was Lala Shri Krishna Dass Gurwala and what motivated him to establish Hindu College? Gurwala's grandfather, Lala Ramji Dass, was hanged by the British for his friendship and support to Emperor Bahadur Shah Zafar during the Revolt of 1857. The fortunes of both the Gurwala and Gopal Rai families were linked to the Revolt. Shri Krishna Dass Gurwala's family history has been traced by Colonel Brij Behari Sharan in *Ek Shatabdi*.[1] It begins with Lala Nodhamal, around 1560 in Lalpura, Uttar Pradesh. He was famous for his wealth and philanthropy. The name Gurwala has its genesis in one of his charitable activities. When people went on pilgrimages, Lala Nodhamal and his family arranged for their safety and also bullock carts for their travel. They also distributed *gur* (jaggery) and *chane* (gram) at various shelters for pilgrims. In 1719, one of the descendants, Lala Radhakishan and his brother Lala Chheetarmal, came to Delhi and began their own business after constructing a house in Paharganj. The family became one of the richest in Delhi and perhaps even in North India. According to the British, he had an infinite treasure of diamonds, pearls and jewels and immense wealth. He was a significant name even in European markets from whom not only rajas and nawabs but the

1 Brij Behari Sharan, *Ek Shatabdi*, pp. 66-67. See also Tara Chand, *History of the Freedom Movement in India*, Vol. II, p. 66. For Ramji Dass's involvement with Bahadur Shah Zafar, see H.L.O. Garrett, *The Trial of Bahadurshah Zafar* (New Delhi: Roli Books, 1932, rpt 2007), p. 134. Reprinted with an introduction by M.J. Akbar. See also Tara Chand, Ibid., pp. 166-167.

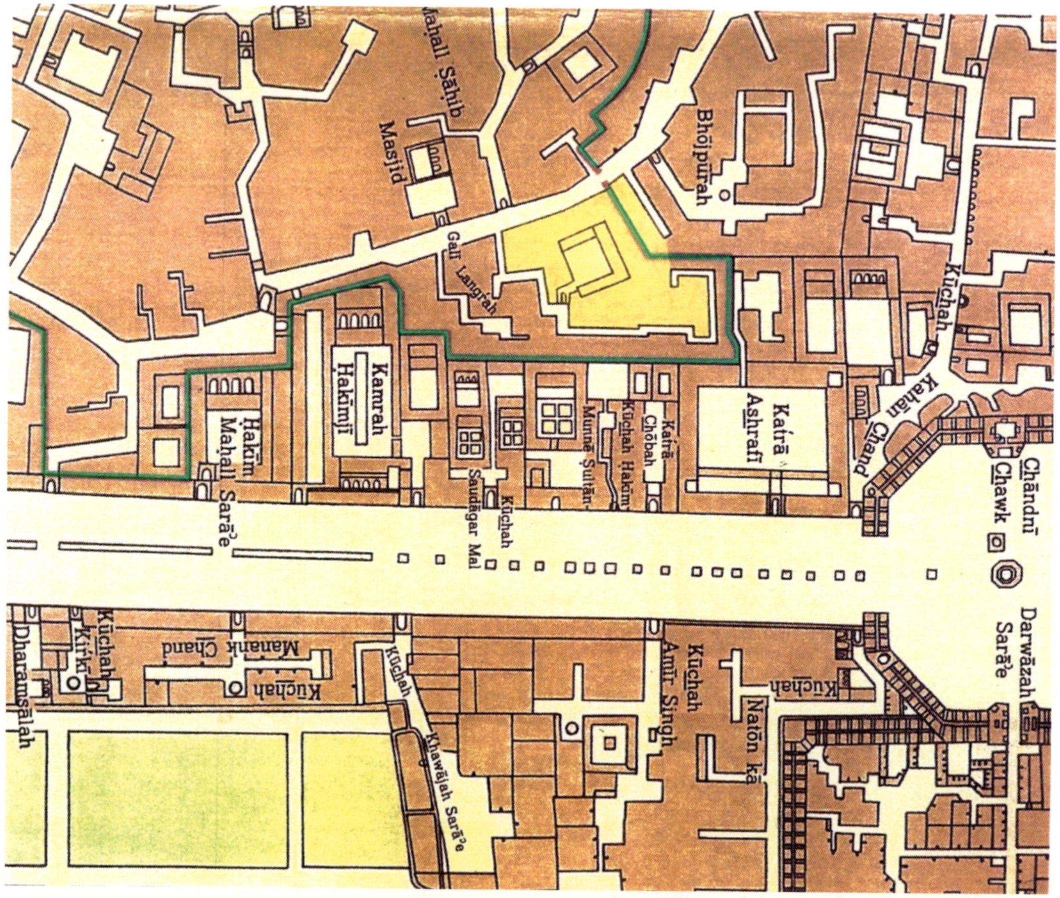

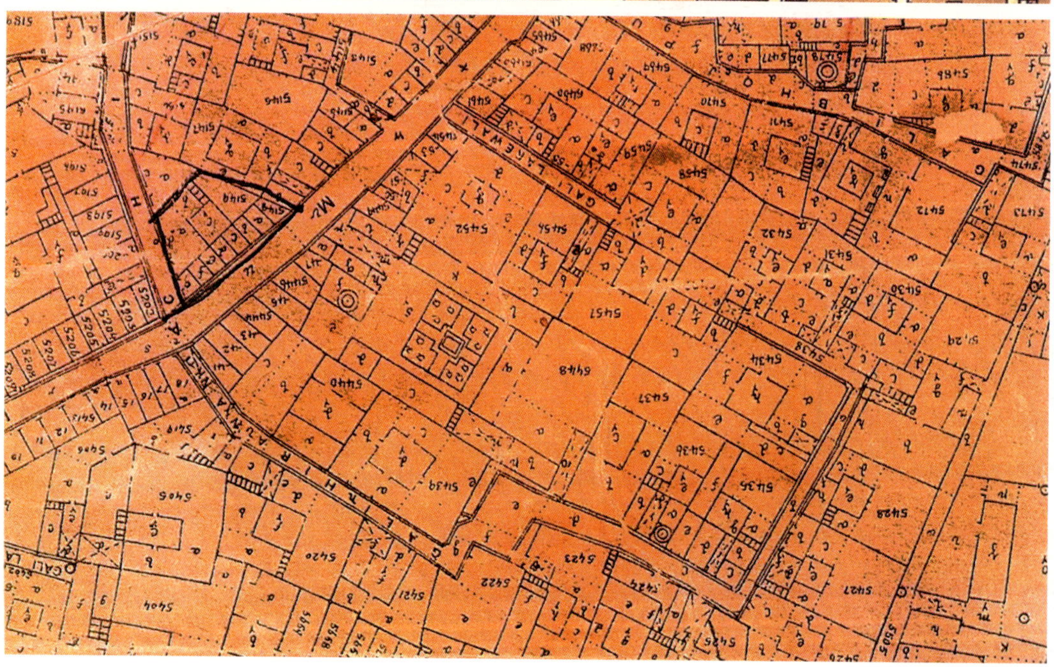

Location of Shri Rai Bahadur Gurwala's Haveli in Shahjahanabad, Delhi around 1850 (marked out in green)

Right: *Detailed plan of Rai Bahadur Gurwala's Haveli in an 1887 survey map by Mr Wilson showing the typical 'Charbagh' in the central courtyard*

Facing page: *Present condition of the main door of Gurwala house (above); Current state of Gurwala house (below); A view of the dilapidated Gurwala house from the other side (below right)*

king himself took huge sums of money on loan. Lala Ramji Dass Gurwala, whom Lord Egerton described as the 'Rothschild' of India in 1821, was a personal friend of Bahadur Shah Zafar.

According to *Ek Shatabdi*, the friendship and respect between Lala Ramji Dass and Zafar was so great that Ramji Dass was accorded the rare honour of being allowed to sit in the royal *durbar* whereas everybody else, including rajas, nawabs and even the British officers had to remain standing. He could also ride on an elephant, a privilege reserved only for the king.

Lala Ramji Dass not only gave a large amount of wealth to Bahadur Shah at the time of the uprising but also encouraged him to play a leading role in it. Ramji Dass himself plunged into the movement helping raise an army and collect information. He had immense organisational abilities and his activities became a source of anxiety for the British. When he was finally caught, hounds were set upon him, and he was tortured and hanged in front of the police station in Chandni Chowk. His house was ransacked and his property confiscated.

The Gurwalas were the worst off among the prominent families of Delhi after the Revolt. However, they still had money as a branch of their firm Bakshi Ram and Mohan Lal was in Lucknow managed by Nannemal, a relative of Ramji Dass. Lala Ramji Dass's son, Lala Narain Dass restarted his business and re-established himself. He succeeded in placating the government through his philanthropic activities and once again the family became influential. He served as an honorary magistrate and municipal commissioner for fifteen years.

Lala Narain Dass adopted Lala Shri Krishna Dass Gurwala, the youngest son of Lala Nannemal, his Lucknow partner, but passed away when his adopted son was barely fifteen years old. This left Lala Shri Krishna Dass one of the richest men in Delhi. His affairs were run by his two uncles and Lala Nannemal until he came of age in the early 1880s. In 1888, together with Gopal Rai, he founded the Delhi Cloth and General Mills and then Hindu College in 1899.[2]

2 Arun Joshi, op. cit., pp. 32–52. See also Khushwant Singh and Arun Joshi, op. cit., pp. 31–41.

AN OBITUARY

We feel deeply aggrieved at the sudden demise of the worthy Founder of our College, Rai Bahadur Lala Sri Krishan Dass Gurwalle. He it was who first conceived the idea of founding a separate college for the people of Delhi on non-sectarian basis and donated a princely sum of Rs. 65,000 to Rs. 70,000 for the same purpose. Besides this, Lalaji has been very distinctly noted as a great philanthropist whose gifts range between two to three Lacs of Rupees to various institutions in the City of Delhi. Born with a silver spoon in his mouth, Lalaji led a life of plain living and high thinking in the daily discharge of the duties assigned to him by God, towards the suffering humanity. A capitalist of a very high rank and distinction, Lalaji very ungrudgingly mixed himself with the poorest, the lowliest and the lost and always stood forth as an infinite source of inspiration to the budding generation of India. His services were so great and so very outspoken that no words of ours will convey adequately any idea concerning them.

The college, its growth, its development, and its evolution were the perpetual theme of Lalaji's thought and even upto the last moments of his life he solemnly wished welfare and wellbeing to the institution of which he was the founder. May his soul live in eternal peace and bliss in the abodes of the Most High.

A condolence meeting of the Hindu College students and staff was held on Wednesday, 28th October to mourn the death of the College Founder, Rai Bahadur Lala Shri Krishan Das Gurwalle. Principal S. K. Sen was in chair. Pandit Harnarain Shartri, the College Sanskrit Professor and an associate of the Rai Bahadur and also an early worker in the cause of the College, spoke quite feelingly about the high qualities of head and heart of the Lalaji and his great philanthropic activities in general.

Obituary of Krishna Dass Gurwala published in the college magazine

Right: *A note in 1922 from Shri Madan Mohan Malaviya praising Sat Narain Gurwala*

I have had the pleasure of knowing Lala Satya Narain Gurwala since he was a boy. He is the son of my esteemed friend, Rai Srikrishnadas Bahadur, of the well-known old firm of the Gurwalas of Delhi, which long enjoyed eminence and opulence in Delhi, and the credit of which extended far and wide. Besides taking part in promoting many other objects of public good, Rai Srikrishnadas Bahadur founded the Hindu College at Delhi and maintained it for many years at his own expense. And I cannot wish anything better for Lala Satya Narain than that he should walk in the footsteps of his father in working for the well-being for his fellow-men, and build up by his own efforts a position for himself in no way inferior to that of his esteemed father.

Delhi,
12th March 1922.

Madan Mohan Malaviya.

In 1895, Lala Shri Krishna Dass set up Krishna Mills, near Mithai-ka-Pul. He became its founder, the managing director and the biggest shareholder as in the case of Delhi Cloth and General Mills. This necessitated his resignation from the Board of Directors of DCM as the company's articles of association laid down that any director who associated himself, without the consent of the Board, with another company doing the 'same nature of business' would forfeit his post. He rejoined the DCM Board in 1905 when the mill was in serious trouble and continued till 1912, when his own financial difficulties became enormous.

Shri Krishna Dass Gurwala, suffered huge losses in the several contracts that he took for the *durbar* that was held in 1911. His firm Bakshi Ram and Mohan Lal closed down after June 1911. Though at one time he was among the richest men in Delhi, now Gurwala had to mortgage his goods, including his shares in DCM, for a loan of Rs 4 lakh from the Upper India Bank. The loan was for a new beginning but he died in 1915, in debt. One of the DCM shares, the first-ever issued, was bought by his son, Sat Narain Gurwala.

Shri Krishna Dass Gurwala was also one of the founders of the Anglo Sanskrit Victoria Jubilee Senior Secondary School presently located in Daryaganj. It is interesting that many associated with the founding of this school were also on the Board of Hindu College, not necessarily at the time of its inception but a few years later. They were a small group of enlightened and far-sighted philanthropists. Lala Amba Prasad, Rai Sahib Ishri Parshad, Rai Bahadur Lala Sheo

Below: *Sat Narain Gurwala (sitting 4th from left) in an NCC group photo*

Lala Amba Prasad's portrait from around 1915

Lala Shiv Shankar Lall (son of Rai Bahadur Amba Prasad) reading an address to the Marchioness of Willingdon (Lady Willingdon). Sir Shankar Lal sitting with her on the left, R.B. Amba Prasad on her right

Above right: *Lala Shiv Shankar Lall and his young son Bhawani Shankar with Marquess of Linlithgow, Viceroy of India (centre)*

Lala Lachhman Das

Pershad and Rai Bahadur Shri Krishna Dass Gurwala were on the Board of Hindu College at different points of time.

In Loving Memory Of Sh.Lachhman Das Garg 22.Oct.1887-16.Oct.1963

An Eminent Freedom Fighter. Worked with Mahatma Gandhi as president Harijan Sewak Sangh, Delhi, 1931-1939, Served as Municipal Commissioner MCD 1924-1939. Founder SD Public Senior Secondary School Chirakhana Nai Sarak Delhi. Dharmshala Janglimal, Pannalal Chhatta Madan Gopal, Delhi. Shri Lakshmi Narain Temple Samalkha Panipat (Haryana). Founder Member Shri Dharmik Lila Committee, Delhi. He took up Vanaprastha in 1940 & lived at Rishikesh on the Bank of River Ganga. **Lt. Col Brij Behari Sharan. # 9818071177.**

Lala Amba Prasad offered to construct the building of the school in 1916 on a land measuring 780 square yards with roads on all the three sides. The school building was built at a cost of Rs 80,000 and shifted to its present premises in Daryaganj in November 1920. Amba Cinema in Old Delhi is named after him as is the Ambadeep building in Connaught Place. After Lala Amba Prasad, his son Shri Shiv Shankar Lall joined the Board. He was followed by his son Bhawani Shankar who left a few years ago to make way for his son Ashwini Shankar. It is interesting to note that this family's association had begun in the second decade of 1900s with Lala Amba Prasad who was Ashwini Shankar's great-grandfather.

Gurwala also helped establish the Victoria Zenana Hospital but his most lasting achievement remained Hindu College. Given his deep involvement with the college, it is not surprising that after him his son Sat Narain Gurwala and his son-in-law Lachhman Das served on the Board of Hindu College Trust. While his father had served as honorary magistrate and municipal commissioner for thirty-three years being made Rai Bahadur by Lord Curzon in 1900, Sat Narain served as municipal commissioner for twelve years. He was, perhaps, the last in his family to gain prominence and take part in the polity of the city.

Whatever Lala Lachhman Das earned, he spent on building wells, ponds, ghats, temples, dharamshalas, *pathshalas*, hostels and old age ashrams.[3] Gradually he earned a name for himself

3 Lala Lachhman Das left behind an unfinished autobiography in Urdu which has been translated by his son, Col Brij Behari Sharan. *Lala Lachhman Das Garg: Atmakatha* (New Delhi, 1991).

and was the municipal commissioner of Delhi for almost eighteen years. He established the Shri Dharmic Leela Committee, Sanatana Dharma Kanya Pathshala and the Mandir Raksha Committee. He was the head of the Delhi chapter of the Harijan Sewak Sangh of which the national head was Mahatma Gandhi.

When he was fifty years old, Lala Lachhman Das handed over the business and family responsibilities to his eldest son, Shri Brij Bhushan Sharan, and renounced the material world. During the twenty-five years of *vanaprastha* he lived in a hut on the banks of river Ganga at Rishikesh, where he studied Vedanta and several religious texts. He also wrote a book. In the last years of his life, he lived on the banks of river Yamuna in an ashram. On 16 October 1963, he breathed his last. His wife Ganga Bhagirathi, Krishna Dass Gurwala's daughter, died at the age of ninety-six at her residence in Nizammuddin on 12 October 1990.

Sanatana Dharma School, Kundewalan, Ajmeri Gate

Facing page: *Obituary of Lala Lachhman Das*

Gopal Rai and his Family History

The trajectory of Gopal Rai's family provides a contrast to that of the Gurwala family.[4] His great-grandfather Ratan Chand had a confectionery business in Jhajjar, where several generations of his family had lived. He was a manufacturer, trader and moneylender all rolled into one. After the famine of 1782 life was difficult for the family. By 1803, Jhajjar and Delhi had been taken over by the East India Company, and their administration placed under the principal officer designated as the resident and chief commissioner of Delhi. The situation at this time was so bad that the arrival of the British was welcomed, particularly by tradesmen and merchants, who wanted some security.

Ratan Chand himself did not become an employee of the British, but he secured a job for his English-speaking young son Badri Dass in the British camp at Karnal in 1821 when he became treasurer in the Karnal Commissariat; he continued on this post up to 1840. From November 1838 to 30 April 1839 he was transferred to the second division of the Army of the Indus as *gomastha* of godown and stores, evidently a responsible and demanding position.

He was offered the job of *kotwal* for the civil shopping area, Sadar Bazaar, at the new military station that the British were setting up at Ferozepore. As a *kotwal* he kept accounts and ensured the procurement of whatever was required by the authorities. While he must have done his job well, Badri Dass apparently saw no conflict of interest in pursuing a commercial career simultaneously and by 1854 he owned more than half the shops in Sadar Bazaar as well as several bungalows in the cantonment which he let out to British officers for Rs 60 a month. Badri Dass came to Delhi with his son, Bishamber Dass, the son's wife and their boys Gopal

4 Khushwant Singh and Arun Joshi, op. cit., pp. 1–15; Arun Joshi, op. cit., pp. 24–45.

Rai and Girdhari Lal. It was because of the position of *kotwal* that he served, that his branch of the family came to be known as *Kotwalwale*. Subsequently another branch of the family that bought orchards outside the city came to be known as *Baghwaley*.

When Delhi fell to the soldiers at Meerut on 11 May 1857, Badri Dass had a narrow escape as he was seen as a 'collaborator' of British rule. He had to swim for his life across the Yamuna carrying with him an English couple, a remarkable physical feat for someone who was nearing sixty at that time. For this effort, Badri Dass was given a reward of Rs 50,000 with some land and property. With the reward he developed a banking business in Ferozepore that was run by two of his sons who were settled there. Badri Dass returned to Ferozepore in 1869, the seat of most of his property and business interests. He also became a shareholder in the Lahore branch of the Bank of Bengal.

Badri Dass died in 1874 leaving a small fortune. This was divided evenly between his four sons. The three elder sons, Raghunath Dass, Kishan Dass and Bhagwan Dass had extensive business interests, but the youngest Bishamber Dass was not inclined towards business and apparently found his inheritance sufficient for his needs. He had three sons. Two of them—Gopal Rai and Girdhari Lal—were close in age. Madan Mohan Lal was about twenty-five years younger. He was sent to the Anglo-Sanskrit School, which Chunnamal had founded in 1869 and then he spent one year at St. Stephen's College, the only college of higher education in the city in those days.

Facing page: *Lala Sher Singh, Shri Om Prakash, Lala Raghu Mal, Lala Hans Raj Gupta (from top to bottom)*

Gopal Rai probably attended school till he was fourteen or sixteen years old and around the mid-1860s entered the service of Ram Kishan Dass as *munim* at Chunnamal Saligram's. Around this time he married Benarsi Dass's sister who later became the head of a prominent jewellers' firm in Delhi, Ishri Dass Benarsi Dass. Gopal Rai had only one daughter; Girdhari Lal had no children. Madan Mohan Lal married Chando Devi and on 27 April 1884, a son was born to them, who was named Shri Ram.

Right: *Ashok Kumar is one of the trustees of Hindu College*

Ishwar Chand, father of Ashok Kumar

In 1896, when Shri Ram was twelve years old, Girdhari Lal died. Gopal Rai, who had a daughter, ordained that Girdhari Lal's widow, who was childless, should be provided with a child. Hence, as was customary among Agarwal *banias*, on the last day of mourning Shri Ram was seated on her lap to symbolise that she had adopted him. Shri Ram did his matriculation in 1897 from the Anglo-Sanskrit School and joined Hindu College in 1899 as one of its first students. He remained in the

college for less than one year when he left to look after the family business. Little did he know at that time that one day he would become the chairman of the same college.

Another branch of the *Kotwalwale* family came from Raghunath Dass, elder brother of Bishamber Dass. He too, was the *kotwal* of Ferozepur as was his son Govind Parshad. The latter had his hands full with his business and his duties as the last *kotwal* of Ferozepur. He did such good work that he was given two villages in Delhi—Laxmi and Manckpur—both of which he later sold. The latter is today's Model Town. Govind Parshad's son, Ishwar Chand was on the Board of Hindu College in the 1960s and the line continues with Ashok Kumar who is one of the trustees. Four temples were made in the name of Raghunath Dass at Jalandhar, Amritsar, Delhi and Ferozepur.

***Lala Sher Singh*:** With him, another strand of Shri Ram's family joined the Hindu College Trust. Sher Singh was married to Shri Ram's sister Kalavati. His brother Ranbir Singh was married to Shri Ram's second sister. Their children Shri Om Prakash and Shri Atma Prakash were part of the Hindu College Trust in the 1940s and 1950s respectively. Shruti Gupta, daughter-in-law of Shri Atma Prakash joined the Governing Body while her husband became a trustree. Lala Sher Singh owned Madura Mills. He was a big financier and even financed the Delhi Cloth Mill (DCM) at one point of time.

***Lala Raghu Mal and his descendants*:** In the second decade of the 1900s, Lala Raghu Mal, a well-known iron merchant joined the Board of Hindu College.[5] He was deeply involved in social work. A follower of Swami Dayanand Saraswati, he was one of the leading figures of the Arya Samaj movement. He got a big hostel made as 'Gurukul Indraprastha', which exists on a hillock near the Tughlaqabad station. Lala Raghu Mal also established the Indraprastha Vedic Library in Kucha Dayaram.

Lala Raghu Mal established the Raghu Mal Trust with Rs 1 lakh which runs the Raghu Mal Arya Kanya Middle School in New Delhi. In memory of Swami Shraddhananda who was shot in his own house, Raghu Mal gave the house to the Arya Public Trust. Bhagwati Devi Shishu Mandir in Ajmere Gate is named after his wife. This was apparently a publishing house.

Lala Raghu Mal's legacy in Hindu College continued with his son-in-law, Lala Hans Raj Gupta in the 1940s, and today with the latter's son Desh Raj Gupta. In February 1924, Lala Raghu Mal's daughter Angira was married to Lala Hans Raj Gupta who came from a family of freedom fighters. After the marriage, Lala Hans Raj returned to Allahabad to do an MA in Economics while simultaneously pursuing his LLB. As Lala Hans Raj was trying to decide his future course of action, his father-in-law asked him to join his business in Calcutta. He wanted to become a

5 *Vinay Aur Vivek—'Shri Hansraj Gupta ki Bahumukhi Sevaon ke Uplakshya Mein Samarpit Abhinandan Granth',* ch. ed. Yashpal Jain (New Delhi: Shri Hansraj Gupta Abhinandan Granth Samaroh Samriti Prakashan, 1972).

Facing page: *Board of Directors & Managing Agents DCM 1957 (above); Board of Directors and Managing Agents of DCM, 1960-61 (below)*

Board of Directors and Managing Agents of The Delhi Cloth & General Mills Co. Ltd (DCM), 1954-55

Chartered Accountant but this he could only do by going to England. Three or four days before the date of departure his father-in-law fell ill and he had to abandon his plans. He returned to Calcutta. Raghu Mal died and Hans Raj Gupta had to devote himself to the business. Disputes arose between the beneficiaries of Lala Raghu Mal and the next fourteen years of Lala Hans Raj Gupta's life were spent in litigation. When the court appointed a receiver who auctioned Lala Raghu Mal's entire estate, Hans Raj Gupta bought it and established his business.

After consolidating the business Hans Raj Gupta moved to Delhi. He built on his share of his father-in-law's business. In 1937 Hans Raj Gupta also started looking after the Delhi Iron Syndicate and got involved not only in the business of iron but also other allied businesses that his father-in-law had been involved in, especially in the business of jaggery under his firm called Madhoram Budhsingh.

Hindu College and DCM

Since many people overlapped on the boards of DCM and the Hindu College Trust, the events in one impacted those in the other. This can be seen in the case of people like Gopal Rai, Madan Mohan Lal, Lala Hardhian Singh, Shri Ram, Shri Radha Kishan, Sardar Boota Singh, Rai Bahadur Lala Sultan Singh, Lala Chandu Lal, Sat Narain Gurwala, Lala Ram Roop and his son Shri Jagannath, Lala Hans Raj Gupta, Lala Hanuman Parshad and Lala Bhiku Ram Jain to

Front Row: Shri Ram Kishan Das · Rai Sahib Sri Ram · Shri Bhiku Ram Jain · Sir Shri Ram (*Chairman*) · Shri S. L. Kirloskar · Shri Hanuman Pershad Gupta · Shri Kamalnayan Bajaj · Shri Bishan Chandra

Back Row: Shri Jagan Nath · Shri Narain Prasad · Shri Bharat Ram · Shri Ram Pershad · Shri Uma Charan

name some who not only served on both the boards but also made active contributions to both DCM and Hindu College.

For example, the most important problem faced by DCM in 1903 was the procurement of cotton and how to raise money to pay the bills. These problems were compounded by Gopal Rai's illness and a cotton famine towards the end of 1903, which made quality cotton impossible to get. Madan Mohan Lal had to take on greater responsibilities because of his brother's ill health. In 1904, the Board set up a committee under Hardhian Singh to supervise the work and to provide him general assistance.

Members common to both the college and the business, like Sardar Boota Singh, Rai Bahadur Sultan Singh and advocates Sri Ram and Chandu Lal, worked together. They also had their share of differences especially when times were hard during the period of World War I.

Below: *Skinner's bungalow*

Lala Raghubir Singh

And Others Followed

Rai Bahadur Lala Sultan Singh joined the Board of Hindu College around 1910. He was also very interested in girls' education and was one of the founders of the first girls' school in Delhi, the Indraprastha School in the Jama Masjid area.

Sultan Singh, a doyen of the Jain community, was a vibrant personality and got along famously with the British. He was accorded *Quaiser-e-Hind*, the highest honour the British bestowed on Indians at that time. However, he got involved with Motilal Nehru, Mahatma Gandhi, Bal Gangadhar Tilak and others in the national movement which led him to return the honour to the British saying that he may not be able to accept their colonial vision any more. Sultan Singh sold his house in Kashmere Gate, which was earlier Colonel Skinner's bungalow, to Hindu College from where the college functioned till it moved to its own building in the university campus in 1952.

After Sultan Singh, his son Raghubir Singh joined the Hindu College Trust. While the father was involved with the concept of education and donated to institutions like Indraprastha and Hindu colleges, in reality he was not an educationist; his son Raghubir Singh was. He founded Modern School at the young age of twenty-five.[6] He strongly believed that India would be free one day and it

6 As told by Shri Ashok Pratap Singh, Honorary President, Board of Trustees, Modern School, New Delhi.
See Khushwant Singh and Syeda Saiydain Hameed (eds), *A Dream Turns Seventy Five: The Modern School 1920–1995* (New Delhi: Allied Publishers Limited, 1995).

would then need people who could combine the best of British administrative abilities with a great deal of understanding of India. Annie Besant was very close to him and he believed in her and followed her. After Raghubir Singh, his son Major General Virendra Singh was an active member of the Trust. Now his daughter-in-law, Meera Virendra Singh is a trustee.

***Lala Hanuman Parshad*:** He facilitated Hindu College's move from Kashmere Gate to the university campus. He joined the Hindu College Board in the 1940s while the college was functioning from Kashmere Gate. He arranged a government loan and had the college building constructed at its present location in the university area.

Lala Hanuman Parshad was a friend of Lala Shri Ram and got deeply involved in education. He was the only child of Lala Chunni Lal, one of the oldest families of Delhi popularly known as *Topkhanewale*. The family was called *Topkhanewale* because during the Mughal period Hanuman Parshad's ancestors were in charge of ammunition stores for which they were given this title.

Lala Hanuman Parshad graduated from St. Stephen's College then read Law from Delhi University. He came in close contact with Mahatma Gandhi, Jawaharlal Nehru and other stalwarts of the freedom movement through Brij Krishna Chandiwale, his Gandhian maternal uncle. In his own way he helped the movement by contributing generously in jewellery and cash. It is said that he also went to England as part of the delegation to attend the Round Table conferences.

Although a businessman, social service and education were Hanuman Parshad's passion. He was deeply involved as a member of the Board of Trustees with Modern School, Indraprastha

Above left: *Major General Virendra Singh (right) with Dr Kavita A. Sharma (left)*

Above right: *Lala Hanuman Parshad*

School, Ramjas School, Ramjas College, Indraprastha College, Lady Shri Ram College, Janki Devi Mahavidyalaya and Hindu College of which he was the treasurer. Lala Hanuman Parshad donated around Rs 5 lakh to Modern School for a gymnasium named after his father Lala Chunni Lal.

In the 1910s and 1920s two names emerged, of Lala Kedar Nath better known as Rai Kedar Nath and Seth Laxmi Narain Gadodia.[7]

***Lala Kedar Nath*:** His most significant contribution was establishing the Ramjas group of educational institutions. His work for education in Delhi was pioneering, progressive and invaluable as he concentrated on serving the poor, the backward and the less privileged sections of society.

Kedar Nath graduated from Lahore when the Government College was shifted there from Delhi. After doing his Masters from Calcutta, he taught in the Government School in Delhi in 1884. In 1885 he married Ganga Devi, daughter of Lala Murlidhar of Roorkee. In the same year he passed the Punjab Provincial Competitive Examination and was posted as deputy commissioner in Multan in Punjab. Meanwhile, he opted for judicial service and soon became a district judge. Kedar Nath was deeply influenced by the life and work of Swami Dayanand Saraswati. Wherever he was posted, he engaged in social work. His death-defying work during the plague epidemic of 1904-05 in Jhung-Maghiana bears witness to his spirit of social service.

Early deaths of all his children ended Kedar Nath's lineage. However, Kedar Nath picked up courage, sought voluntary retirement in 1911 and devoted himself to social work. He wanted to work in Punjab but when he heard of the financial crisis at Hindu College he shifted to Delhi and made it the base for his social work. He became the secretary of the College Trust in January 1912 and soon collected Rs 52,000 for it thus putting it on a sound financial footing at least for the time being.

In 1912, Lala Kedar Nath founded a school in memory of his father in Kucha Ghasi Ram, Fatehpuri, Delhi which is today known as Ramjas School No. 1 in Daryaganj. He founded Ramjas School No. 2 at Anand Parvat in 1916 largely for the underprivileged and the marginalised. Anand Parvat was almost a desolate and deserted place during those days but here he laid the foundation for his future cultural and educational projects to be undertaken by the Ramjas Foundation.

On 25 December 1916, Kedar Nath gave away everything to the Ramjas institutions. This gave them new momentum and the Ramjas College Society was founded. Ramjas College came into existence in 1917. The act of renunciation on the part of Kedar Nath touched Lala Laxmi Narain Gadodia who too donated generously to the Ramjas institutions.

---

7 Ram Chandra Pradhan, *Bhagavadgita, a Primer and Life-Sketch of Karmayogi Lala Rai Kedarnath* (Noida: Bhagavadgita International Foundation, 1995, 4th edn 2004).

Seth Laxmi Narain Gadodia:[8] He was a close associate of Shri Jamnalal Bajaj and Mahatma Gandhi and was a great nationalist, philanthropist and a strong proponent of education; he was also on the Board of Hindu College. He established the Nandgram Gadodia Library in the name of his father, with the objective of making books available to poor students. He was an active member of several education trusts that ran Ramjas College, Hindu College, Commercial College and Indraprastha Girls College and School. The importance of girls' education was accelerated by the reform movement of the nineteenth century. It received special attention from Hindu religious organisations. The efforts were to provide both religious and secular education. Realising the importance of girls' education Seth Laxmi Narain Gadodia opened the Gadodia Girls School at Kucha Natwan in 1907.

Seth Laxmi Narain Gadodia

Gadodia's Swadeshi Store was attacked by Chandrashekhar Azad whose close associate, Vishwambhar Dayal, worked there. Dayal told Azad that the cash was locked up at around 10 pm and that there was about Rs 14,000 in the shop at that time. When Azad attacked the store, Vishwambhar Dayal not only slid the bag of cash towards him but also opened the iron safes and placed the bag of gold ornaments in front of him. Azad said that they were revolutionaries, not professional robbers and would not touch the jewellery of their mothers and sisters.[9]

Azad and his associates decamped with three bags of cash containing about Rs 14,000. Azad gave Vishwambhar Dayal some money to procure arms from Rajasthan. On hearing Azad's statement, Seth Laxmi Narain was so impressed that he denied that he had faced any loss. The police could not clinch the case against Vishwambhar Dayal and had to acquit him.

> *Among the other founders*: Lala Bala Parshad, a well-known trader, financier and an accounting wizard and Rai Sahib Lala Ganesh Das, a cloth merchant whose family is still in the same business in Chandni Chowk. Jivan Mal Kakkar another original founder trustee came from Peshawar and settled initially in Shimla before coming to Delhi.

Narottam Morarji Gokuldas: He joined the Hindu College Board around 1903, and was an eminent businessman with major interests in shipping. His father, Morarji Gokuldas was

8 Manudutt Sharma (ed.), 36th no. of *Agrawal Itihas Granth Samuchchay* (Hissar: Shri Durbar Karyalaya, 2001).

9 Oral Interview of Professor N.K. Nigam, Oral History Transcript No. 70, Nehru Memorial Museum and Library, recorded on 1 March 1968. See also N.K. Nigam, *Balidan: Chandrashekhar Azad ki Romanchkari Jeevani,* pp. 70-71.

a textile magnate. Narottam Morarji managed two mills—Morarji Gokuldas Mill of Bombay and Sholapur Mill of Sholapur—while studying at Elphinstone College. He later came in close contact with Mahatma Gandhi, Dr Annie Besant, Dadabhai Naoroji, Rabindranath Tagore, Sarojini Naidu and Motilal Nehru. He established the Scindia Steam Navigation Company Ltd. on 27 March 1919. On 5 April 1919, Scindia's first ship, S.S. *Loyalty*, sailed from Bombay to the United Kingdom and unfurled the Indian shipping flag in international waters. Narottam Morarji died on 5 November 1929. The Government of India issued a postage stamp in his honour in 1977.

Shops owned by Hazarimal Jewellers, one of the founder trustees and of Lala Bulakidas Gotewala who joined around 1911 still exist.

In the late 1930s, Behari Lal Jaipuria of the firm Behari Lal Beni Prasad, and the son of Chunnilal Jaipuria came on board. Lala Har Prasad Agarwal, the elder brother of Shri Ram Charan Agarwal—Shri Prakash and Jai Prakash Agarwal's father—joined in the mid-1940s. In the 1940s and 1950s came Shri Virendra Swarup Mathur of Atlas Cycles, R.B. Janki Dass, the owner of Janaki Dass and Sons in Connaught Place and Shri Bhiku Ram Jain of the Jain Motor Car Company. Jain was an active Congressman who became the mayor of Delhi and was a member of Parliament from the Chandni Chowk area. Shri Ram Kumar Gupta with his hardware business called Modern Hardware in front of Super Bazaar in Connaught Place joined the Board in the late 1950s. He had a long association with the Ramjas Trust as did his cousin Shri Satya Narain Gupta, who was the chairman of the Hindu College Trust for about fifty years along with being a member of the Governing Body and later its chairman.

Below: *Ghanshyam Das Birla*

Narottam Morarji

***Ghanshyam Das Birla*:** The most prominent industrialist to join the Board of Hindu College in the mid-1940s, Ghanshyam Das Birla belonged to the influential Birla family. Born in 1894 in Jaipur state in one of the richest and most prosperous merchant families of India, Ghanshyam Das had little formal education but later, through newspapers, books and dictionaries he learnt a lot of History, Economics, English, Sanskrit and one or two other Indian languages. He was a voracious reader. He was a nationalist who was closely associated with Mahadev Desai and Rajendra Prasad, with whom he corresponded regularly on various subjects of national importance. He came under Sardar Patel's influence eight years before the latter's death and the mutual attachment continued to the end. Lala Lajpat Rai and Pandit Madan Mohan Malaviya were among Birla's earliest associates; they were also responsible for his brief incursion into politics as a member of their party. Gandhiji's sincerity and search for truth was the dominant influence in Birla's life. An active participant in the freedom struggle in the 1930s and 1940s, Ghanshyam Das Birla was a visionary. He firmly believed that India needed industrialisation as a means for creating and raising the standard of living for an average Indian. For this, he was even willing to seek the cooperation of the British.

Ghanshyam Das Birla founded and maintained public and educational institutions in various parts of the country, the best being at Pilani where the Gandhian scheme of basic education found a place in the curriculum. The Birla Education Trust gave impetus to the emancipation of women and the upliftment of Harijans. Ghanshyam Das Birla was honoured with a Padma Vibhushan in 1957 by the Government of India and with the degree of Honorary Doctor of Law by Banaras Hindu University in 1967.

Religious Reinvigoration

Just as the strand of nationalist industrialisation and a wealthy civil society found its way to the Hindu College Education Trust, so did religious reinvigoration after 1857. Both the Sanatana Dharma and Arya Samaj tried to exert their influence and they found their representatives on the Board. In 1877-78, Swami Dayanand made a whirlwind tour of Punjab and Delhi. He spoke vehemently against social and caste prejudices and called for a new systematic education system based on Vedanta with emphasis on Hindu revivalism. This stimulated the founding of the Arya Samaj on 1 November 1878. As it began to gain in influence from the 1880s, the Arya Samaj spurred a reaction among orthodox Hindu organisations. Religious societies sprang up to promote the *sanatana* religion and to keep a check on Arya Samajists and the proselytising activities of the missionaries.

The Sanatana Dharma organisation, Bharata Dharma Mahamandala, founded by Pandit Din Dayal Sharma, reached Delhi in 1890-91. Din Dayal Sharma had a project of establishing a Sanskrit Mahavidyalaya or college in Delhi. In 1893, the Mahamandala's most important issue was the projected Sanskrit College; a resolution for this was reaffirmed in 1895. Controversy over social customs erupted in Delhi in December 1898 at a meeting of the Vaish conference. The proponents of radical reforms clashed with the more traditionally minded. This generated considerable support among orthodox Vaish and Aggarwal communities for the Sanskrit College.

The controversy at the Vaish conference provided support for a college based on Hindu ideals. In 1899, Pandit Din Dayal was successful in getting support for Hindu College. Din Dayal and the Mahamandala opened the college on 15 May 1899, adding an orthodox institution to the city's educational establishment. The main financial support for the college came from members of the Sanatana Dharma Sabha of Delhi. Krishna Dass Gurwala was the chief financier who supported the college with permanent grants and rent for five years. Other members like Narain Das, Munshi Jivan Lal, Pearey Lal, R.B. Lala Hardhian Singh and R.B. Pandit Janki Nath raised subscriptions. In 1900, the Maharaja of Darbhanga was also called on to support the college.

Pandit Raghubar Dayal Shastri**:** Born in a *kayastha* family, he was always called 'Pandit ji' thus shattering the myth that the term was reserved for Brahmins only. The Sanatana Dharma stream of thought found its expression when Pandit Shastri joined the Board of Hindu College Trust in the second decade of the 1900s. He was Professor of Sanskrit at St. Stephen's College. He became the bursar of the St. Stephen's College and for a short time was also its vice principal under Mr S.K. Rudra. This showed the high level of confidence that the Cambridge

Mission authorities had in him. He was an ardent nationalist and together with C.F. Andrews was kept under surveillance by the CID.[10]

Raghubar Dayal Shastri bore the humiliation of being under police watch without a murmur. He stood firm in his vision and belief in the Sanatana Dharma. At St. Stephen's, he founded the Hindu Religious Association, delivered lectures on Hinduism to the whole college thus bringing awareness about the classic documents of Hinduism. But there was no trace of proselytising or communal antagonism.

After about eighteen years at St. Stephen's, Raghubar Dayal Shastri left to become the vice principal of the Oriental College in Lahore for a short time. He then became the principal of the Sanatan Dharma College, Lahore in June 1917, a year after it was established. He wanted to make Sanatan Dharma College an ideal Hindu institution. His dream was to plant such Hindu institutions throughout the length and breadth of the country where young Hindu men would be trained to go out into the world ready to sacrifice for the sake of their dharma.

***Master Amir Chand*:** Another strand that emerged in the Hindu College Board, although briefly, was an active revolutionary one. Amir Chand was born in an Agarwal (*vaish*) family in Delhi. His exact date of birth is not known but at the time of his execution in 1915 he was nearly fifty years old. Before the uprising his ancestors had a thriving trade and owned considerable property in Dariba in Delhi. Amir Chand's father, Hukam Chand, was first a district magistrate in Lahore, then a High Court judge in Hyderabad and finally a legal adviser to the Nizam. In terms of social status, his was an orthodox upper-middle-class family. Amir Chand was married at the age of twelve but became a widower after about five years. A protagonist of women's rights, Amir Chand took a vow not to remarry because widows were generally not allowed the right to remarry. The family lost everything in the 1857 uprising.

Amir Chand was a student of St. Stephen's School and St. Stephen's College. A teacher by profession, he had a good circle of friends. Among them were engineers, professors and English missionaries teaching at St. Stephen's College. Hanumant Sahay, Avadh Behari, Bal Mukand and Basant Kumar Biswas were his associates in the revolutionary group. He had direct contact with his students, Lala Hardayal and Ras Behari Bose. The Partition of Bengal and the repressive measures of the government made Amir Chand a staunch revolutionary. He was fully engaged in the Swadeshi and Boycott movements. He sent copies of his boycott speeches to the police. In 1908, he brought out an Urdu weekly, *Akash*, which was edited by Ram Chandra, a revolutionary from the North-West Frontier Province. However, this public platform had to be abandoned soon because of bureaucratic repression.

With Lala Hardayal, Master Amir Chand organised the Revolutionary Party. Meanwhile the government decided to shift the capital from Calcutta to Delhi. Bengal extremists and the

10 Sanatan Dharma College magazine 1928-29 Lahore, brought out in his memory after his death on 13 April 1929.

Delhi revolutionary group joined hands and in 1912, at the signal of Ras Behari Bose, Basant Kumar Biswas, dressed as a woman, threw a bomb at Lord Hardinge from the roof of the Punjab National Bank building, as the viceregal procession was passing near Chandni Chowk.

Opinions differ as to how the police got a clue about Amir Chand and his revolutionary associates. Large-scale hunts led to Amir Chand and several of his associates being arrested. The case was conducted on the evidence of two approvers and he seems to have been defended by Babu Moti Sagar, Lala Sagar Chand's son and a leading lawyer on the Board of Hindu College. However, Amir Chand was sentenced to death in 1914. Appeals to the High Court and the Privy Council were rejected, and he was hanged in April 1915. Apparently the building from which the bomb was thrown belonged to Sultan Singh and Amir Chand had been a tutor to Raghubir Singh recommended by C.F. Andrews whom Sultan Singh regarded as his close friend.

The Independent Professionals

The rise of independent professionals was an important phenomenon of the time. Among the original trustees were Lala Girdhari Lal, Babu Pearey Lal, Lala Basheshar Nath, Munshi Tota Ram and Pandit Jagan Nath Parshad who were pleaders, while Lala Kanahiya Lal was an engineer. More professionals joined over time like Rai Sahib Sri Ram in the 1930s. He was also legal adviser to DCM as was Premjus Roy who joined in the late 1950s. Chandu Lal, Bar-at-Law came in the 1940s. His daughter married Shyam Nath who became the mayor of Delhi and their daughter Veena also studied at Hindu College. Raj Narain's son, Shiv Raj Bahadur remained the chairman of the Hindu College Governing Body for several years. Their best-known descendant today is Sheila Dhar née Bahadur, granddaughter of Raj Narain and niece of Shivraj Bahadur. Rameshwar Nath, a leading advocate of the Supreme Court and owner of the Kashi House in Connaught Place joined the Trust in the 1960s.

Premjus Roy

Pandit Madan Mohan Malaviya: He was a founder trustee and remained with the Trust for the first ten years. Born in Allahabad on 25 December 1861 in a Brahmin family, which was poor but of a good social status, Malaviya's grandfather Pandit Pran Dhar and father Pandit Braj Nath were known for their Sanskrit scholarship. Young Madan Mohan was sent to Pandit Hardeva's Dharma Gyanopadesh Pathshala at the age of five where the emphasis was on discipline and religion rather than on formal education. He left the *pathshala* and joined the third class of the Zilla School in 1869. He matriculated in 1879 and joined Muir Central College, Allahabad. Here he came under the influence of Pandit Aditya Ram Bhattacharya, a Professor of Sanskrit whom he revered.

Madan Mohan Malaviya wanted to study further but poverty compelled him to take up a teaching job in his old school. Public life attracted him so he attended the second Congress session held in Calcutta in 1886 with his Sanskrit Professor, Pandit Aditya Ram Bhattacharya. He delivered such an impressive speech there that A.O. Hume, General Secretary of the Congress, mentioned it appreciatively in his annual report. Soon, Raja Rampal Singh, an enlightened *taluqdar* of Oudh who had heard his Calcutta speech offered Madan Mohan editorship of the Hindi weekly, *Hindustan*, for a salary of Rs 300 a month. Malaviya edited the paper from July 1887 to the end of 1889, during which period it was converted into a daily. Raja Rampal Singh continued to give him Rs 100 per month even after he left the paper and became a lawyer passing his LLB examination in 1891. He was also the editor of the weekly, *Indian Union*, started by Pandit Aditya Ram Bhattacharya from 1885 to 1890.

Madan Mohan Malaviya started practising in the High Court in 1893 but clients had begun approaching him even while he was studying. His fame as a lawyer spread quickly through the province. Although he had to look after a large family, Malaviya preferred public work to his legal practice. He gradually suspended his legal practice to devote time to collect funds for the Mac-Donnell University Boarding House, which was built in 1903. He virtually withdrew from the legal profession in 1909, but in 1922 he took up the defence of 225 persons condemned to death in connection with the Chauri Chaura riots because of which Mahatma Gandhi had suspended the Civil Disobedience Movement. He saved 153 accused from the gallows.

Malaviya's zeal for public work made him realise the necessity of starting newspapers, particularly in Hindi, for the education of the public. He started the Hindi weekly, *Abhyudaya*, in 1907 and made it a daily in 1915. He also started *Maryada*, a Hindi monthly, in 1910 and when questions relating to the peasants of Oudh came to the fore, he started *Kisan*, a Hindi monthly, in 1921. He started *Leader*, an English daily on 24 October 1909. He was mainly responsible for the collection of funds needed to keep the papers alive. Both *Abhyudaya* and *Leader* rendered valuable service to the cause of the national freedom for nearly half a century. Madan Mohan Malaviya was the chairman of the Board of Directors of the *Hindustan Times* from 1924 to 1946.

Although a strong supporter of the Congress, Madan Mohan Malaviya founded the Hindu Mahasabha in 1906. According to his supporters, he was not trying to oppose the just claims of the Muslim community but the 'divide and rule' policy of the British government. Banaras Hindu University was Malaviya's greatest achievement. It emerged from his deep love for Hindu culture and the spiritual ideas embodied in Hindu religious books. The scheme for the university was drawn up through discussions with his friends and the cooperation of Annie Besant, the Maharajadhiraj of Darbhanga and the Maharaja of Banaras. The importance of the economic development of the country made Malaviya combine the teaching of science and technology with that of religion. Colleges of agriculture, engineering, mining, metallurgy and geology, the Ayurvedic College and an allopathic hospital, which was named after Pandit Sunder Lal, the first vice chancellor of the Banaras Hindu University, were started soon after its establishment. This made the Banaras Hindu University pre-eminent among the then existing Indian universities.

Jugal Kishore Khanna: He followed in the same tradition of being a professional deeply embedded in the freedom movement and social work. He was a freedom fighter who went on to become a member of the Constituent Assembly where he served actively in the drafting of the Constitution. He can be seen in the first photographs of the Parliament of 1947. Jugal Kishore was also a member of the Governing Body of Ramjas College and of the Trust for Ramjas schools. He entered into the political arena as a college student and joined Mahatma Gandhi's Independence movement in May 1918. He played a prominent part in the Swadeshi movement and the Satyagraha and Quit India movements. His whole family including his wife, Rama Rani, daughter Sheila, and nephew Ved Prakash Khanna made immense sacrifices in the struggle of 1942. His residence in Katra Neel in Old Delhi functioned as the high command from where all the directions and guidelines were issued.

As a leading lawyer and the secretary of the Bar Council, Jugal Kishore often defended those who were politically accused during the freedom struggle. He was member of the defence council of Netaji Subhash Chandra Bose's historic INA trial. He was the secretary of the INA Relief and Rehabilitation Committee for more than three decades. At the time of India's Partition in 1947 Jugal Kishore served as an honorary special magistrate to prevent riots and disturbance.

Jugal Kishore was remarkable for providing selfless service for the welfare of the people. In 1918 when cholera and influenza epidemics were raging, wiping off hundreds of lives daily, Jugal Kishore, a young man of eighteen years, came forward and organised treatment centres in various parts of the city. The monsoon months of July to September brought sorrow and grief to people living in the low-lying areas along the Yamuna because of the devastation caused by the flooding of the river which was followed by disease. Jugal Kishore was instrumental in erecting a protective dam to keep off the floodwaters. This was done under his guidance as the chairman of the Construction Services of the Bharat Sevak Samaj. The dam or *bandh* still serves the people of Delhi.

The Movers and Shakers

Among the builders of the college, apart from Lala Shri Krishna Dass Gurwala, the two who stand out most prominently are Sir Shri Ram and his son Dr Bharat Ram.

Sir Shri Ram ensured that the college grew in stature to compete with the best without being elitist. The kind of leadership he provided can be best recalled through the eyes of those who were closely associated with him. Apart from fighting the cause of Hindu College with university authorities, Lala Shri Ram knew how to recognise talent and retain it. As Dr B.M. Bhatia,[11] who served as a principal under him, pointed out, he selected people for the job carefully and then gave them complete confidence and trust so that they could discharge their responsibilities without fear or favour. He was a strict disciplinarian but never a bureaucrat. Austere in his own living, Lala Shri Ram was lavish in his hospitality to his guests. In spite of

Sir Shri Ram

11 Arun Joshi (ed.), *Remembering Lala Shri Ram: Reminiscences on his 100th Birthday* (Delhi: DCM Limited, 1983), p. 270.

his hands being full with work, he found time to give close attention to institutions under his care. For him, tiredness was a mental state. Lala Shri Ram could work for twelve hours a day because he did not immerse himself in one subject or problem for a long stretch of time. After working for an hour or two on one organisation he would switch to another. This gave him the necessary relaxation and prevented boredom.

Dr Sarup Singh, who began life as a lecturer in English at Hindu College, also has a lot to say about Lala Shri Ram's leadership, his understanding of the world and his commitment to institution building. He could accept valid criticism even if it came from a young lecturer. But what stands out is a remarkable incident that gives an insight into the values that Lala Shri Ram stood for.

Dr Sarup Singh as the warden of the Hindu College Hostel decided to impose some discipline. He passed an order that every boarder should be in his room latest by 10 pm. Since the hostel had no gate and was anyway housed in a dilapidated building, he had no choice but to send an employee of the hostel to go around and report the absentees. He found that there was one hosteller who went out every day and rarely returned before 11 pm. The following evening when the boy returned in a fancy car, Dr Sarup Singh confronted him and threatened him with expulsion. No one told him till later that he was Lala Shri Ram's grandson.

Below: *Dr Bharat Ram*

Dr Sarup Singh

The following day Lala Shri Ram came to the college at around 5 pm and Sarup Singh was called to the principal's room. Expecting the worst, he arrived there with great trepidation only to find a smiling Sri Shri Ram who explained that he had come to apologise on behalf of his grandson. He said that since the boy was a darling of the family, no one ever reprimanded him and so it was good that someone had disciplined him. This one incident, recalled Sarup Singh, led to deep affection and regard for Sir Shri Ram.[12]

Examples of Sir Shri Ram's hard work, generosity, insight into character and ability to arouse loyalty abound. He died on 11 January 1963, which was a sad day for the college. He had been an old student of the college although only for six months. An industrialist, educationist and philanthropist, to use Professor Prem Chand's words, Sir Shri Ram passed away with the satisfaction of knowing that he had paid his debt to society and had returned to life more than he had taken from it.

***Dr Bharat Ram*:** He took his father, Sir Shri Ram's place, in 1963. He steered the destiny of the college till his death in 2007 with great involvement and commitment. During his forty-year association, the college went from strength to strength adding Honours courses in Science in the 1970s when a new science block was made. The student strength increased and the college became an extended college in 1989. A new auditorium replaced the old one that had burnt down because of short-circuiting in 1966; a new sports complex and canteen; and several houses for teaching and non-teaching staff members were also added. With his encouragement

12 Ibid., pp. 15–20.

and support a new Students' Centre was built entirely out of the college's own resources. The college marked its Centenary in 1999 with Shri Atal Bihari Vajpayee, the prime minister of India at that time as the chief guest.

Probably all those who came into contact with Dr Bharat Ram will acknowledge that he touched their lives in more ways than one. He was a wise man with a vision, but extremely grounded and practical. He was firm, had the capacity to take bold decisions and was also full of charm and fun at the same time. He guided with a gentle hand and gave plenty of space to the principal to grow, innovate and deal with challenges. He taught a lot without even knowing that he was doing so.

***Bhiku Ram Jain*:** He was a member of the Lok Sabha, and an old student of Hindu College during the tenures of S.K. Sen and N.V. Thadani. Bhiku Ram Jain was the treasurer of the Hindu College Governing Body for thirty years. He spent a lot of time in steering the college. He contributed to the development of an institution that had helped him 'become a better and worthy citizen'. His deep interest in the university led him to become a member of both the Delhi University Court and Council.

***Satya Narain Gupta*:** He studied in the college and later headed the Governing Body, after Dr Bharat Ram passed away. He served the Trust for over fifty years, first as its secretary and then as its chairman. He is respected for his management skills and philanthropic activities. Satya Narain Gupta was deeply involved in the field of education. Besides being the chairman of the college Governing Body, he was associated with the Ramjas Foundation till he retired as its chairman.

Satya Narain Gupta knew the college well and understood its ethos completely having been its student in the 1940s. He graduated in 1943, when the college was in Kashmere Gate and N.V. Thadani was the principal. He recalls his association with the college, during his student days when the student strength was about 800 compared to over 3,000 now. It was an egalitarian college in which the elite were uncomfortable because they were different from the rest of the students. Satya Narain Gupta belonged to this group and was embarrassed to use the car when it came to pick him up from college. Most students came by bus or on bicycles. Satya Narain Gupta's car often travelled empty while he took the bus home. Hindu College then was a nationalist college in which the vibrant spirit of the Independence movement was palpable. During the Quit India Movement many national leaders like K.M. Munshi and Rajagopalachari came to address the students through the parliament and Satya Narain Gupta reflects with amusement on how he also wore khadi on these occassions.[13]

Bhiku Ram Jain

13 *Centenary Souvenir*, 1999, then chairman of the College Trust and member of the Governing Body in his Centenary message.

***Dr N.V. Thadani*:** Although N.V. Thadani's name keeps coming up as students, teachers and his contemporaries cannot but re-emphasise his invaluable contribution to the college for about twenty-six years, during two tenures, we must also not forget Professor Phani Bhushan Adhikari and his attempts to steady the college, find a more suitable place for it and a better residence for its students while carrying on a heavy load of teaching.

Dr Thadani continuously raised the bar, building the prestige of the college to the level that it came to be regarded as one of the premier institutions of North India. What helped was his large heartedness and commitment to education without biases and prejudices. For example, in spite of the rivalry between Hindu College and St. Stephen's, largely because of the opposing visions that formed the basis of their establishment, they collaborated with each other in teaching activities. In the early 1920s, students from St. Stephen's College were granted permission to attend Biology classes at the Hindu College. When a similar request was made by Ramjas College, this practice had to be stopped as the resources of Hindu College were already stretched and it was difficult to cope with numbers.[14]

Facing page: *Professor S.K. Sen (above right); Dedication of the college magazine* The Indraprastha *(below left); Cover of college magazine dedicated to S.K. Sen (below middle); Essay by Principal N.V. Thadani on Late Mr S.K. Sen (below right)*

Right: *Dr N.V. Thandani*

Satya Narain Gupta

***Professor S.K. Sen*:** Dr Thadani's two tenures were separated by the tenure of Professor S.K. Sen, an Oxford graduate in History with a well-established reputation as a teacher. He administered with gentleness and sincere concern for the welfare of his students. S.K. Sen's term of office came to an unfortunate and tragic end on 1 October 1934 when he died of a sudden heart attack on the opening day of the college after the vacations. He was addressing the students and announcing with great pride and pleasure the names of the two students who had been selected for the Indian Civil Service—Khub Chand and Nakul Sen—when he collapsed. Kanwar Lal Sharma recalls it as the saddest day of his life.[15] As S.K. Sen fell, Sharma recalls how he tried in vain to hold him. He asked for 'water' and everyone ran helter-skelter to get him some but it was too late: 'He had already passed into history. A cloud of gloom

14 F.F. Monk, *A History of St.Stephen's College, Delhi* (Calcutta: YMCA Publishing House, 1935), pp. 221-222. This is also recorded in the minutes of the Hindu Education Trust of the period.

15 Kanwar Lal Sharma, 'Hindu College in My Days', *The Indraprastha*, 1983-84.

hung over the college and tears burst out of everyone's eyes.' Everyone was shocked and the tragic news brought the entire college and half of Delhi to the cremation ground to pay their last respects to Professor Sen.

***N.V. Thadani again*:** The post of the principal remained vacant for about a year when Dr Thadani returned to the college in his old capacity. Not only did he guide the college through the Quit India Movement but also helped mitigate the hardships of the Partition as best as he could. Jivat Thadani, his son tells us, that as Delhi was flooded with refugees from Punjab and Sind colleges of Delhi University were needed to absorb as many as they could among those who had been studying in colleges on the other side of the border. Of course, there were not only students but also teachers and professors. The real crunch was physical accommodation and the challenge was one of organisation and resources. Hindu College decided to organise a 'second shift' of staff and students. The Ministry of Education was requested to provide resources to deal with the emergency which it did although reluctantly. Teaching staff were hastily reruited on a temporary basis and students had to be accepted for various courses of study, largely on the basis of their own statements regarding prior preparation, in the absence of proper documentation. There were a few unfortunate but unavoidable errors of judgement in the process, which had to be corrected when they came to light.

THE

INDRAPRASTHA

Vol. XVII } NOVERMBER 1934. { No. 5

The Present Issue.

This issue of the Indraprastha is dedicated to Late Mr. S.K. Sen. His death is our real loss and no amount of expression can give vent to our feelings. It is purely with the intention of paying our humble tributes to the memory of the "Great Dead" that the present issue is published. This year has been particularly unfortunate for this institution since it has lost two of the strongest pillars upon which the beams of success were laid. Principal S. K. Sen and Prof. H.L. Chablani rendered invaluable service to the cause of education, and their loss is mourned not only by our College but by the University as a whole.

In conclusion we thank all those who have helped in bringing out this issue, particularly Mr. Ved Prakash of the 3rd year, who has been of considerable service in procuring the photo blocks.

Editor.

The Indraprastha

The Hindu College Magazine.

Regd. No. L. 3105.
Vol. XVII.
No. Special
November, 1934.

MUSIC OF TRUTH

SPECIAL NUMBER

IN MEMORY OF

THE

LATE PRINCIPAL S.K. SEN.

Editor:—BHIM SAIN SABBARWAL.

Late Mr. S. K. Sen.

(By Principal N. V. Thadani)

Principal S. K. Sen was one of the gentlest and most amiable of men I knew, and I had a very happy recollection of our association together for seven or eight years. He was a sound teacher of English and History, a fine organizer, a capable administrator, and a good man. In him the student community has lost a trusted guide, the University a distinguished educationalist the City of Delhi a genial personality, and I an old friend. He was a gentleman in a very real sense of the term, and should long be missed by his students, Colleagues, friends and associates. His sudden death leaves a gap which will not easily be filled.

The character of the Kashmere Gate campus changed rather quickly, under the extreme pressure for space, and some activities had to be sacrificed to make way for higher short-term priorities. The need for resources to enable the construction of new premises on the University campus site was felt more sorely than ever before.[16]

Unfortunately towards the end, Dr Thadani developed serious health problems, but he continued to serve the college that he had done so much to build until he retired in 1950. Dr Sarup Singh recalls his remarkable courage and integrity. The principals of both St. Stephen's and Hindu colleges were offered the title of Rai Bahadur by the British. While Mr Mukarji of St. Stephen's accepted it, Dr Thadani did not. It needed great courage to refuse and perhaps that is why Dr Thadani was so highly respected.

Another incident recalled by Ashok Jaitly in *St. Stephen's College: A History* bears witness to Thadani's sagacity and courage. As August 1947 approached, there was exhilaration at the coming of Independence but also trepidation as communal tempers were building up to a frenzy. An attempt was made by some rowdies to set fire to the laboratory at St. Stephen's College. And then Jaitly narrates, 'as if out of a medieval romance, the College was saved from a riotous mob armed with kerosene tins and rags by the courageous act of the head of its age-old rival. Principal N.V. Thadani of Hindu College, along with a couple of his staff, stood boldly at the gates of St. Stephen's and shamed the mob by asking them to burn his college first (Hindu was still at Kashmere Gate) before attacking the "Mission College".'[17]

16 Unpublished notes of Mr Jivat Thadani.

17 Ashok Jaitly, *St. Stephen's College: A History* (New Delhi: Lotus Collection, Roli Books, 2006), pp. 39-40.

Shri Jivat Thadani, Principal N.V. Thadani's son who helped ferrying many to the safety of camps and other protected spaces during the mob frenzy of the Partition, recalls, 'The Principal of Anglo-Arabic College (renamed Delhi College some time after Independence) approached Principal Thadani for help, as his home was located in an extremely vulnerable area. A way had to be found, under cover of darkness, to move him and his family to Principal Thadani's home and to place a caretaker family in the vacated house, so that the premises may not be vandalised. The Principal's House in Hindu College had acquired the characteristics of a small "Refugee Camp" in any case, because of the influx of Principal Thadani's own extended family from Sind; and the reinforcements from within Delhi went unnoticed for a while. But word got round, somehow, that Hindu College was harbouring some Muslims; and miscreants mobilised a substantial crowd of people, drawn mostly from areas beyond the immediate vicinity, who threatened to "burn down" the house unless its Muslim guests were surrendered to them.

As he was at the time, Principal Thadani went out to the Compound Gate to face the hostile crowd and talk to them. He told them that his house was full at the time of innocent people who had come to him for shelter from hostile crowds in various parts of the country, far and near, and it was his bounden duty, as a host, to protect them from all danger. They would have to kill him before they crossed the boundary of decent behaviour and harmed any of his innocent and unarmed guests who had placed their faith in the Hindu traditions of hospitality.

The appeal to decency did not fall on deaf ears. Some among the crowd, which by then included a few students and staff of the College who had inconspicuously joined the hostile outsiders, appealed for trust in his judgment and actions; others argued that time must be allowed in any case to resolve the issues involved—for a nationalist and a host. Slowly, passionate

Hindu College Hostel

anger gave way to murmured hesitation and doubt; the tension was palpably reduced and the crowd agreed to disperse peacefully.

Later in the day, Principal Thadani was able to arrange, in consultation with Mr Zahid Hussain, the newly appointed High Commssioner for Pakistan, (who had earlier been an officer of the Government of India and treasurer of the University of Delhi) for the transfer of his Muslim guests to the High Commission compound in New Delhi and thence to the airport for a flight to Karachi.'[18]

Dr Sarup Singh was the warden of the Hindu College Hostel at that time and it was he who had brought out a number of hostel residents to join the crowd outside the residence of Principal Thadani so that his appeal may not fall on deaf ears and the crowd could be deflected from its aggressive purpose.

Principal Thadani's retirement after almost twenty-five years of service (1917–50) with a term of about six years in between of Professor S.K. Sen, meant the end of an epoch. In his tribute to Dr Thadani, Dr Bool Chand says in the college magazine: 'He was an academic architect with the insight of a scientist, the foresight of a statesman and the finish of a jeweller; brilliant debater, always cool headed with friends and foe.'

***Professor A. Bhattacharya*:** Head of the English Department in the college and in the university, Professor Bhattacharya succeeded Dr Thadani. Fondly recalled as a teacher by his old students like K.G. Khosla and K.K. Birla, his leadership enabled the Governing Body to complete the construction of the college building and shift to the university campus in 1953-54. Principal Bhattacharya faced great odds, the chief one being the lack of readily available finances. But due to his courage and zeal, the E-shaped college building in the university campus was completed in 1953 together with a hostel having about 160 rooms. A new Assembly Hall with a small stage too was constructed. Unfortunately, Principal Bhattacharya's health began to fail and he resigned in March 1958.

> Principals Sen, Thadani and Bhattacharya, the three successive principals in the pre-Independence days served as role models for faculty members both as teachers and scholars.

Raj Narain Mathur

***Dr Raj Narain Mathur*:** He took over as principal in July 1958. He had the distinction of being the first old student of the college to be appointed its principal. Dr Raj Narain Mathur had taught Economics in the college. He left to become the principal of Government College, Mandi in Himachal Pradesh and then returned to head his alma mater. During his tenure the

18 Unpublished notes of Mr Jivat Thadani.

college celebrated its Diamond Jubilee in 1959. He left in 1964 and in May of the same year Dr B.M. Bhatia took over.

***Dr B.M. Bhatia*:** He was another institution builder. He provided leadership during the Indo-Pak conflict in 1965 and inspired everyone to donate to the National Defence Fund. The college steadily grew under his guidance. Due to an unfortunate incident in 1966-67 the college hall was gutted by a fire caused by a short circuit of electric wires. Although heartbroken, Dr Bhatia rose to the occasion. The students gave all the cooperation. When the University Grants Commission was tardy in releasing money for constructing a new hall, Dr Bhatia led a demonstration of students to the vice chancellor for funds. Donations were collected through door-to-door and shop-to-shop visits, apart from what was sanctioned by the UGC and a state-of-the-art auditorium was constructed. M.J. Bhatt designed it with Dr Ebrahim Alkazi, former director of the National School of Drama, doing the stage. The acoustics were done by Dr Pancholi of NPL and lights by Shri Mookerji and eminent theatre personality Mrs Sheila Bhatia.[19]

When Dr Bhatia went on study leave from 1971–73, Mr P.C. Sood of the Department of English officiated in his place. Even in his short tenure, P.C. Sood added a new science block to the college building to enable the Honours classes to shift from the university to the college. Dr Bhatia returned in September 1973 and under his leadership the college celebrated its 75th Founder's Day on 15 February 1974. The celebrations were surprisingly simple. As Dr Bhatia

Above: *One side of the Hindu College Auditorium*

Dr B.M. Bhatia

19 Dr B.M. Bhatia, 'College Auditorium: How it was Built', *The Indraprastha*, 1983.

explained in his speech, 'The country is facing an economic crisis, it becomes our duty to help it and bring it out from the crisis. That is why we decided not to waste any money and contribute whatsoever we can in the service of the country.' In July 1977, Dr B.M. Bhatia became the vice chancellor of Jodhpur University and Shri V.M. Misra, lecturer in Physics, was appointed the officiating principal of Hindu College. But Dr Bhatia returned in just four months and continued till August 1980, when he retired.

Above left: *Sanjay Chauhan (who received the Mark of Honour in 1988) with a friend, B.D. Saini*

Above right: *Shri P.C. Verma*

Principal's bungalow in earlier days

***Shri P.C. Verma*:** He was from the Department of English and was appointed principal after Dr Bhatia retired. Many development projects were sought to be undertaken during his tenure. He motivated the alumni of the college to help in renovating the college café and constructing a sports complex. During his tenure, six classrooms were added and several staff quarters

were built. P.C. Verma also had to cope with the emerging financial crises in the college as UGC threatened to reduce grants by creating three special funds—the Endowment Fund, the Development Fund and the Establishment Fund—to meet contingency expenses. Academically the college did well. For the first time in its history, students of Hindu College were awarded the prestigious Rhodes scholarship, not once but over three years—Animesh Srivastava, an Economics student in 1984, Mahesh Rangarajan, a History student in 1985 and Sanjay Chauhan, an Economics student in 1988.

Dr Kavita A. Sharma: The tenure of the next principal, Dr S.N. Maheshwari was short-lived as he left in 1997. After two officiating principals, Dr Mandhata Ojha and Dr K.P. Sarabhai, who were both well-respected senior teachers in the college, Dr Kavita A. Sharma became the second 'old student' to become its principal. She was appointed in January 1998. This was a landmark as she was the first lady principal of not only the college but also of any co-educational college in Delhi University. Endowed with restlessness and full of energy and the determination to do something for the college, Dr Kavita Sharma overcame all odds and brought glory to the college in both academics as well as extracurricular activities. During her tenure houses were built for non-teaching staff, hostel facilities were upgraded, computer labs came up and a modern students centre was built with a seminar hall, common room, computer facilities, a bookshop, photocopying facilities and a bank. During her term the college celebrated its Centenary.

Above: *Dr Kavita A. Sharma*

The college led in environmental consciousness as solar lights were installed together with solar water heating for the hostel and parts of the college, and exclusive rainwater harvesting was introduced over the sprawling twenty-five-acre campus. A heritage grant ensured that the

Principal's bungalow at present

Dr B.N. Ganguli

Right: *Guard house built in 1825*

whole building was repaired and renovated and a guard house of 1825 vintage, one of the only remaining three in Delhi situated in the college campus was repaired and restored to become a small art gallery for students. After Dr Bharat Ram's passing away the guard house was named after him. Dr Kavita Sharma's popularity among the students and her colleagues created a rare amalgamation of efforts to achieve greater heights. Her relentless efforts to ensure a healthy financial base for the college and support to the Managing Committee have been recognised by one and all.

Since then has followed a period of some uncertainty as after two officiating principals, Dr D.N. Gupta and Dr Subhash Chaudhry, Professor Vinay Srivastava from the department of Anthropology at Delhi University was appointed the college's principal in 2010. But he left in 2012 to rejoin the department and once again there was an officiating principal, Dr Pradumn Kumar from the Department of Physics who had earlier been appointed vice principal for the first time in the history of the college.

> "At least five of the teachers of Hindu College rose to vice chancellorship of universities. Two of them—Dr B.N. Ganguli and Dr Sarup Singh of Delhi University itself. Dr B.R. Seth, who was the head of the Mathematics department in the college became vice chancellor of Dibrugarh University in Assam and Dr J.N. Kapur of the same department, of Meerut University in Uttar Pradesh. Dr B.M. Bhatia had a short stint as vice chancellor of Jodhpur University in Rajasthan."

Creation and Evolution of Democratic Spaces

Was it an unspoken commitment or an undercurrent that prompted students and teachers of Hindu College to become involved in the national movement? Was this nationalistic consciousness motivated by a concern for the marginalised or those excluded from the power structures? Societies such as Tarun Samaj and the Harijan Service League kept alive the vision of the founders of the college that opportunities, particularly for education, must be made available to all sections of society, especially to its weaker sections. The nationalist sentiment was visible from the formative years in the seriousness with which the college parliament and a formidable Literary Union took root. These two institutions prepared the students as nationalists, great public speakers and political analysts. The college, with the endeavours of its various principals and teachers, created democratic spaces which gave room to all sections of society to grow.

Previous page: *Ms Indira Sachdev (3rd from left), Assistant Manager Magazine and Ms Ruby Joseph (5th from left), Joint Secretary Literary Union with Principal Thadani (centre) in Office Bearers 1939-40 group photo*

Right: *An Act to institute a parliament in Hindu College*

Kamala studied in Hindu College from 1936–38

APPENDIX A.

An Act to institute a Parliament in the Hindu College, Delhi.

WHEREAS it is expedient to institute a Parliament in the Hindu College, Delhi, be it hereby enacted:—

I that the General Body of the students and teachers of the College shall constitute the Parliament of the College :

II that all students of the College shall be ordinary members and all teachers Honorary members of the Parliament :

III that the Principal of the College for the time being shall represent "His Majesty" :

IV that the Parliament shall have the following powers, namely—

(1) to provide for debates and discussions by such persons and under such conditions as may be permitted by "His Majesty" ;

(2) Subject to the previous approval of "His Majesty" to enrol persons of distinction other than members of the general body of the College as Temporary or Honorary Members of the Parliament ;

(3) Subject to the previous approval of "His Majesty" to pass such legislation as may concern the ordinary members of the Parliament :

(4) to receive reports of the working of the different societies of the College :

(5) to do all other acts and things as may be required to further the objects of the Parliament as a body corporate of the College :

OFFICES OF THE PARLIAMENT

V that the following shall be the officers of the Parliament

(1) The Speaker,

(2) The Prime Minister,

(3) The Cabinet Ministers,

(4) The Cabinet Secretaries,

(5) The Deputy Speaker,

(6) The Secretary to Parliament,

" HIS MAJESTY "

VI that the Principal of the College for the time being in office shall represent "His Majesty".

(a) that the Principal shall have the right to inspect or cause an inspection to be made in the working of the Parliament, and make such changes

Tarun Samaj

Tarun Samaj was wedded to social reform and concern for the downtrodden. It invited prominent leaders to address and inspire students. In March 1930, Sarojini Naidu, attending one of its functions, talked about the dream of a free India:

> In a few years there will be no room left for communal wrangling or indication for stupid quarrels and watertight compartments. When Tarun Samaj would become Swaraj Samaj in free India it would cross even the narrow channels of nationalism. My message to the youth is dream splendidly, dream proudly and without fear, but with every thrill of your dream remember that you are to give testimony of the acceptance of responsibility. In responsibility lies the glory of youth.[1]

Harijan Service League

Gandhiji's Harijan movement inspired the students of the college to start the Harijan Service League in 1932. Actively aided by G.D. Birla, the league worked out plans for including mass education, improving the condition of slums and fighting commonplace caste prejudices.

The nationalist character among the students was strengthened by listening to eminent leaders among whom were Lokmanya Tilak, Annie Besant, British Labour MP Oswald Moslay, Mahatma Gandhi, Rabindranath Tagore, Madan Mohan Malaviya, Sarojini Naidu, Mohammed Ali Jinnah, Shaukat Ali and Mohammed Ali of the Khilafat movement, Moti Lal Nehru, Jawaharlal Nehru, Sardar Patel, Jai Prakash Narayan, K.M. Panicker, B.R. Ambedkar and K.M. Munshi.

Women in Hindu College

The college opened its doors to girls when Indian society was just coming out of decades of conservatism and orthodoxy. Parents could hardly imagine their daughters going to college, that to a co-educational college, sitting in a class dominated by boys. It required some courage to allow daughters to join colleges for higher studies. Hindu College, despite its religious fervour, was progressive and opened its doors for girls although mindsets changed slowly. However, it did not take long for girls to start taking active part in college activities as editors of the college magazine, as debaters, actors in theatre groups, performers in music and dance competitions and subsequently as teachers. The college organised arts and crafts competitions and exhibitions. Skills in embroidery, sewing, arts and similar activities were promoted through these competitions.

Most of the girls were admitted in faculties not available elsewhere. Thus, since Indraprastha College was not equipped for honours

Sheila Bahadur (Dhar) was a fiercely independent person, participating in debating and the Literary Union in college. Later she made a name for herself as a classical singer

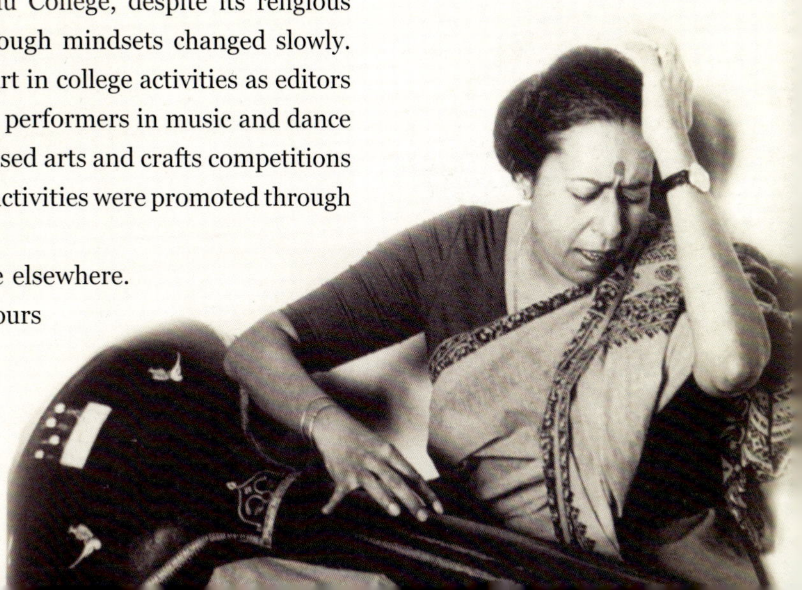

1 *The Indraprastha,* 1930.

and post-graduate courses in Science, girls were admitted to these courses in Hindu College. There was strict segregation as girls sat on the front benches and were expected to enter from the front door of the classroom. Teachers paid special attention to them but the library was out of bounds. Preet Chablani recalls a telling incident, which is amusing in retrospect. A girl had come from outside Delhi to do her Masters from Delhi University. She wanted admission in Hindu College but Principal Thadani said she could not get admission if she arrived riding a bicycle from the new YMCA, where she proposed to stay. So she had to shift to the old YMCA so that she could demurely walk to college.[2]

P.C. Sood's analysis of Principal Thadani's attitude was: 'He was, undoubtedly, a man of learning and inspired awe in others. There was, however, a striking contradiction in his otherwise wholesome personality. He was pronouncedly conservative in matters of sex and this appeared hugely odd in the head of a co-educational institution. I am not sure if he equated sex with sin but his efforts to keep boys and girls separate amounted to obsession almost.'[3] Girls compulsorily sat together on the front benches. The boys' and girls' common rooms were at the opposite ends of the building; they could not mingle even during functions. In fact, being within speaking distance of one another in the compound could attract punishment. This enforced segregation despite the changing times, especially after the country won Independence with the joint struggle of men and women, was sure to raise a reaction. Some high-spirited students were bound to storm the principal's citadel of orthodoxy. This happened sooner rather than later.

Professor Balkishan Das, the head of the Department of Biology, was the staff president of the Hindustani Dramatics Society. Every year the society staged a play, with boys playing

2 *In Retrospect*, p. 60.

3 P.C. Sood, 'Hindu College—things many do not know', *The Indraprastha*, 1983-84, p. 20.

Biology Group, Hindu College, Delhi, 1942-43. Damyanti Bhasker, Taravati Bahl, Chander Kanta Rajani, Gargi Kalsi, Prof. Balkishan Das, MSc (In-charge), Mr Pindi Das (BSc, LLB), Shiela Chopra, Sneh Lata Ghoshal, Sudershan Kumari (Left to right of first row)

the roles of girls. Not only that, girls were not permitted to see the performance. In 1944, Kapila (Vatsyayan) Malik, reading in English Honours, rebelled and demanded that the girls be associated with the dramatic society. Principal Thadani defied cajolery, threats and demonstrations but finally he conceded that the girls could stage their own production and their parents could be the audience. It was at best a half victory at this stage.[4]

At the time of Sheila Bahadur and Kapila Malik, there were about a dozen girls in the college where almost 1,000 boys were enrolled. They were the pioneers because of whom the doors opened for others. Their early struggles are instructive of the difficulties faced in a conservative society. Dr Sarup Singh recalls how when Sheila Bahadur once came to perform on stage, a ruffian from Kashmere Gate appeared from nowhere and said something nasty. She left the stage in tears. Dr Sarup Singh protested and called her back. The programme continued and the principal hauled the man up the following day for his conduct.

Hindu College gave girls like Sheila Bahadur room to grow and find their wings. From the well-known family of Barrister Raj Narain, Sheila Bahadur made a name for herself as a classical singer. A fiercely independent person, she was involved in debating and the Literary Union in the college. Married to well-known economist and academician, Professor P.N. Dhar, Sheila Bahadur was the chief editor in NCERT and had a long stint in the Publications Division of the Government of India. She was also the director of Bal Bhavan. L.C. Jain, an alumnus of the college, later India's high commissioner to South Africa, Magsaysay Award winner and a Padma Vibhushan, also recalled how girl students gradually participated in college activities in spite of the isolation enforced by Principal Thadani.

4 Ibid.

Left: *Women in Sports: Govt XI Founder's Day cricket match with President Raj Narain Mathur seated (centre)*

Right: *L.C. Jain presenting credentials to Nelson Mandela as high commissioner of India to South Africa*

Above:
Left to Right (standing): Ashwani Arora, Ram Mohan, Shyla Rao, Ashok Ahuja, Manjit Bawa, M.S. Azaad, Bobby Mathur; Left to Right (sitting): Laxmi Bharadwaj, P.C. Verma, Principal Raj N. Mathur and Jagdish Sarin were members of the Hindustani Dramatics Society

Below:
Dramatics Club, 1936-37, Hindu College, Delhi. Cast of the play Harijan*: Bhadra Puri (in sari) and Madan Puri (in achkan) can be seen standing 3rd and 4th from left*

Left:
Left to Right: Meenakshi Mittal, Manoj Bajpai, Gupta, Sharmishtha Chakraborti, Arun Kumar and Rahul Priyadarshi

Left below:
Left to Right (standing): Manoj Bajpai, Sandeep Gupta, Ravi Kant Sharma, Rahul Priyadarshi, Alok Ranjan, Alok Mishra, Parimoo, Muktesh Pardeshi;
Left to Right (sitting): Sharmishtha Chakraborti, Meenakshi Mittal, Vishal Bhardwaj (4th from left), Arun Kumar, Gupta, Shabbir (extreme right)

Dramatics Club, 1935-36: Bhadra Puri dressed as a woman in the play Shankh ki Shararat

The girls were supposed to stay in their common room when not in class, where they remained confined behind a *chik* with a guard outside. So, as Sheila (Bahadur) Dhar recounted humorously, if a boy wanted to speak to a girl, he would give an excuse about some matter concerning the Literary Union for example, and the girl would come out and talk to him in the courtyard in full view of everyone.[5]

These restrictions gradually changed as the girls began to contest college elections and women students like Sheila Bahadur were prominent at the Boat Club while Kapila Malik in all literary events. Daya Krishna fondly recalls those times, 'Who would imagine Kapila in those days going to bat as a young college girl in a friendly match with boys?'[6] Kapila (Malik) Vatsyayan also remembers the journey from behind the '*chiked* screen' of the ladies room to the classroom, which would have tested the sinews of the most hardy. Among the first challenges to this 'gender apartheid' was thrown by Kapila Malik herself. As she recalls, 'Once there was an altercation. I was heatedly debating something with a group of boys. There was to be a parliament session. Principal Thadani walked up majestically and said, "Very interested in talking to boys, aren't you?" Furious and red in the face I shot back, "Of course, that is why I have joined Hindu College."'

The repercussions were instantaneous and spontaneous. A strike was organised to protest against the principal's remarks. Teachers were roped in. The college came to a halt. Dr S.K. Saxena, lecturer in Philosophy walked up to the principal and convinced him that the girls could no longer be confined to the ladies room beyond class hours. They needed to be given the freedom to converse with boys on the campus. He advised the principal to take some of the students, particularly girls, into confidence in running the college. Principal Thadani took note of the counsel and from then on he and Kapila (Malik) Vatsyayan remained friends till the end. Looking back, Dr Vatsyayan says that at one level it was a battle of sorts that had been won. As she says, 'The incident remains in my mind as one of great learning.'[7]

Above: *Prof. Prem Chand (sitting 2nd from left), Mrs Khurshid, A. Bhattacharya (centre), Dr S.K. Saxena and Ustad Chand Khan with the participants of a music competition held in Hindu College on 18 March, 1952*

***Other women of substance*:** During the 1930s and 1940s, there were some other girls who participated in different activities. A few showed merit and became editors or assistant

5 *In Retrospect*, p. 80.

6 Ibid., p. 57.

7 Ibid., pp. 71-72.

editors of the college magazine, which was of a very high standard with faculty members also contributing articles regularly.

As early as 1932-33, there were two girls on the editorial board, Kunta Kumari in Hindi and Amina Muaim-ud-Din in Urdu.

In 1936, Nirmala Joshi was the student general editor. In her editorial she talked of national freedom and regeneration of students and politics. She asked the girls to come out of the common room and assert their rights.

Tila Joshi and Mira Mukherji were actively involved in the all-important Literary Union.

In 1939, Reba Roy was in the college cabinet. The parliament saw a deputy leader of the opposition, Farkhanda Akhtar.

The debaters: At a time when girls were thought to be shy and withdrawn, the college had women debaters of all-India merit. Amina Muaim-ud-Din won the second prize in an all-India debate in Urdu. In 1930, at an all-India debate in memory of the college's founder, Krishna Dass Gurwala, Sushila Devi won the first prize in the ladies group. She was later in the college parliament as a minister in the cabinet. Indrani Devi won the second prize in English. Kunta Kumari represented Delhi University when a team from Oxford University visited. Shanta Sen Roy was another debater who performed very well.

Women in academics and other fields: Raj Kumari Pari topped in Sanskrit Honours; Swaran Lata Sehgal topped in Philosophy while in Intermediate Medical, Urmila Sharma stood first. This was in 1939. All this was considered unusual as boys dominated virtually all the fields of activities.

Dr Satya Rai pioneered as the first lady lecturer to be appointed in the college in the 1959-60 session. She was not an alumnus and her appointment created a stir in the teaching

Above left: *Left to Right (standing): P.K. Mukherjee (Bengali Editor), M.S. Masud (Urdu Editor), R.S. Ahluwalia (Punjabi Editor); Left to Right (sitting): R.K. Gupta (Manager), Mr B.N. Ganguli (Prof. In-charge), Principal Thadani, Ms Indrani Bournwall (Hindi Editor) in the Editorial Board of Hindu College, 1937*

Above right: *Tila Joshi (4th from right) and Mira Mukherji (6th from right) were in the Literary Union in the Office Bearers 1937-38 group photo. Purshottam Lal (3rd from right) was a great debater and was then the prime minister in the college parliament*

Dr Savita Datta—first lady prime minister of the college parliament

Above: *Dr Satya Rai (centre)—first lady lecturer to be appointed in 1959-60*

Centre: *Dr Kavita A. Sharma—first lady principal of Hindu College in 100 years*

community of the university. Some teachers saw it as an encroachment on the male domain while others appreciated her courage and saw it as a path-breaking step. Some women, who joined later, could not stay long and for almost a decade Dr Satya Rai was the only woman teacher till others such as Dr Kavita A. Sharma, Suchitra Gupta, Dr Saroj Bala and Dr Tripta Wahi joined and stayed on. Satya Rai came from Government College for Women, Amritsar, where she taught Political Science. Dr N.N. Aggarwal, head of the Political Science department of the college, accompanied the nervous new teacher, to introduce her to her class of nearly eighty students. There was pin-drop silence while she was teaching; as she came out she heard the boys saying that they had come prepared to harass her but were so absorbed in her lecture that they could do nothing. 'That was my proudest day in Hindu College,' admits Satya Rai.

In the staff room, while as a novelty she was welcome, her colleagues felt an obvious loss of freedom. Many were uncomfortable interacting with a female colleague, so they left two chairs on either side of her unoccupied! There were a few exceptions who tried to make her feel comfortable. But obviously some gender dynamics had to be settled as preconceived notions were challenged. Some would raise eyebrows if she accepted a lift from a male colleague while others were just indifferent. However, Satya Rai was self-confident and so was her husband, Lajpat Rai. On the whole she states that she had very cordial relations with her colleagues and being the only female, she defined her relationship with her male colleagues according to her own assessment and understanding. It gave her great pride and satisfaction that after four decades of 'joining this great institution, now nearly 40 per cent of the teaching staff consists of women and the institution is headed by a woman, Dr Kavita Sharma, who very graciously said to me "you opened the door for us".'[8]

In 1998 Dr Kavita A. Sharma became the first lady principal of Hindu College in 100 years and of any co-educational college in Delhi. This was the culmination of the efforts of the pioneering women students and teachers of the college. An alumnus of the college, studying English Honours and later doing her post-graduation in English Literature, Dr Sharma rose to head the prestigious institution. She was visiting honorary lecturer at Tokyo Women's Christian College and also at the University of Indonesia. A prolific writer, a recipient of Shastri Indo Canadian research fellowships, a New Century Fulbright scholar and a winner of the Indira Gandhi Sadbhavana Award, Dr Sharma contributed greatly to her alma mater. After more than ten years as principal, she moved on to become the first woman director of the India International Centre.

In 2004, Dr Savita Datta, another old student of the college and the first lady prime minister of its parliament, became the principal of Maitreyi College, Delhi University and in 2006, the director of Campus of Open Learning. She is also a visiting faculty at the Institute of Informatics and Community in the university. A well-known figure among the present generation of teachers, Dr Savita Datta was the head of a delegation of Delhi University to the

8 *In Retrospect*, pp. 97–99.

Open University in the UK to initiate the Blended Learning Project. Dr Datta has received the World Education and Literacy Award, besides many higher education awards. She has also received the Indira Gandhi Sadbhavana Award.

As we talk of women in academics, Leela Gandhi appears on the scene with significant credentials. An important member of the powerful debating team of the college, she also excelled in studies. She got an Inlaks scholarship and later became a part of the English faculty in the college. She is now a Professor of English in Chicago University. She got her doctorate from Oxford and has several published works to her credit. Among the present women teachers at the college who are also its old students is Dr Anju Srivastava from the Department of Chemistry who did her Chemistry Honours from Hindu College and then pursued her Masters and PhD from IIT Delhi. She has published widely and was amongst the selected few teachers who were given the 'Distinguished Teacher Award' by the former president of India Dr A.P.J. Abdul Kalam when it was introduced for the first time in Delhi University in 2010. In the non-teaching staff, the pioneers were Mrs Rajesh Sharma and Mrs Suman Dutt Sharma, who were the first women to be appointed in the administration in 1989, the year UGC conferred the status of 'extended college' to Hindu College.

Apart from academics, many joined the civil services, became lawyers, doctors, scientists and performing artists and are found in all walks of life. Not all are known or can be listed. The Old Students' Association (OSA) too has tried to recognise their achievements but there are many more who will gradually emerge from the mists of time. While there are many lawyers, Mukta Gupta, a Zoology graduate from Hindu College, has achieved the distinction of being one of the few women judges in the Delhi High Court.

Reva Nayyar, Asha Swaroop and Tuktuk Ghosh were among the many women alumni who went into the civil services. Reva Nayyar, an alumnus of the 1960s, qualified for the IAS at the age of twenty-one years. From the Haryana cadre, she is remembered for her work in the North-Eastern region, and in Haryana as managing director of Haryana Breweries who

converted a loss-incurring venture into a profit-making unit (its share value jumped twelve times). She is the recipient of the Asia International award, the National Citizen award and a Gold Medal for excellence in management given by an organisation in Singapore.

Asha Swaroop, Chief Secretary of Himachal Pradesh was also Secretary, Information and Broadcasting, Government of India. She was honoured with the Bharat Shiromani Award. A post-graduate in English Literature, Asha Swaroop was also a Pearson Fellow of the International Development Research Centre, Canada. In her long bureaucratic career, Asha Swaroop was known for the commitment with which she looked after the various government departments.

Dr Tuktuk Ghosh, graduated in History from Hindu College and also taught here from 1979–81. An ace debater, she had keen interest in literature, arts and travel. A PhD in ancient history and archaeology from the University of Delhi, she published her thesis in 1985 under the title, 'The History of Rice in India: Mythology, Culture and Agriculture'. As an IAS officer of the 1981 West Bengal cadre, Dr Ghosh held key positions both at the Centre and in the states.

Deeksha Suri and Shradha Suri Marwah are two young women entrepreneurs who joined their father's business and carved out their paths to success. Deeksha Suri, a post-graduate in Business Management from the London School of Economics, is the executive director of the Lalit Suri hospitality group. She is one of the three to inherit the hospitality group, perhaps India's only privately owned company which owns sixteen luxury hotels. Shradha Suri Marwah, another member of the Lalit Suri family, holds a Master of Science in International Marketing Management, London and Master of Science in Information Systems from the London School of Economics. She is the managing director of Subros Limited Auto Air Conditioning and the director of Mercantile Capital and Financial Services Pvt. Ltd., Rohan Motors Limited, Prima Telecom Ltd. and Prima Cellular Limited. She is also an executive director of Fibcom India Ltd. She served as a director of Bharat Hotels Ltd. Shradha Suri Marwah started her career with Reebok India before moving to Subros Limited as its managing director, where she has been a critical part of change management and has taken the company to new heights.

The college also had the advantage of providing a pre-medical course and this attracted many girls aspiring to be doctors. Among the many eminent ones is Dr Sudarshana Sabharwal, a well-known gynaecologist in Delhi who graduated in Medicine in 1943, topping in her class. She is the winner of the Hardinge Gold medal and the Willingdon Silver medal. She practised till the age of eighty and performed over one lakh operations in her long career.

Among eminent performing artists is Rani Karnaa, renowned Kathak and Odissi dancer who was a student of the college in 1954–56. Suchitra Gupta who teaches History at Hindu College has made a contribution to the Delhi theatre scene and is a well-reputed artist on television. She guided several students and gave them their initial breaks on stage; she has been on the visiting faculty of the National School of Drama. She has lent her voice for the National

Facing page: *Editorial Board 1958-59 (left); Delhi Students' Arts and Crafts Exhibition 1936, Hindu College, Delhi (right)*

Geographic and History channels. There are many young women from Hindu College in the media: Sapna Rana, Soni Sangwan and Neha Khanna come to mind.

The present crop of film personalities has quite a sprinkling of Hindu College girls who have done extremely well. Tisca Chopra created a place for herself with her performance in the movie *Taare Zameen Par*. She has acted in several films and television serials and has won many awards, including a Filmfare award for her acting. Loveleen Tandon earned kudos as the co-producer of the Oscar-winning *Slumdog Millionnaire*. Rekha Bhardwaj has won the Filmfare award for the best playback singer. Her songs have become a rage amongst the present generation. She is equally comfortable in classical, sufi and ghazal singing. She topped the university in her graduation in Music.

Women in sports have, however, remained a lacuna. Very few Hindu College girls have excelled in sports. Vineeta Malhotra won the national championship in horse riding in 1997-98. However, in recent years, girls have been outshining and outnumbering boys in many fields. They top the college and the university, participate enthusiastically in extracurricular activities and win prizes. The college has had girls as prime ministers, opposition leaders and secretaries of the Literary Union and editors of the magazine. Perhaps it is the egalitarian space in the college that allowed girls to find their wings even when they were in a minority.

The Literary Union, Speakers Association and the College Parliament

A culture and tradition were created for training students in public speaking and inculcating awareness about nationalism. This resulted in a strong Literary Union, which continues to occupy an important place in college life. The Literary Union attracted national leaders like Jawaharlal Nehru, Pattabhi Sitaramayya, Bhulabhai Desai and Sathyamurthy, Rev. C.F. Andrews, Swami Bhawani Dayal (president of the South African Indian Congress), R. Frank Wheatley.

Well-known speakers such as Bool Chand, Kulwant Rai, H.D. Sikand, V.N. Sareen, D.N. Bhasin, S.C. Dutta, D.K. Syal and Purshottam Lal dominated the debating scene. In December 1933, a Speakers Association was formed. The chronicle in the college magazine (February 1935) observed the long-felt need for starting such an association. Even though the Literary Union was doing useful work, it 'could not take the burden of training speakers'. It was patronised by the then principal, S.K. Sen. The association trained students in the art of elocution and gave lessons in public speaking. It was considered a section of the Literary Union.

The college parliament was a natural corollary. The Literary Union and parliament complemented each other as the debaters invariably became good parliamentarians and some of them were elected as prime ministers of the college. The parliament was created on the lines of the British House of Lords and House of Commons and had a similar constitution, paving the way for democratic governance in the college. The upper house had professors as its members; the lower house was constituted by the students. The principal presided over the two houses and was addressed as 'His Majesty'.

When it was started in 1920, the parliament was possibly only meant to be a mock parliament to acquaint students with the parliamentary system and procedures. In 1923, the principal nominated Dasharatha Sharma as the prime minister, as there were no elections. He also appointed P.K. Shanglu as the leader of opposition. Eventually the parliament grew into a giant platform both for students and teachers. At the back of their minds, the college administrators must have been dreaming of a free India and self-governance. The draft constitution of the college's parliament reflected the seriousness attached to it. It was a thoroughly credible exercise! The participating students were well educated about how the Parliament worked in Britain; more so, after India attained freedom and had her own Parliament in 1950.

What is amazing is that with great effort the students succeeded in enrolling Mohammed Ali Jinnah, N.V. Gadgil, Sardar Sant Singh, Bhulabhai Desai, Sathyamurthy, Seth Abdulla Hasan, Maulana Shaukat Ali and many other eminent people and parliamentarians as honorary members of the college parliament. They participated in many sessions of the college's parliament and this was a privilege for both the students as well as the teachers.

Above left: *Dasharatha Sharma was prime minister of the college parliament in 1923*

Below: *Professor Prem Chand was a fierce nationalist and speaker for decades*

Facing page: *Board of Advisors of the Literary Union, 1956-57 (above); Great debaters: H.D. Sikand, Kulwant Rai and V.N. Sareen won the Law Hall and the Lucknow University Union trophies (below)*

Role in the Freedom Movement

Participating in the freedom struggle came naturally to the students and teachers. The significance of the teachers' role is evident even in various debates in the college. The college parliament was the nucleus of all discussions regarding the freedom movement.

Principal N.V. Thadani inculcated a great sense of patriotism among the students during his tenure. A staunch believer in the freedom movement, he was there to support and protect the students. Professor Prem Chand, another fierce nationalist, and speaker for decades, trained students in public speaking and the parliamentary system and procedures.

The all-India debates organised by the college parliament and the Literary Union brought together some of the best talent in debating from other colleges and universities as well. The topics discussed those days were considered 'anti-national' by the British regime.

The college was never insulated from national life and the political atmosphere prevalent in the country. In 1934, the students were discussing progressive topics such as, 'Socialism is the only means of attaining emancipation' and 'Co-education is essential in India at the present moment'. In 1938, in an extraordinary session of the parliament, Prem Chand moved a resolution, 'That in the opinion of this House, all the communal organizations of the country should be dissolved forthwith to join hands with the Congress in the interest of a united Nationalist Programme'.[9]

In his opening remarks, Prem Chand reiterated the humiliation of being a slave nation. He said, ever since we realised that 'Swaraj is our birthright' and 'even a government of angels is no substitute for self-government', we have been making efforts to achieve this much-coveted ideal of freedom. All this was discussed even before the Quit India Movement. The period between the late 1930s and early 1940s could be considered an important landmark in the college's parliament. A debate saw some important political leaders participating in the extraordinary session. The then Speaker of the Orissa Assembly, Mukanda Prasad Dass, moved a resolution: 'In the opinion of this House, the educational reconstruction of India can only be achieved through the Wardha Scheme.' This scheme advocated free and compulsory education for seven

Group photo of the parliament, Hindu College, 1939-40. Bool Chand (4th from right) and Reba Roy (2nd from right) were the Speaker, and Minister for Social Service and Hobbies respectively

9 *The Indraprastha*, 1938-39.

years and the education process to be manual and productive work oriented, with the mother tongue as the medium of instruction. Eminent leaders Khuda Bux, Speaker of the NWFP Assembly, G.S. Gupta, Speaker of the CP Assembly and K. Venkata Swami Naidu, Deputy President of the Madras Council participated in the debate besides Professor N.R. Malkani, N.V. Thadani and J.N. Sahani.

Parliament in the College Magazine

The editorial of the December 1936 issue of the college magazine, *The Indraprastha* read, 'We feel that while the solemnity, the decorum and earnestness displayed in the proceedings of Parliament are educative restraints, sometimes they are oppressive.' However the college was convinced of its usefulness and went ahead to strengthen it. A supplement of the magazine also gave a glimpse of how outsiders were invited to participate in debates after being sworn in as honorary members of parliament. In a special session held on 4 December 1939 in the amphitheatre, Professor M.M. Beg (later the principal of Delhi College) and B. Banerjee, an eminent advocate, were first sworn in as honorary members before they participated in the debate on 'If man is to live, God must go'.

Students' interest in national issues and politics remained alive during this period. The editorial notes in the December 1936 issue of the college magazine observed:

> In Europe the students' movement stands for democracy, peace and culture and has arrayed itself definitely against Fascism and war. In dependent countries the students are actively helping the movement of national freedom and regeneration. What about our own country and our students?
>
> The picture is neither very gloomy nor bright. A beginning has been made and in the right direction too. At Lahore, last month, the foundation of an all India students' federation was laid. Prior to this there have been students' organizations but they existed in name only. They have not prospered. Though they were called students' unions or students' associations, yet in practice they were or became the mere adjuncts of some particular party and thus they no longer remained a students' organization.

Reacting to the cry raised at that time that students should have nothing to do with politics, the magazine asserted that it was an impractical suggestion because 'if students are to become responsible citizens of tomorrow they must know and discuss the political issues which affect the destiny of their country.'

The editorial further said:

> There is certainly a difference between an intelligent interest in politics and active participation therein. We plead for the former and realize that the latter is not possible

> as long as we are students. We certainly should not allow politics to be banned for us, we want to be treated like other citizens, responsible for our acts and the consequences thereof. This is however between the state and individual conscience.

It called for the organisation of the student community and coming to democratic decisions with the participation of all the students.

Significantly, the editorial carried a quote from veteran leader, Bhulabhai Desai, which said, 'The question that I want every Indian student to ask himself is—what is it that accounts for the present position in India today? What is it that has reduced India to the position in which it is today? ...That is the question which requires solution, for on its true solution depends our future near as well as remote.'

A special supplement of the college magazine was published on parliamentary debates where the speaker, Dr Bool Chand drawing from his rich experience of studying abroad wrote an article on 'Questions in Parliament' underlining the importance of the right of the members to ask questions. He profusely quoted from British and French parliaments while elaborating on the procedures followed in accepting the questions and the responsibility of the government to reply to the questions.

The Question Hour

The question hour was described as 'interpellations' and the participation of women students was frequent. The questions were numbered and His Majesty's government was obliged to answer them.

An example:[10]

> Q.No.2 Hon. Leela Awasthi: Is H.M.'s (His Majesty's) Government aware of the fact that certain Hon'ble members including a few professors were insulted by a police sergeant? If so, what action has the Government taken in the matter?
>
> Reply by Hon. Reba Roy: Yes, Sir. We have achieved a definite victory in as-much-as it has been decided that in future, cases under certain sections can never be taken up by the Police and the Magistrate, but by the college authorities.

Assertion of the Parliament and the Creation of the Common Room

Students rightly felt that the parliament was not serving a useful purpose discussing topics like 'Should men have moustaches or not?' or 'How should doves and pigeons be prevented from coming inside the rooms?' They wanted a parliament where students could discuss and decide the budget allocations for different societies in the house, and not mundane issues. The

---

10 Supplement, *The Indraprastha*, 'Parliamentary debates (Winter Term)', December 1939.

parliament needed to pave the way for greater participation of students in college affairs. Sure enough the college parliament prompted the creation of a common room in 1937. This was considered quite an achievement.[11]

After Independence

There is no record of events and parliament sessions after 1940 or whether the college magazine came out because several students were actively participating in events relating to the freedom struggle. But after Independence, particularly after the college moved to its new campus, the parliament apparently was quite rudderless and could not match its old glory.

The magazine published in April 1950 carried an editorial that observed:

> The Parliament still continues to be the pulse-beat of college life, and still draws large crowds. Mr P.C. (referring to Prem Chand) still continues to preside over its sessions. We still go about saying that our Parliament has not its equal in any other College in Delhi.
>
> But it is obvious to the discerning eye that something is missing; that it is crying aloud for some kind of a change. In a free India, fiery speeches are not enough. In one important session, the Speaker said, in tones of great seriousness and solemnity that His Majesty is going to make a very important announcement. We held our breath; something momentous was coming.
>
> We learnt that we are now a Republic that we have a President instead of His Majesty. The Home ministry then garlanded the President and the Speaker, and feted them; the ministers were photographed...
>
> The appointment of a standing Finance Committee is all to the good; we welcome the cooperation given by our teachers. But what about handing more powers to the students? Must the ministers be ministers only in name? Why not give the government and the opposition the right to bring out their wall papers, and thus educate us politically? Why not make our constitution more in accord with the spirit of the times?

The student community restlessly demanded more powers and a hand in the administration. The Literary Union organised an essay competition in 1954 for which the topic was 'The College parliament should be abolished'. The constitution was amended later to adjust to the changing circumstances.[12]

---

11 Kulwant Rai, 'The College Puts on a New Colour!', *The Indraprastha*, December 1937.

12 *The Indraprastha*, 1954-55.

The popularity of the college parliament was so great that a team from the British Broadcasting Corporation (BBC) came to make a documentary on the working of parliamentary institutions in India. Hindu College was among the institutes selected to show the working of democracy at the grass-roots level. Famous Olympic marathon runner, Chris Chataway, who was later a minister in the British government, headed the BBC team.[13]

At some point the existence of the college parliament was in jeopardy because the students were losing interest. They seemed more interested in cultural programmes than in serious debates and attendance in the parliament thinned. Also, in 1961 the college decided to have indirect elections by amending the constitution. There was one MP for every seven students thus restricting the franchise. Now there were only 170 MPs. This had an adverse affect on the college parliament. Students lost interest in the proceedings and decisions of the house because they were not directly involved. Speaker Prem Chand was the first to realise that life had gone out of the college parliament. The then principal, Dr B.M. Bhatia constituted a committee, which recommended a new constitution restoring franchise to all students. This had an electrifying effect and the college appeared to have retrieved its glorious parliament.[14]

However, this was short-lived. Perhaps once the national struggle was over there was no common cause left that could hold the students and teachers together. Gradually politicking became the order of the day and so some of the worst aspects of electoral politics began to vitiate the atmosphere.

When Principal Dr Kavita Sharma was the president and Dr K.P. Sarabhai was the speaker of the college parliament, it was felt that the only interest that the students had was defeating the budget and thus bringing down the government. The result was that every time the government fell, the members (students) lost interest in the proceedings. Nothing much was achieved by the parliament. There was a tendency on the part of the students to be frivolous in their approach to the parliament. Principal P.C. Verma had already scrapped pre-election speeches and the sessions usually descended into chaos. An amendment was made that even if the budget was defeated, the government would not fall. The election for secretaries for some of the societies was done away with and the only electoral offices that remained were that of prime minister and leader of opposition. The prime minister was the highest vote getter and the second was the leader of opposition. The prime minister was free to choose his council of ten ministers with their corresponding secretaries. This brought peace but the substance of the parliament was already largely lost.

As the college grew, departmental societies and other college societies came up with their own festivals of lectures, debates and cultural activities. Students found it easier to concentrate

The Hindu College Parliament at work was televised by technicians from BBC for the audience in England, 1956-57

Facing page above:
Hindu College produced freedom fighters like Dr Kapila Vatsyayan (left) and Brij Mohan Toofan (right)

Facing page below:
Left to Right—Raj K. Oberoi (Secy OSA); Gajraj Bahadur Nagar (Minister of Food, Civil Supplies and Tourism, Haryana); Bhiku Ram Jain (MP); Dr Subramanian Swamy (MP); N.K. Nigam; Amitabh Verma (prime minister of the college parliament)

---

13 *The Indraprastha*, 1956-57.

14 Ibid., 1965 and 1966.

on the opportunities available in these spaces rather than entangling themselves with the university electoral politics. Now the chief focus of the prime minister was watered down to the success of MECCA, the annual winter festival!

Although the parliament declined, the legacy of debating that it and the Literary Union gave remained very strong. These two bodies gave some of the best debaters to Hindu College. The decades of the 1950s and 1960s saw some great debaters—Inder Sharma, Raj Bhargava, Giri Lal Jain, R.W. Desai, K. Thyagraj, Viresh Chaudhry, N.K. Naik, Vijay Jaitley, Lalit Bhasin, Kumud Shankara, Dev Ghatak, Pran Nath Khanna, Kusum Bassi and Sudhakaran. Subsequent years had debaters like Vithal Rao Cowalgi, B. Ghosh and also Aftab Seth and Arun Bhagat. And of course there were T.C.A. Rangachari and Chand Joshi, a formidable team dominating the debating tradition for their entire stay in the college.

The 1970s and 1980s had Hardeep Puri, Pradeep Puri, Ravinder Jassal, Bhasker Chatterjee, Balachandran Nair, Sanjay Srivastava, Deepak Verma, Siddhartha Basu, Mahesh Rangarajan and Anil Shorey who kept the flag high for the college winning several trophies. In Hindi debating there were Jasbir Neerav and Narendra Brahmchari who won dozens of trophies for the college. In the 1980s, Hindu debaters won the Mukarji Memorial trophy instituted by St. Stephen's College, for many years at a stretch.

The college produced parliamentarians like Dr Subramanian Swamy, Bhiku Ram Jain, Charanjit Singh, Hari Kishan Shastri and Vishwabandhu Gupta; ministers from Haryana—Gajraj Bahadur Nagar, Rao Inderjeet Singh and K.L. Poswal; freedom fighters—Professor N.K. Nigam and Professor L.C. Jain along with Kapila Vatsyayan, Brij Mohan Toofan and local leaders like Kanwar Lal Sharma and Kanwar Lal Gupta.

TAGORE'S MESSAGE TO US.

তোমার বীণা আমার মনো মাঝে
কখনো শুনি, কখনো ভুলি, কখনো শুনিনা যে।
আকাশ যবে শিহরি উঠে গানে,
গোপন কথা কহিতে থাকে ধরার কানে কানে,
তাহার মাঝে সহসা মাতে বিষম কোলাহলে
আমার মনে বাঁধনহারা স্বপন দলে দলে।
হে বীণাপাণি তোমার সভাতলে
আকুল হিয়া উন্মাদিয়া বেসুরে হয়ে বাজে
তোমার বাণী কখনো শুনি কখনো শুনি না যে॥

২ মাঘ ১৩৪৩

শ্রীরবীন্দ্রনাথ ঠাকুর

Tagore's Message to Us.

(*Translated into English by B. N. G.*)

The strains of thy *Vina* in the recesses of my heart
Now do I hear, now I do not,
Now I forget and I heed them not.

When the sky quivers with music
And whispers into the ears of Earth its mysterious secrets;
In the midst of this soulful communion
The riotous procession of wayward dreams
Revels in my mind in sudden frenzy
With a terrific din resounding.

In thine audience hall, O *Vinapani,*
My distracted heart pours forth
Discordant notes in a mad impulse.
Now I hear thy voice, now I do not,
Now I forget and I heed it not.

2nd Magh, 1343.

Sri Rabindranath Tagore

Reminiscences

Daya Krishna (1938–45) recalls the days when noted journalist Giri Lal Jain was the prime minister of the college and there were other brilliant students like Sita Ram Goel, Raj Krishna, J.N. Kapur, Madan Mohan Mathur, J.P. Guha, K.K. Kaul, Vivek Dutta, L.C. Jain, Som Benegal, Brij Mohan Toofan and Kapila Malik (Kapila Vatsyayan).

A prominent student of the fifth year and a keen debater himself, Kulwant Rai described the parliament as, 'A remarkable piece of innovation'. He further wrote, 'I am not sure whether this parliament is a revival of some old and dead institution which existed in this college in the days gone by. However, it has received a fresh lease of life at the hands of His Majesty, Principal Thadani, if I may be permitted to use a parliamentary phrase.'

'With small and general reform of parliament, its latent capacity to act as the greatest instrument of the students shall reveal itself. Thus the students will be able to prove their work as organisers as well as they have done as speakers,' he added.

Kulwant Rai gives an interesting account of how some of the demands made by the parliament were met. A considerable sum of money was sanctioned to build an amphitheatre in 1937 on an old unused water tank in the college. College elections were held here with a show of hands. In the amphitheatre apart from various other activities, classes were also held even in inclement weather and the cold winter in spite of the stone seats and lecturers straining to make themselves heard.[15]

L.C. Jain (1940–47) described the parliament as, 'an excellent forum for rousing interest in public affairs in the general body of the students as well as giving what could be called training to some of the students elected as the prime minister or the leader of the opposition. The college parliament would frequently invite leaders who were members of the Central Assembly as it was called, personalities like Sathyamurthy, C. Rajagopalachari and N.G. Ranga.'[16]

Dr Kapila Vatsyayan (1942–45) reminisces, 'Prem Chand was the maker of debaters. He taught us to argue well, to take positions and defend our stand. Kumar Dev with his husky voice was the supreme debater with D.K. Syal as the most vociferous one. Parliament elections were a training ground for the future. We fought elections but without a tinge of real politics outside influencing us. There were the Students Federation and the Students Union but without the strings. We were first and last all nationalist and minor players in the struggle for freedom.'[17]

Sheila Dhar (1943–50) recalls, 'The College parliament used to be held in an amphitheatre. All this was in the Westminster House style politics. "My Hon'ble friend on the side opposite," etc., all this Victorian style of political oratory.'[18]

---

15 *The Indraprastha*, 1937.

16 *In Retrospect*, p. 66.

17 Ibid., p. 74.

18 Ibid., p. 79.

Facing page:
Rabindranath Tagore's message when he visited Hindu College in 1936

Preet Chablani, daughter of Principal N.V. Thadani, was a student of the college (1938–41) and she vividly recalls Rabindranath Tagore's visit to the college.[19]

K.L. Madhok (1951–54) who had the good fortune of seeing both the Kashmere Gate and university campus, proudly recalled the parliamentary proceedings that were watched by students in the round amphitheatre. As years passed, there was an emphasis on decorum and discipline and the students were expected to understand the rules and procedures of the house. Professor Prem Chand, the speaker for many decades, gave a new dimension to the college parliament, adding wit and humour to the proceedings.[20]

Kanwar Lal Sharma, a senior advocate and a political leader involved in Delhi's affairs, joined the college in 1929-30. He was the first elected prime minister of the Hindu College parliament. While talking about his involvement in the freedom movement, Kanwar Lal Sharma talked about how he organised the Delhi Student Federation and was its first president. He recalled Asaf Ali, Achyut Patwardhan and C.F. Andrews coming to the college to address the students and how the parliament received wide publicity not only in Delhi but also outside. In an article[21] he describes how fortunate he was to hear Mahatma Gandhi and Jawaharlal Nehru addressing the students on their visits to the college. He and Preet Chablani recalled the magical evening of poetry with Rabindranath Tagore and Sarojini Naidu reciting their poems. Preet Chablani remembers Tagore seated on the dais impressive in his stately presence. After a few introductory remarks when he started reciting his poems in a commanding voice the students were overawed. He became a different man, alive with the fire of his inward joy. He was in tune with the images he had created and lifted them all into the world of his imagination.[22]

Mark of Honour

This is the highest honour that the college bestows on any student for all round excellence. No wonder it comes once in a blue moon for the standards set by the college for this award are so high that students do not qualify for it frequently. In its history of more than 110 years, barely half a dozen students have been honoured with this award. However, it can be a point of argument that many more, worthy of this award were left out.

Shyam Sunder Mathur got the MOH in 1938, for excelling in cricket and meritorious service rendered to the college

Above: *Tilak Raj was the first student to receive the Mark of Honour (called MOH here) for being a tennis star in 1935-36. He was the best tennis player in the university since 1932*

Sports

Sports were an integral part of college life from the beginning providing opportunities to students from all sections of society to grow and excel. In keeping with its ethos, the college had elections for the posts of General Secretary, Games and for captains and secretaries for

19 Ibid., p. 59.

20 'Hindu College in My Time', *The Indraprastha*, 1983-84.

21 Ibid.

22 *In Retrospect*, p. 59.

each game. While hockey, tennis and volleyball drew quite a few talented students, it was cricket that dominated the psyche of students, teachers and other staff members. The players turned into icons for the students and the college authorities showed enough indulgence. In the early 1930s, besides cricket, hockey and volleyball were quite popular and dominated university tournaments. The leading players of these years were K.D. Bhasin, Sardar Bahadur, Kiran Bahadur, Hemchandra, Abdul Hayee and Shyam Sunder Mathur (Cricket) and many of them captained the university team. Rameshwar Dayal was the university hockey captain; Suraj Prakash, Tilak Raj and Rajinder Singh excelled in tennis. Kiran Bahadur played in the Ranji Trophy for Delhi. In the 1940s, other Ranji players, Ravi Vaide, Lakshmi Chand Saxena and Mohammed Rauf were the mainstay of the college cricket team, the university champions.

The cricket rivalry with St. Stephen's College is legendary and continued for almost half a century. However, as old timers point out, the rivalry had a healthy tradition; the two teams would treat each other to dinner regardless of the winner.

The two colleges played the finals for years, with no one dominating. Each college vied to admit talented sportsmen. Former Ranji player and alumnus of the college, Late Dr Ravi Vaide, once wrote, 'Even during those days a mini-*Mahabharata* was fought between Hindu and St Stephen's on the cricket field...' He added, 'Only the battle royal involved everyone those days. Mercifully this great rivalry between the two colleges, which constituted the bulk of the Delhi University and Delhi Ranji teams in later years, continued in subsequent years with great friendship between the two.'[23]

The 1950–60 decade and some years after that saw the phenomenal rise of cricket in the university and the dominance of Hindu-St. Stephen's in the sport. This period provided Ranji players for Delhi in large numbers. At one time, the Delhi team consisted almost entirely of Hindu and Stephen's players. This period also saw Prakash Bhandari make his test debut, being the first from Delhi to represent the country.

The Inter-College Cricket finals drew massive crowds, whenever these two colleges clashed. Hindu won the trophy for nine consecutive years from 1952 onwards. Before that for a number of years, St. Stephen's had been the winners.

Indian cricket icon Gautam Gambhir needs no introduction. Before Gautam joined the elite list of test players from the college, his predecessors were Prakash Bhandari, Manmohan Sood, Rajinder Pal, Surinder Khanna, Sunil Valson, Rakesh Shukla, Saba Karim, Gursharan Singh, Deep Das Gupta, Nikhil Chopra, Rahul Sanghvi, Murali Karthik and Akash Chopra.

The college was also in the forefront in basketball, hockey, shooting, swimming, football and athletics. Shooters from the college include M.S. Rathore, N.S. Rathore, Ajay Pratap Singh, Rupinder Singh, M. Uthappa and Zorawar Singh. The college displayed its supremacy in swimming and water polo by winning the Delhi University Aquatics Meet six times in a row from

Roshan Abbas, the recipient of the MOH in 1991, is now an eminent personality in the entertainment industry

Middle: *Sundeep Khanna received the MOH in 1972 for academic excellence*

Above: *Raj K. Bhargava got the MOH in 1957 for being an all rounder*

23 Dr Ravi Vaide, *Total Recall in Chronicles of Time* (Delhi: OSA, Hindu College, 2011).

1967-68 to 1973-74. In athletics, the college produced Pramod Kumar who won the gold medal in 5,000 metres and silver in 10,000 metres in the All-India Athletics Meet in Trivandrum in 1983-84. In swimming, Nand Kishore Bansal, Ramesh Lal, Madan Lal, Bhudev Sharma, Umesh Talwar, Vinod Bansal, Ajay Singh, Balbir Singh and Bharat Merchant represented the country in various international events.

The table tennis flag was held aloft by Manjit Dua, the national champion and Sudhir Phadke. They were also members of the four-member Indian team that took part in the international table tennis competition on the American continent. Devinder Puri and Inder Prakash dominated the all-India rankings.

Vikramjit Singh, five-time national golf champion, represented the country for twenty-five years. He won the Asia-Pacific Seniors Golf Championship. After winning the Sri Lanka championship in 1967, he won the same title after a gap of twenty-five years in 1992.

Raj Bhargava recalls the ever-popular president of games of his time, Mr D.S. Mathur who was also the head of Department of Physics. With his disarming smile he always parried the thrusts from other people on cricketers and saw them through not only in the cricket finals but also their examinations. It was partly his association with Mr Mathur and partly his own interest in sports that prompted Ashok Mittal of the Department of Commerce, to involve himself in the organisation of sports in Hindu College.

Sports persons of the late 1960s will not easily forget Ashok Mittal and G.C. Soni, the sports in-charges, who provided mature and timely guidance. Soni always said, 'We should concentrate on producing good sportsmen and not merely good players.' Soni was

Right: *Prakash Bhandari made his Test debut from Hindu College*

Facing page: *Centenary dinner in Hindu College: S.P.S. Chauhan, Vinay Lamba and Anil Shorey (left to right)*

Below: *Cricket match between old students and present students (extreme right); Balaji Rao playing a shot (centre); Hindu College Cricket Team, 1942-43 (left)*

succeeded by Mr O.P. Dutta and with him the college was in reckoning for fourteen out of seventeen games in which inter-college tournaments were organised. The college also won the Chancellor's Trophy consecutively for three years during 1966–1972. All major sports championships were bagged by Hindu College during this time under the stewardship of the President of Games, Dr A.K. Mittal.

Vinay Lamba, a well-known cricketer got news of his admission to Hindu College when he was attending the All-India Schools Cricket Coaching camp in Hyderabad. He fondly remembers the Physical Director, Soni Saheb who taught him discipline and hard work. Perseverance, diligence and punctuality were a few traits that got ingrained under his guidance and support. And, of course, how could the sportsmen forget S.P.S. Chauhan, popularly known as 'Babuji'. Vinay Lamba pays his tribute to him: 'Mr Chauhan was a great sports fan and would go out of his way to do anything to help a sports person.'[24]

The college produced several cricketers of national repute who could not play in the national team but were involved in various championships including the Ranji Trophy and Dalip Trophy. Many of them are remembered even today.

For the founders of the college, it was imperative to provide education to those who were not part of the privileged elite and to create a nationalist milieu where students would be encouraged to fearlessly express themselves, fight foreign rule and always be aware that they had to lend a helping hand to the less privileged. Inducting girls from the beginning was part of the founding vision of the college that sought to provide educational opportunities to all sections of society, especially to those to whom it was not easily available.

24 *In Retrospect*, pp. 121-122.

As time passed, participation in college debates, parliament sessions and other public events like sports came naturally to the students. The secular and democratic character of the college started right from its inception with English, Sanskrit, Urdu and Persian teachers being inducted and the college being thrown open not only to Hindu but also Muslim students who were given the freedom to stay away from Hindu prayers and the study of Hindu scriptures. The college parliament with its democratic character was unique for any educational institution. It brought democratic norms to students naturally. As Dr Subramanian Swamy, an alumnus, aptly summed it, the college taught him to think freely.

From the Mists of Time

Hindu College today is a large multi-disciplinary institution with students from every part of the country and from every station of life. They go on to do exceedingly well in all the spheres be it the government, judiciary, law, industry, the corporate world, theatre, cinema or performing arts. There are also several foreign students, particularly from developing countries who studied here and then returned to hold high positions in their respective countries. The college can truly claim to be a microcosm of the macrocosm of India stemming from the vision and aim of its founders—a nationalist college to serve the common man, making higher education available to those who were not a part of the elite. While there was a desire to educate Hindus and to encourage the study of Hindu texts, the outlook was essentially secular. Lacking support from the establishment at least for the first fifty years of its existence, the college preceded Delhi University and even when it became a part of it, its relationship with the university was often rocky at least in its initial years.

That the college was a people's movement can be seen from the fact that society at large came to its support and made contributions big and small at different times whenever the college found itself in financial difficulties. The business community of Delhi periodically rose to the occasion and eventually wholesale cloth merchants as a body decided to collect two pice (paise) per bale of cloth by way of contribution to the college. This continued to bring in a substantial sum of money for quite a number of years. Pandit Harnarayan Shastri of the Sanskrit department is still remembered for his great efforts to tide over the financial difficulties of the college and how he inspired the whole staff not to draw their monthly salaries until the finances of the college had improved. During the Centenary year of the college, Jivan Lal Seth at the age of ninety-four fondly recalled Pandit Harnarayan Shastri. What an impact he must have had on the students![1]

Locations and People

It is amazing how locations live on in the memories of old students and some people have become institutions in themselves. Inder Sharma talks of the time when the college was located in Kashmere Gate, opposite the famous 'St. James Church' and adjacent to an old historical mosque. He nostalgically remembers the *imli* (tamarind) tree under which the boys sat and watched girls. Its place has been taken by the virgin tree in the present campus and the rites associated with it have lost their innocence in the last ten to fifteen years. Then there was the amphitheatre where all kinds of activities took place—morning prayers, students' parliament, variety entertainment functions and even classes. Inder Sharma waxes lyrical about it: 'Who can forget "that great pit" ... "that swimming pool" turned into "that immortal amphitheatre," the scene of historic speeches by eminent public men of the times and the grooming of the

1 *In Retrospect*, p. 29.

Part of Skinner's building with a mosque near Hindu College

Previous page: *Both ex-students Jivan Lal Seth (left) 96 years and B.D. Gupta (right) 92 years with Principal Kavita A. Sharma—two special guests*

leadership of tomorrow's India. That resounding voice of a frail, meek-looking Prem Chand, demanding and commanding, "when the Chair stands there shall be absolute silence". How many of us owe so much to him and to friends like R.R.G.? (R.R. Gupta).'[2]

The present Inter State Bus Terminus (ISBT) was the cricket and athletic ground, both for Hindu and St. Stephen's colleges. Football was played where the Ladakh Buddha Vihar is situated at present on the bank of the Yamuna. Bhiku Ram Jain recalls that there was also a Boat Club and the students could enjoy a nice boat ride on the river.[3] In the Kashmere Gate building, Raj Bhargava remembers the thirty steps of the iron ladder which took pre-medical students to the Biology lab. Raj Bhargava chuckles that irreparable harm was done to the Ritz and Minerva cinemas when the college shifted to the university campus. In the new location, as Sukhbir Singh of the college office was heard to remark, attendance in the classes suddenly went up.[4]

Bhiku Ram Jain speaks nostalgically about Mithan Halwai with his *bedmi* lassi and *halwa*, which cost a princely sum of four annas. For Preet Chablani, it was the delicious breakfast of *jalebis* with milk, which brought all students together irrespective of college affiliations. Students converged at Mithan Halwai's shop for breakfast. Motilal, well-known film actor and an alumnus, did not forget to drop in there for a round of *bedmi aloo* and *chhole* to top it all with a sip of coffee at Carlton Café, another favourite haunt, whenever he visited the college. Today most of the Kashmere Gate building which was sold to the government has been demolished to give way to a modern one in which are housed the offices of the Municipal Corporation. However, some remnants of the old building can still be found at the back.

Banwari, the keeper of the cycle stand, was an institution in himself. The uncrowned king of the cycle stand for almost five decades, his love for the college and his childlike curiosity

2 Inder Mohan Sharma, 'Banwari's Bench', in Raj K. Oberoi (ed.), *The Hinduites*, p. 55.

3 *In Retrospect*, pp. 31-32.

4 Raj Bhargava, *Souvenir on the Occasion of Diamond Jubilee of Hindu College*, Delhi (1899–1959).

Lala Mithan Lal

Left: *Mithan Halwai has now been converted into a motor market*

Above: *Motilal, one of the finest actors of the Indian film industry, was considered a daredevil as a young man in college*

BOAT CLUB

HINDU COLLEGE DELHI.

Session :- 1951-52

Left to Right: *Sitting*: Suresh Kapoor, W. N. Khanna, K. C. Gupta, Y. P. Chopra.

Chairs : Kishan Sarup, Man Mohan Bedi, (*Joint Secretary*) Prof. G. C. Rampal (*President*), Principal A. Bhatacharya, Manohar Lal (*Secretary*), D. I. Yadve, B. P. Nautiyal.

Standing : *1st Row* : Jasbir Singh, Raj Kumar, R. C. Gupta, S. K. Bhalla, A. P. Chaudhry, Gurdip Singh, Kanwar Harkishan Singh, T. P. Singh, K. L. Aggarwal, T. C. Gupta, Sarwan Khanna.

2nd Row : U.C. Jain, T.C. Gupta, K.S. Chohan, Dharam Pal, Amarjit Singh, Rajinder Kumar, Kuldip Bahadur, Rajinder Kumar, J. K. Jain.

Photo by :
BERRY STUDIO
DELHI.

BOAT CLUB

Hindu College, Delhi. 1952-53.

Chairs (left to right)—Ranbir Singh, Harbans Singh, T. C. Gupta (Joint Secretary), Shri Gyan Chand (President), Shri A. Bhattacharya (Principal), Man Mc n Bedi (Secretary), Surinder Paul Singh Pruthi (Chief Adviser), Wishva Nath Khanna (Adviser), Rajinder Vaid (Adviser).

Standing 1st row (left to right)—Bawa, Santosh, Krishen, Jain, Gupta, Grover, Irani, Kulwant Singh, Munjal,

Standing 2nd row (left to right). Taddy, Basant, Suri, Chaudhri, Singal, Ram, Ram Krishen Malhotra, Goel, Harmesh, Baldev Singh, Surinder.

Photo by :
BERRY STUDIO,
Kashmere Gate, Delhi.

Today, most of the Kashmere Gate building of Hindu College has been demolished and houses the offices of the Municipal Corporation

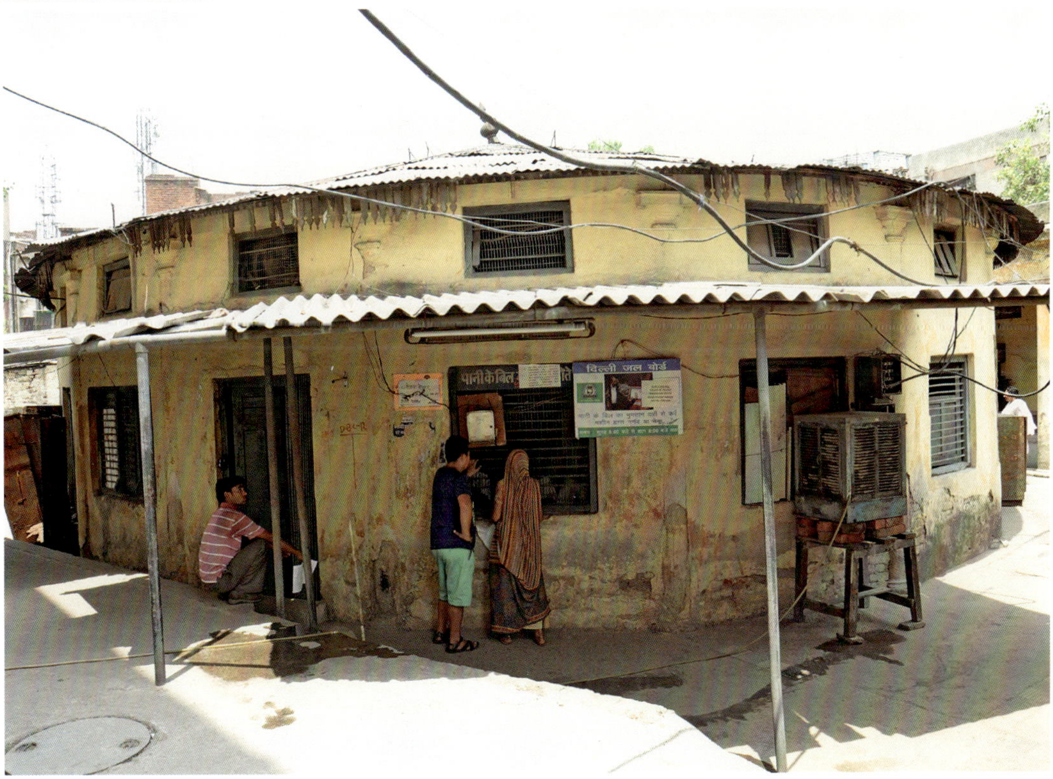

The circular building, once a baradari is presently the collection department of Delhi Jal Board

Above: *Remnants of Skinner's mansion now used as a storehouse of the Delhi Jal Board*

made him a darling. H.D. Sikand, a fourth year student in 1937, wrote in the college magazine (June 1937):

> Banwari is not a Lilliputian. He belongs to the Sisodia clan of Gihlote Rajputs.... He has served the college faithfully for the last eleven years. During his period of office several principals have come and gone, several students have become professors, and many professors have sold their bicycles and bought cars. When Banwari joined, there was no Parliament in the college, the education of girls was in its infancy and 'social service' was a new phrase.
>
> Banwari was a great authority on hats, water-proofs, attaché cases, umbrellas, tyres, cycle-lamps, pumps and tennis shoes. All old boys of the college sought Banwari's advice before going in for a new cycle. He could be often found exhorting some fourth year student, 'There is not much to think, Mister, go and buy a Humber. Dr Indra Sen always rides a Humber. If you want durability go in for a Hercules. Dr Umrao Bahadur uses it. Nothing like a Hercules.'

Even in the late 1950s and early 1960s, Banwari did not lose his inquisitiveness. He knew all the students who participated in any activity in the college, whether it was dance, drama, music or debating. But cricketers were Banwari's favourite because he loved the game and fondly

Present-day location of Carlton Café, so evident from the showroom's name in the motor market

recounted the exploits of all those who had played in front of him. 'Banwari's bench' fondly provided a student with *bidis* when he ran out of cigarettes; or a new basket for his cycle from a first year student's bike where a student could keep his books safely during examinations. According to Inder Sharma, Banwari was the 'information post, the trusted keeper of our secrets and bags, who used to keep a close watch on the movement of students and outsiders. He was an encyclopedia by himself.' In 1960, Satyavir Tyagi, Hindi editor of *The Indraprastha*, described Banwari as: 'Ordinary height, fair complexion, a pointed nose conveying the sharp mind, lines on the face, some light and some deep, sunken blurred eyes, a *bidi* in hand, a khaki pant—more like a pyjama, a long coat and the cap.' A great lover of cricket, he would know the minute to minute score sitting on his bench. When the college lost, he would remark philosophically 'defeat or victory is a part of the game' yet one could see the pain in his eyes.

Paanji sold paan (betel leaves) and cigarettes and Jai Singh sold tea. The lawn in which he sat is still popularly known as the Jai Singh Lawn. 'Chaat wale kaka' or Panditji sold his wares from the gate of Hindu College and Sardarji vended 'Caryhom' ice cream. The road in front of the college was a roadside club for exchanging daily, weekly and fortnightly gossip. Bhola and the washerman's father, Ram Singh served when the college was still at Kashmere Gate and moved with the college to the university campus.

For well-known film director, Imtiaz Ali, the wall separating Jai Singh Lawn from the entrance to the college taught him some precious lessons for life. He would sit for long hours on that wall with Paanji stationed by it, not too far away from him. He could not really understand why this wall existed as it did not separate anything from anything. You could go to the Jai Singh Lawn, from the opening on the side, for tea or xeroxes or even for a meeting of the 'Frusto Samaj'.

Anyone entering the college could see both Paanji and Imtiaz Ali sitting on the wall. The only difference between them, says Imtiaz sardonically, was that while his young eyes would be constantly moving and responding to those entering through the college gate, Paanji's experienced eyes took notice of only those who came up to his box-shop. The rest of the time, he stared indifferently into space with a faraway look and people could come and go as they pleased. As Imtiaz sat on the wall he saw each person come in, 'with a different song playing in his mind. Each body had a different tune. And the same person on different days would have different rhythms. Rigorous exercise of sitting on the wall and a new belief was forming in my head. That I could discern people, approximate their thoughts. That, like most other college beliefs, fell by the wayside after a week or so.'

This made Imtiaz think about why he and Paanji responded so differently. It was because he realised that while he was interested and expectant, Paanji had seen all that life could show. So it occurred to him that it was only a matter of time and he too could turn into a

Paanji was felicitated during the Centenary celebrations of Hindu College

Paanji. That thought served to galvanise him into building a future for himself. It broke his addiction to the wall. But he does acknowledge that 'all that gaping at people helps me today in my profession as a director. I have to explain people to people. I couldn't have done that well if I hadn't sat on the wall.'[5]

Immortalised in the Chronicles

The Indraprastha, the college magazine which has been in existence for more or less seventy-five years is the chronicler of the life and times of the college. Its covers follow the interesting journey of the Hindu College logo as it evolved with the growth of the college. The first logo in January 1930 had Saraswati, the goddess of learning with her veena and *Vande Matram* written under it. It had a Sanskrit quote and its translation which read, 'A golden veil is thrown over the face of truth. O, *Pushan*! Dost thou uncover it for the comprehension of right *dharma*.' The 1931 issue shows 'Bharat Mata' within a map of India. Two lions flank her. The words *Vande Matram* are inscribed in the middle. The cover of the November 1932 issue shows the logo as 'a rising sun' and 'a lotus flower.' The words 'Music of Truth' are inscribed in the logo and the bold alphabets H.C.D. are written below it. On the cover of the February 1935 issue, the logo is retained as such but the letters H.C.D. are omitted. The same cover design was repeated in almost all the issues till the late 1960s. After that, the cover designs were different every year. The logo has now got crystallised into a water lily with the rising sun on top and the words 'Music of Truth' below.

Many Hinduites live in the pages of *The Indraprastha*. As J.K. Anand, a former librarian says, the magazine is virtually a treasure-trove of a wide range of articles, stories and poems written by both teachers and students. Apart from recording the visit of Mahatma Gandhi in February 1930 and his speech, *The Indraprastha* also talks of the shifting of the college from Kashmere Gate to its present building in

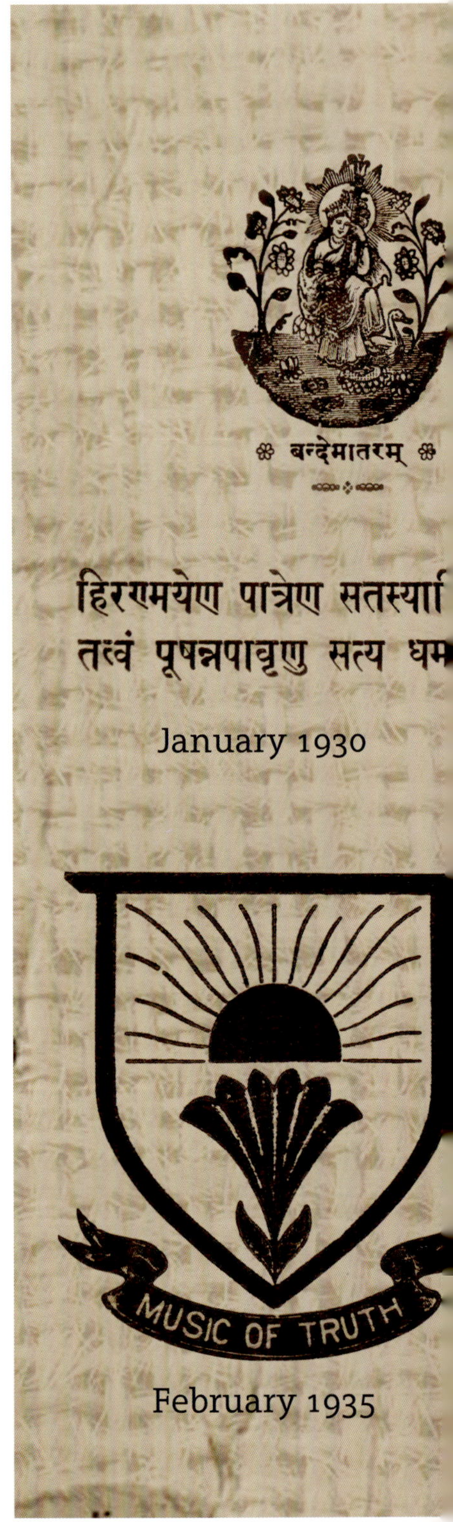

Facing page: *Hindu College logo over the years*

5 *In Retrospect*, pp. 139–141.

1931

November 1932

1957

Present Logo

1953. It describes the various landmarks of the college: Diamond Jubilee Year celebrations in 1959; the Platinum Jubilee and the Centenary, together with the starting of the annual MECCA festival in 1973 when Sanjay Srivastava was the prime minister. Prior to this festival, cultural programmes were held every fortnight in which only students from Hindu College participated.

Apart from *The Indraprastha*, the memories of many others are recorded in the various souvenirs as well as in a book *In Retrospect* published at the time of the Centenary. The Old Students' Association has been publishing an annual newsletter since 2000, which reports on its various activities. In addition, some members of the families associated with Hindu College have published books and monographs. Some of these are *Ek Shatabdi* and *Lala Lachhman Das Garg: Atmakatha* by Col Brij Behari Sharan, and *Yogeshwar Dayal Aur Dilli* by Mrs Usha Kumar, Yogeshwar Dayal's daughter.

The July 1966 Disaster

Dr B.M. Bhatia recalls the fire caused by a short circuit that gutted the old hall together with the entire stage equipment and furniture. This was a stunning blow to the college but when Dr Bharat Ram, the chairman of the Governing Body was informed about this, he assured all help in rebuilding the auditorium. The vice chancellor was equally sympathetic and promised to try his best to secure a grant from UGC.

When the college reopened on 18 of July that year, Dr Bhatia, in a voice choked with emotion promised 'a better, bigger and more beautiful hall'. Donations were invited and a beginning was made with a small sum of Rs 350 which included Rs 100 sent by Mr Sudhir Bose of St. Stephen's College and Rs 50 from Rajiv Khanna, an old student and by then a lecturer in the Law faculty. A year was spent in trying to get private donations which did not go beyond a mere trickle, getting mandatory sanctions for constructing the hall and struggling with the UGC which at first turned down the application for funds.

In the 1967-68 academic session things suddenly began to happen. Anil P. Vijaya was elected prime minister of the college parliament and the first thing he did was to serve a notice of strike to protest against the UGC for refusing to sanction the required grant for building the hall. A procession of students went to the vice chancellor to present a memorandum. Dr Bhatia accompanied them. Hindu College students had asserted themselves for a good cause and they met with success.

Facing page: *M.A.K. Pataudi at a Fund raising dinner in Hindu College for development of the sports complex, 1985 (above); Amitabh Bachchan on the occasion of Fund raising for the building of the sports complex (middle); Visit of President Giani Zail Singh to inaugurate the new college canteen*

Donations poured in from old and current students due to the vigorous efforts of the Fund Collection Committee of the college. On a single day Dr Bhatia and his senior colleagues collected Rs 10,000 from one *katra* in Chandni Chowk with the help of Madan Mohan Sharan. Funds were also raised through a concert by noted singer M.S. Subbulakshmi who performed free of charge. For laying the wooden planks on the stage, advice was sought from famous dancers Indrani Rahman, Sonal Mansingh and Rani Karnaa. The chairs were especially acoustically treated so that even when the hall was relatively empty, there was no echo from the vacant seats. Everyone gave their advice and service free of cost.

Dr V.K.R.V. Rao, Union Minister of Education inaugurated the new hall on 14 February 1970. On this occasion, apart from others, two distinguished old students, Robert Odero, the Kenyan high commissioner in Delhi and Nakul Sen, Lieutenant Governor of Goa, addressed the gathering of over 2,000 who crammed into an auditorium meant for 750.[6]

Sports Complex and Canteen

Another memorable occasion is described by Principal P.C. Verma. In 1986 Raj Bhargava proposed to Dr Bharat Ram that the alumni would like to build a new canteen and sports complex for Hindu College. Dr Bharat Ram was chairman of the Organising Committee, Principal Verma was the vice chairman and Mr Raj Bhargava and Arun Pandya were the secretary and treasurer respectively. The estimated cost was Rs 10 lakh. This committee saw the complex through the drawing board to its full construction and completion, raising Rs 15 lakh for it through direct donations, a souvenir and a celebrity dinner with Amitabh Bachchan as the chief guest. Vinod Khanna, Charanjit Singh, N.K. Jain, Gurdial and Chaman Mahajan and K.M. Bijli donated substantial sums for it. Alumni like Inder Sharma, Ranvir Tyagi, Prakash Bhandari, D.N. Gupta and others contributed their willing and substantial help. Thus a magnificent complex came up without any help from UGC.

The drama that accompanied the foundation stone laying of the canteen is best described by Principal Verma himself:

> We wanted some prominent personality to lay the foundation stone of the complex. Some Hinduites who were senior bureaucrats took me to request the then vice president of India, Mr R. Venkatraman to do the honour. But he declined saying that since he was the chancellor of Delhi University he could not possibly come to such a small function. Soon thereafter, at a dinner hosted by Mr Ranbir Tiwari, I mentioned Mr Venkatraman's decision to Mr Charanjit Singh. Charanjit assured me, 'Sir, don't worry. Now we will get the President of India.' True to his word, he arranged for Giani Zail Singh, the then president of India and the visitor of Delhi University, to lay the foundation stone of the complex on March 20, 1986. Gianiji inquired of me, 'Vermaji, *ab chai pilaoge ya nahin*?' I replied, 'Sir, your Military Secretary forbade us to arrange tea for you for security reasons.' Not amused, Gianiji said, '*Arey mere se kyon nahin kaha, main sab theek kar daita*.' And then when Dr Bharat

6 Dr B.M. Bhatia, 'College Auditorium: How it was Built', *The Indraprastha*, 1983.

Hindu College grounds or Pavilion behind the main building

Above: *Turning the first sod for the canteen and sports complex. Dutta, the Sports director with Sanjay Chauhan*

The last item Fishpond *performed on Annual Day in college (L-R): College prime minister Ashwani Arora, Bobby Mathur and B. Ghosh*

Above: *English Dramatic Society (Globe Society), Hindu College, 1956-57*

Ram and I were seeing Gianiji off, remarking on Gianiji's impeccable dress sense, Dr Bharat Ram remarked, '*Aap bahaut khubsoorat lag rahe hain.*' Pat came Gianiji's reply, '*Khubsoorti aap lay leejeye aur apni daulat mujhe de deejeye.*' We could not have asked for a better person to start us off on the project.

Mrs Margaret Alva, the then Minister of State for Youth Affairs, Sports and Women's Welfare inaugurated the complex on 20 October 1986 amid much fanfare. The inaugural procession was led by the famous film personality Joginder, an alumnus of the college.[7]

The Early Achievers

Khub Chand, Nakul Sen and Ram Bhadran were ICS officers; Giri Lal Jain, was the editor of the *Times of India*; H.K. Dua the editor of *The Hindustan Times* and *Tribune*; Dr Raj Krishna was an internationally-known economist at the Delhi School of Economics. In as early as 1945, five students of the college stood first in the MA examination held by Delhi University in their respective subjects and won gold medals: Giri Lal Jain (History), Raj Krishna (Economics), Sita Ram (English), J.N. Kapur (Mathematics) and Daya Krishna (Philosophy). L.C. Jain, Ambassador in South Africa and Magsaysay Award winner, was in the same batch as Giri Lal Jain, Raj Krishna and J.N. Kapur.

7 *The Indraprastha*, 1993.

Right: *Khub Chand receiving the Distingushed Alumni Award from Justice J.S. Verma*

Nakul Sen

Recollections

Professor Daya Krishna, one of the best known philosophers of the country recalls Brij Mohan Toofan in college, coming dressed as a Naga sadhu for a fancy dress show. When the enraged principal tried to throw him out, he staunchly refused saying, 'Sir I represent one of the oldest and noblest sects of sadhus in India.' Says Daya Krishna, 'Toofan is no more, but the memory of his innumerable pranks, imaginatively conceived and boldly executed, regale his friends even now when they talk about him. Or in a different vein, who can imagine Kapila in those days going to bat as a young college girl in a friendly match with the boys?'[8]

Yogeshwar Dayal

Mrs Usha Kumar writes of another eminent old student, Yogeshwar Dayal, her father, who was in the college in the early 1930s. He was very active in extracurricular activities like the Historical Society and the Literary Union. He belonged to Chandni Chowk and became known for his contribution to communal harmony in the city through an event of great significance called '*Phool Waalon Ki Sair*'. A society was formed and it got registered as Anjuman Sair-e-Gul Faroshan under the Societies Registration Act and the long lost festival of communal harmony was revived. It was an annual event where eminent representatives of Hindu and Muslim communities jointly participated—Hindus offering floral *chaadar* at the Dargah of Khwaja Bhakhtiar Kaaki and Muslims offering floral *pankhas* at the Hindu temple of Jogmayaji, both in Mehrauli.

This festival was started in the times of Mughal king Akbar Shah II, father of Bahadur Shah Zafar fulfilling a vow of the queen, Begum Mumtaz Mahal and was continued even during British period. It was stopped in 1942 when the Quit India Movement started. In 1961, Prime Minister Jawaharlal Nehru asked Yogeshwar Dayal (from an eminent family of Old Delhi) and the then Mayor, Nuruddin Ahmed, to revive this festival. This prestigious festival lasting three to five days still continues.[9]

On Theatre's Map

Professor R.W. Desai tried to put Hindu College on the map of the capital in 'theatre in English'. This was an uphill and challenging task in 1957 when he formed the Globe Society. It ran for five years from 1957–62 during which time it had two secretaries both of whose terms ran consecutively: Yaduvansh Mathur, small built, gentle, soft spoken and inoffensive who, unfortunately died a year after passing out from the college with his BA degree; and the tall and strapping Satendra Nandan from Fiji, who went on to become the Education minister in his country.

8 *In Retrospect*, p. 56.

9 Usha Kumar, *Yogeshwar Dayal Aur Dilli* (New Delhi: Bani Publications, 2005, 2nd edn 2006).

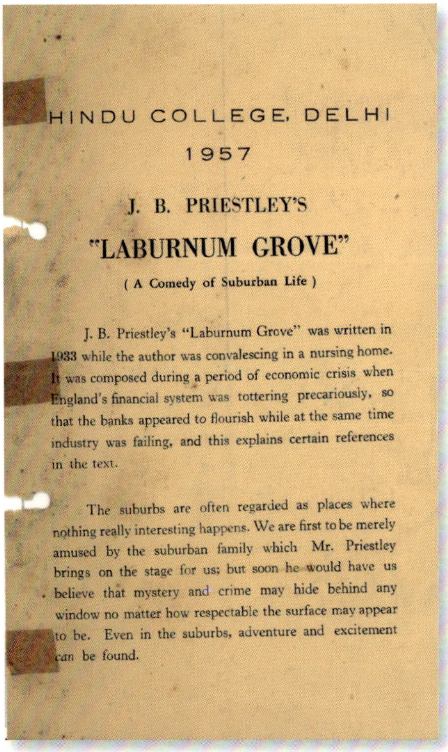

HINDU COLLEGE, DELHI

1957

J. B. PRIESTLEY'S

"LABURNUM GROVE"

(A Comedy of Suburban Life)

J. B. Priestley's "Laburnum Grove" was written in 1933 while the author was convalescing in a nursing home. It was composed during a period of economic crisis when England's financial system was tottering precariously, so that the banks appeared to flourish while at the same time industry was failing, and this explains certain references in the text.

The suburbs are often regarded as places where nothing really interesting happens. We are first to be merely amused by the suburban family which Mr. Priestley brings on the stage for us; but soon he would have us believe that mystery and crime may hide behind any window no matter how respectable the surface may appear to be. Even in the suburbs, adventure and excitement can be found.

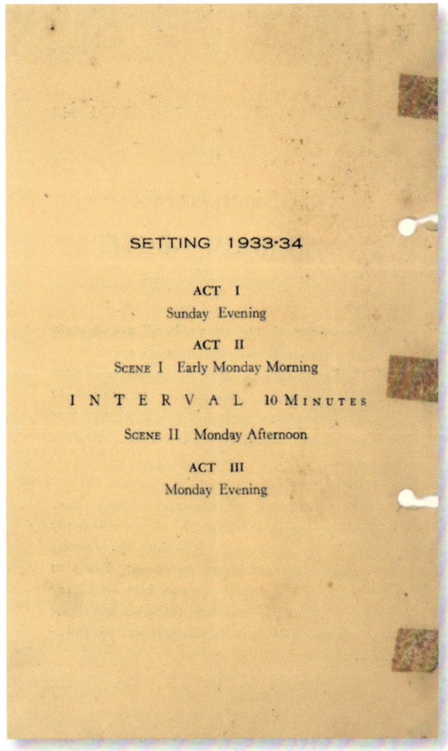

SETTING 1933-34

ACT I

Sunday Evening

ACT II

SCENE I Early Monday Morning

INTERVAL 10 MINUTES

SCENE II Monday Afternoon

ACT III

Monday Evening

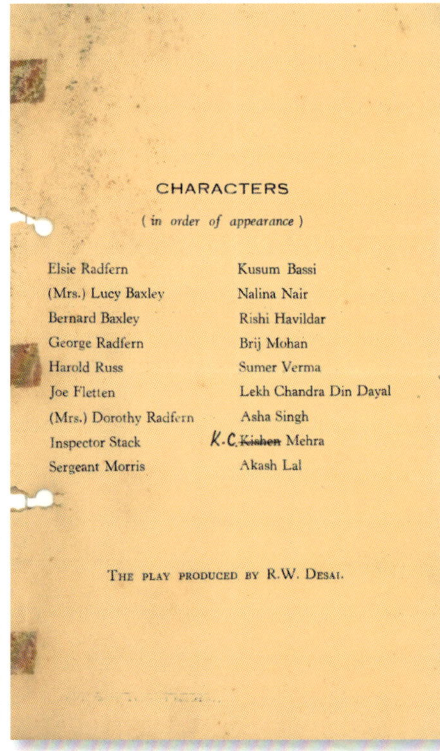

CHARACTERS

(in order of appearance)

Elsie Radfern	Kusum Bassi
(Mrs.) Lucy Baxley	Nalina Nair
Bernard Baxley	Rishi Havildar
George Radfern	Brij Mohan
Harold Russ	Sumer Verma
Joe Fletten	Lekh Chandra Din Dayal
(Mrs.) Dorothy Radfern	Asha Singh
Inspector Stack	K.C. ~~Kishen~~ Mehra
Sergeant Morris	Akash Lal

THE PLAY PRODUCED BY R.W. DESAI.

The first production of the Globe Society was J.B. Priestley's *Laburnum Grove*. It relied to a great extent on subtle variations in lighting effects to suggest different time slots. It was, feels R.W. Desai in *In Retrospect*, a good 'first play' with which to venture into hitherto unchartered waters. The cast of six was not unmanageably large; most of them belonged to the pre-medical first and third year classes, a course long since abolished, but which was in those years a compulsory pre-requisite for those intending to study Medicine.

The next production in the following year, was Shakespeare's *As You Like It*, a far more daunting and challenging endeavour. In spite of commendable performances by K.C. Mehra, Preeti Singh, Leela Rangaswami, Dev Ghatak and Din Dayal, the production was not very successful. This led to introspection. The college authorities had to be persuaded to equip the stage with necessary mechanical devices so that the production did not go through ludicrous pitfalls like the curtain refusing to close at the end of a scene!

This was followed by *Macbeth* with K.C. Mehra in the title role. Like the previous one, this production too got a mixed response. Perhaps attempting Shakespeare was too ambitious at this point of time but the Globe Society plodded on and in 1962 presented *Julius Caesar*. According to Desai, Rangachari as Antony, Dev Ghatak as Brutus, Sudhir Agarwal as Cassius and Gul Kapadia as Portia were outstanding.

Above: *Globe Society's first play* Laburnum Grove, *1956-57 (all)*

But why did Desai persist? It was a challenge. There was a desire to demonstrate that no single institution had a monopoly over plays in English, and that given sufficient zeal and

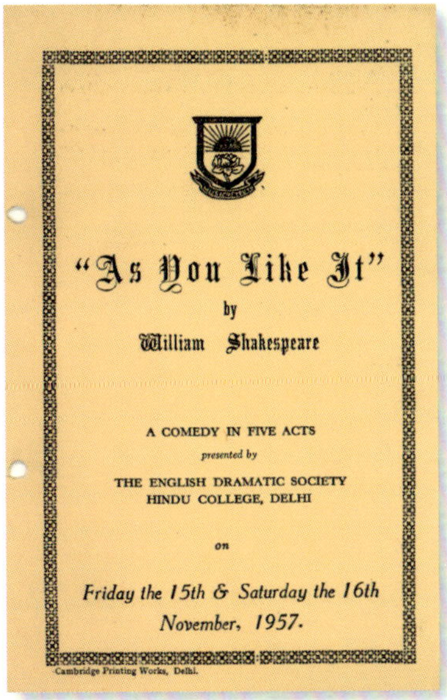

"As You Like It"

by

William Shakespeare

A COMEDY IN FIVE ACTS

presented by

THE ENGLISH DRAMATIC SOCIETY
HINDU COLLEGE, DELHI

on

Friday the 15th & Saturday the 16th
November, 1957.

Cambridge Printing Works, Delhi.

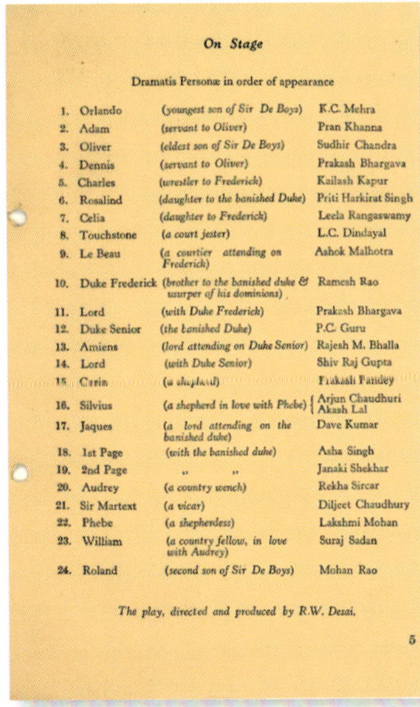

On Stage

Dramatis Personæ in order of appearance

1.	Orlando	*(youngest son of Sir De Boys)*	K.C. Mehra
2.	Adam	*(servant to Oliver)*	Pran Khanna
3.	Oliver	*(eldest son of Sir De Boys)*	Sudhir Chandra
4.	Dennis	*(servant to Oliver)*	Prakash Bhargava
5.	Charles	*(wrestler to Frederick)*	Kailash Kapur
6.	Rosalind	*(daughter to the banished Duke)*	Priti Harkirat Singh
7.	Celia	*(daughter to Frederick)*	Leela Rangaswamy
8.	Touchstone	*(a court jester)*	L.C. Dindayal
9.	Le Beau	*(a courtier attending on Frederick)*	Ashok Malhotra
10.	Duke Frederick	*(brother to the banished duke & usurper of his dominions)*	Ramesh Rao
11.	Lord	*(with Duke Frederick)*	Prakash Bhargava
12.	Duke Senior	*(the banished Duke)*	P.C. Guru
13.	Amiens	*(lord attending on Duke Senior)*	Rajesh M. Bhalla
14.	Lord	*(with Duke Senior)*	Shiv Raj Gupta
15.	Corin	*(a shepherd)*	Prakash Pandey
16.	Silvius	*(a shepherd in love with Phebe)*	Arjun Chaudhuri Akash Lal
17.	Jaques	*(a lord attending on the banished duke)*	Dave Kumar
18.	1st Page	*(with the banished duke)*	Asha Singh
19.	2nd Page	,, ,,	Janaki Shekhar
20.	Audrey	*(a country wench)*	Rekha Sircar
21.	Sir Martext	*(a vicar)*	Diljeet Chaudhury
22.	Phebe	*(a shepherdess)*	Lakshmi Mohan
23.	William	*(a country fellow, in love with Audrey)*	Suraj Sadan
24.	Roland	*(second son of Sir De Boys)*	Mohan Rao

The play, directed and produced by R.W. Desai.

5

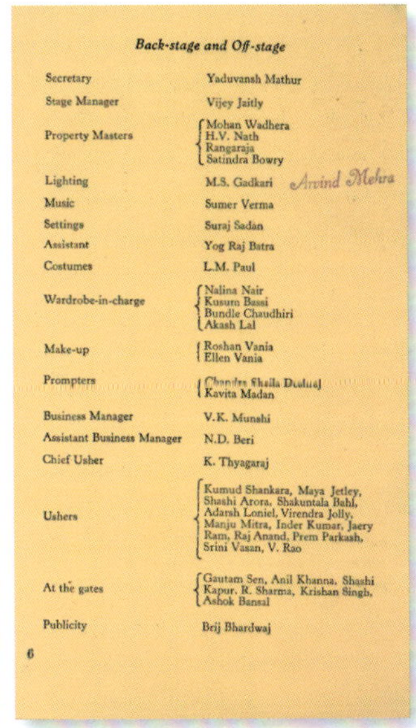

Back-stage and Off-stage

Secretary	Yaduvansh Mathur
Stage Manager	Vijey Jaitly
Property Masters	Mohan Wadhera H.V. Nath Rangaraja Satindra Bowry
Lighting	M.S. Gadkari Arvind Mehra
Music	Sumer Verma
Settings	Suraj Sadan
Assistant	Yog Raj Batra
Costumes	L.M. Paul
Wardrobe-in-charge	Nalina Nair Kusum Bassi Bundle Chaudhiri Akash Lal
Make-up	Roshan Vania Ellen Vania
Prompters	Chandra Shaila [illegible] Kavita Madan
Business Manager	V.K. Munshi
Assistant Business Manager	N.D. Beri
Chief Usher	K. Thyagaraj
Ushers	Kumud Shankara, Maya Jetley, Shashi Arora, Shakuntala Bahl, Adarsh Loniel, Virendra Jolly, Manju Mitra, Inder Kumar, Jaery Ram, Raj Anand, Prem Parkash, Srini Vasan, V. Rao
At the gates	Gautam Sen, Anil Khanna, Shashi Kapur, R. Sharma, Krishan Singh, Ashok Bansal
Publicity	Brij Bhardwaj

6

Group photo from the play Laburnum Grove. *Sitting left to right: Asha Singh, Kusum Bassi, Nalina Nair. Standing left to right: L.C. Dindayal, K.C. Mehra, R.W. Desai, Sumer Verma, Brij Mohan, Rishi Havildar, Akash Lal*

Above: *Globe Society's second play was Shakespeare's* As You Like It, *1957-58 (all)*

Right: *Act II, Scene VII*

Below right: *Act V, Scene I (L-R): Audrey, Touchstone and William*

Below: *Act I, Scene III—Rosalind and Celia*

Group photo from the play As You Like It. *Suraj Sadan, P.C. Bhargava, S.R. Gupta, Arjun Chowdhury, Ashok Malhotra, Prakash Panday and Rajesh Bhalla (last row left to right); Rekha Sircar, Mohan Rao, Sudhir Chandra, Pran Khanna, Kailash Kapur, Yaduvansh Mathur, Ramesh Rao, Dave Kumar, P.C. Guru (middle row left to right); Lakshmi Ram Mohan, Leela Rangaswamy, K.C. Mehra, Priti Singh, R.W. Desai, Asha Singh, Janaki Shekhar (sitting left to right); L.C. Dindayal (sitting on the floor)*

Above: *Act III, Scene II (L-R): Rosalind, Celia and Orlando*

macbeth

On Stage

Dramatis Personæ in order of appearance

1.	1st Witch		Leela Rangaswamy
2.	2nd Witch		Kumud Shankara
3.	3rd Witch		Shashi Arora
4.	Duncan	*(King of Scotland)*	Pran Khanna
5.	Malcolm	*(Sons to Duncan)*	Sudhir Chandra
6.	Donalbain		S. Swami
7.	Lennox	*(Noblemen of Scotland)*	N. Gopal
8.	Angus		Arun Chaddah
9.	Ross		S.P. Dewan
10.	Macbeth	*(generals of the King's army.)*	K.C. Mehra
11.	Banquo		Dave Kumar
12.	Lady Macbeth		Sudha Mohindra
13.	1st Messenger		Ashok Bhandari
14.	Fleance	*(son to Banquo)*	Shashi Nanda
15.	Porter		Ashok Malhotra
16.	Macduff	*(a nobleman of Scotland)*	Baljit Ahluwalia
17.	Old Man		Anil Kashyap
18.	1st Murderer		Kailash Kapur
19.	2nd Murderer		Sudarshan Oberoi
20.	Lady Macduff		Ina Dhanda
21.	Her Son		Maher Parekh
22.	2nd Messenger		Suresh Khanna
23.	Doctor		Vinay Mushran
24.	Gentlewoman	*(attending on Lady Macbeth)*	Janaki Shekhar
25.	Seyton	*(an officer attending on Macbeth)*	Ramesh Rao
26.	Old Siward	*(Earl of Northumberland, general of the English force)*	Mahajit Chowdhury
27.	Young Siward	*(his son)*	Brij Suri

The play directed and produced by R. W. Desai.

Back-stage & Off-stage

Stage Manager	Mohan Wadhera
Choreography (witch scenes)	Kumud Shankara
Music	Sumer Verma M.S. Gadkari
Lighting	K.C. Dhawan
Costumes	L.M. Paul
Settings	Ranjan Sen
Make-up	Harbans Bahadur
Prompters	Lakshmi Rammohan Kalika Bhandari
Property Masters	R.A. Shukla, R. Bhattacharyya, P. Bhargava, P. P. Banta, P.C. Guru.
Business Manager	Arvind Mehra
Ushers	Herminder Mohini, Adarsh Mohini, Kusum Narayan, Maya Jetley, Prem Sood, Man Singh, Krishna Singh, R.N. Sachdeva, Anil Khanna, Kuldip Shanker, Shapoor Parekh. Deepak Mehra, P.N. Nat, Gautam Sen.
Vice-President	Yaduvansh Mathur
Secretary	Shiv Raj Gupta

JULIUS CÆSAR

by

WILLIAM SHAKESPEARE

Cassius: "How many ages hence
Shall this our lofty scene be acted over,
In states unborn and accents yet unknown !"

Brutus: "How many times shall Caesar bleed in sport,
That now on Pompey's basis lies along
No worthier than the dust !"

—*Act III Sc. I*

Dramatis Personae in order of appearance

First Citizen	Arvind Baweja
Second Citizen	Chander Prakash
Third Citizen	Arun Bhagat
Fourth Citizen	Anand Vaid
Other Citizens	Falguni Chakravarty Vinod Kumar, Shayam Sunder, Sakta Chowdhry Santosh Sharma Laxmi Narain Jose Moutia,
Flavius	Pervez Mistry
Marullus	Aroon Chaddha
Caesar	Burjor Cooper
Casca	Ashok Marwah
Calphurnia	Janaki Shekhar
Antony	Ranga Chari
Soothsayer	Chander Prakash
Brutus	Dave Kumar
Cassius	Sudhir Chandra
Cicero	Narendra Prakash
Cinna	Arvind Karmarkar
Lucius	Anil Sharma
Decius	Nipender Khanna
Cimber	Pramod Sahni
Trebonius	Shyam Malhotra
Portia	Gool Kapadia
Servant to Cæsar	Rajender Pal
Ligarius	Ramesh Rao
Publius	Shashi Nanda
Artemidorus	Harinder Shourie
Popilius Lena	Inder Chhitwal
Cinna, a poet	Deepak Seth
Octavius Caesar	Anand Vaid
Lepidus	Harinder Shourie
Lucilius	Baljit Ahluwalia
Pindarus	Shashi Nanda
Poet	Chander Prakash
Messala	Aroon Chhadha
Titinius	Nipender Khanna
Varro	Arvind Baweja
Claudius	Inder Chhitwal
Cato	Atul Kapoor
Clitus	Pervez Mistry
Dardinius	Brij Mehra
Volumnius	Satish Chawla
Strato	Rajender Pal

The play, directed and produced by
R. W. Desai

Back-Stage & Off-Stage

Stage Managers	Sohan Wadera Jaisaj Puri
Costume designing	Janaki Shekhar
Wardrobe-in-charge	Gool Kapadia
Settings	Promindera Batra
Lighting	Ramesh Rao
Music	Sumer Verma Harinder Shourie
Business Manager	Arvind Mehra
Ushers	Sudha Mahendra Prem Sood, Shashi Arora Ashok Kapoor Brij Ghosh, Robin Nath Davy Joshi, Jasbir Kochar, Umesh Dayal Nirmal Kapoor
Secretary	Satendra Pratap

expertise on the part of the faculty, Hindu College students could also put up such plays if they wanted to. They could produce plays in English that were both enjoyable and were of acceptable standards measured by the modest yardstick of a college production.[10]

It was not just theatre that attracted college students. In Bollywood, Hindu alumni have played a significant role from very early stages. Actor Motilal was a popular student of the college and was known for exploits that were considered sacrilege at that time. Madan Puri, known for his varied roles, was a very active participant in college theatre at a time when boys played the roles of girls. Manoj Kumar, another alumnus of the college, contributed very significantly not only as an actor but also as a producer to the Mumbai film industry. In contemporary cinema one can see Imtiaz Ali, Arjun Rampal, Vishal Bhardwaj and Ashish Vidyarthi to name a few along with Tisca Chopra and Loveleen Tandon.

Madan Puri actively participated in college theatre and later joined the Bombay film industry

The college also produced Urdu poets like Gulzar Dehlvi, Hindi poets Bal Swarup Rahi, Ram Avtar Tyagi, Ramesh Gaur—the last two also eminent journalists—well-known singers like Madhup Mudgal, Tejpal Singh of the Singh Bandhu Duo, Rekha Bhardwaj and Sudeep Bannerji.

In this context it would be good to recall the vibrant Hindi Sahitya Sabha. In existence as an active society even in the 1930, this was the Hindi avatar of the Literary Union except that it does not seem to have organised debates which it left to the Literary Union. It had the distinction of organising many litereary events including essay, short story and poetry competitions besides inviting Hindi literary giants to address the students.

Left: *Urdu poet, Gulzar Dehlvi was an alumnus of the college*

According to Dr Kamal Kishore Goenka, a former professor and an eminent scholar, the Hindu College Sahitya Sabha was fortunate to have Munshi Premchand, the great Hindi novelist address the students on 9 March 1936. His interaction with them made it a memorable event for the college.[11]

In later years, the eminent poet, Harivansh Rai Bachchan, participated in a 'Kavi Sammelan' in the present college premises where he recited many of his poems including the famous *Madhushala* to a packed hall. Another well-known Hindi writer and critic, Vishnu Prabhakar came to the college to be the judge for a short story competition. The Hindi Sahitya Sabha also organised a ballet, *Urvashi* written by the famous poet, Ramdhari Singh 'Dinkar'. Till today the college has a strong literary

Facing page: *Globe Society's third play was* Macbeth, *1958-59 (above all); Group photo of the on-stage players from the play* Macbeth *(middle left); Group photo of the off-stage and back-stage people from the same play (middle right); Globe Society came back in 1962 with the play* Julius Caesar, *which was highly appreciated (below all)*

10 *In Retrospect*, pp. 84–86.

11 Dr K.K. Goenka, *Premchand Vishwakosh*, Vol. 1 (New Delhi: Prabhat Prakashan, 1981).

tradition both in Hindi and English and the students benefit from many of the best-known writers in both the languages who find it worth their while to come to the college to interact with the students.

The College, a Stepping Stone

For some, the college provided an opportunity to take active steps towards their careers helped by the friendships they formed here. Kumar Rajesh recalls how Hindu College set the ball rolling for his journalistic career. For an article for *The Indraprastha*, he interviewed BJP's L.K. Advani, Madhu Dandavate from the Janata Party and the Late Hemvati Nandan Bahuguna of Lok Dal. Rajiv Gandhi had won with a huge majority. Kumar Rajesh was attempting to enlist the opinion of the opposition parties on the major issues facing the country like terrorism in Punjab, rural and caste violence in Bihar and others. Principal P.C. Verma was understandably not keen on such a volatile story in the magazine but agreed. Kumar Rajesh became the magazine manager subsequently. Shruti Prasad who was working for TV Today got him a break with *Newstrack*. This marked his entry into the world of journalism.[12]

An important aspect of the college faculty has been the appointment of some prominent students as teachers who became extremely popular among the students commanding their respect and love. For instance, Professor J.N. Kapur, Dr Bool Chand, Professor Daya Krishna and Professor Prem Chand were all students of the college. Dr Ram Ashray Sharma, Dr Mandhata Ojha, Dr Harish Naval, Dr Suresh Rituparna, Dr D.N. Gupta and Dr Kavita A. Sharma are among those who were students of the college and who later returned to teach here. Even today twenty-seven members of the faculty are former students of the college, the senior-most perhaps being Mrs Suchitra Gupta.

Professor Prem Chand taught Philosophy in college

The earliest issues of *The Indraprastha* in the 1930s and 1940s fondly talk of Dr N.V. Thadani, Principal S.K. Sen, Dr Bool Chand, Dr Indra Sen, Dr B.R. Seth, Pandit Harnarayan Shastri, Professor Prem Chand, Professor S.K. Saxena, Professor A. Bhattacharya, Dr Umrao Bahadur, Professor Shree Ram, Professor J.N. Kapur, Professor Ganpat Rai and Professor A.N. Puri, to name just a few.

K.K. Birla recalled that the standard of teaching was good. Apart from the scholarship of Professor Bhattacharya, he remembered Professor Arjun Lal Agarwal of Chemistry, Professor A.N. Puri of the Physics department and Professor Shree Ram of Mathematics as being excellent teachers. Professor Agarwal and Professor Puri's books were read by generations of students, while Professor Hriday Narayan and Professor Bansi Lal supervised Chemistry practicals.[13]

A.N. Puri has his memories of the time when he joined Hindu College in 1927 as head of the Physics department with Mr S.K. Sen as the principal. Babu Pearey Lal was the chairman and R.B. Suraj Narain the secretary of the Governing Body. It was a highly qualified faculty with

12 *In Retrospect*, pp. 133–135.

13 *In Retrospect*, pp. 37–43.

luminaries like Dr Sarup Singh in English, Mr A.T. Bannerji and Dr B.R. Seth in Mathematics, Mr C.C. Mitra and Mr Prem Chand in Philosophy, Mr B.K. Das in Biology, Mr A.L. Aggarwal in Chemistry, Dr B.N. Ganguli in Economics and Mahamahopadhyaya Harnarayan Shastri and Mr K.N. Kaul in Sanskrit and Hindi.[14]

It was a different era when teachers and students enjoyed a different relationship as compared to today. Classes were attended and while students wrote tutorials industriously, teachers corrected them painstakingly taking time to discuss them. Kapila Vatsyayan remembers the classes that would go on for long hours. Students went to teachers' homes and teachers came to their homes. 'There was no dearth of attention and care,' she says.[15] As Daya Krishna, an alumnus of the college, who later became one of the well-known professors of Philosophy points out, 'There was a constant dialogue between some of the brightest students from different disciplines and they had the active support and encouragement from the faculty in all subjects. To name but a few, there were Giri Lal Jain and Sita Ram Goel from History, Raj Krishna and Ram Swarup from Economics, J.N. Kapur from Mathematics, Madan Mohan Mathur, J.P. Guha and K.K. Kaul from English and Vivek Dutta in Philosophy.'[16]

Professor J.N. Kapur, an alumnus recalls that when he finished his High School exam in 1938 he was in a quandary on whether to join St. Stephen's or Hindu. His headmaster told him that if he wanted to do well in life and join a top administrative position, then he should join St. Stephen's and if he wanted to be a nationalist and pursue scientific studies, Hindu would be the college for him. He offered to give a letter for Professor Ganpat Rai of Hindu College and for Principal Mukarji of St. Stephen's. Principal Mukarji's indifference and the contrasting welcome by Professor Ganpat Rai and Professor Puri together with Principal Thadani's happiness tilted the balance towards Hindu College in Kapur's mind.[17]

Giri Lal Jain

Dr Thadani, apart from being the principal, was an excellent teacher of English as were Professor R.R. Gupta and Dr Sarup Singh. Dr Saxena whom Prem Chand called a 'good Pagan', 'the soul of wit and humour' was a great teacher of Philosophy as was Dr Indra Sen dubbed in contrast, 'a good Puritan'. Indra Sen later joined the Aurobindo Ashram. As Daya Krishna said, 'To be taught by persons like Dr Indra Sen, Dr S.K. Saxena and Professor Prem Chand was the privilege of a lifetime; it was a living experience and we looked forward to their classes, wondering what new portions would unfold that day.'[18] Philosophy students would then talk about what they had been taught with other students and some of them started attending their classes regularly even though they were formally enrolled in other subjects.

14 *The Indraprastha*, 1983.

15 *In Retrospect*, p. 74.

16 Ibid., p. 56.

17 *The Indraprastha*, 1983.

18 *In Retrospect*, p. 56.

Teachers like Dr B.N. Ganguli in Economics, Dr Hari Dutt Sharma in Sanskrit, Dr S.L. Poplai in History and Dr B.R. Seth in Mathematics were well known even among students who were not studying their subjects.

R.R. Gupta, a younger teacher of English at this time who had been involved with the revolutionary activities of Bhagat Singh, also remembered these outstanding colleagues and added some others like Dr Ganpat Rai of History who was also in charge of sports, Dr Umrao Bahadur and Dr Bool Chand who left for Banaras in 1940.[19] R.R. Gupta himself left a deep impact on many of his students. For Inder Sharma, who was a student of Economics, R.R. Gupta did not teach him only English but also imbued him with a sense of idealism. He was a romanticist who followed Keats and Shelley in his daily life.

Dr Sarup Singh is also fondly remembered by Sheila Bahadur, who studied English Literature. What impressed her as a student was that he never tried to be an all-knowing person. He approached every piece of literature as a research project. The tutorials were held in the open, under a tree and sometimes in the university garden. Occasionally he would say, '*Bore ho gai, chalo zara aaj gana sunado*' (Are you bored? Let's have a song from you).[20]

Professor Prem Chand of course left an indelible stamp on all the students of the college irrespective of the subjects that they were studying because to use Inder Sharma's phrase, he 'was a teacher of LIFE'. He imbued the students with confidence, gave them the courage to stand up and speak and debate fearlessly in public. It was training that stood them in good stead.

For Lalit Bhasin, three teachers remain etched in memory: Dr Dasharatha Sharma, head of the History department; Professor Prem Chand; and Dr S.K. Sexena. Dr Saxena, although a teacher of Philosophy, is also one of the best music critics in the country. He is also a great lover of classical music who inspired the students to participate in music festivals and inter-college and inter-university competitions. As prime minister of the Hindu College parliament in 1958-59 defeating the veteran Brij Bhardwaj, Lalit Bhasin celebrated the Diamond Jubilee of the college. It was a week-long celebration of sports, dramatics, music (when Talat Mehmood came to the college), debates, a students' day with events ending on Founder's Day. This may have been the biggest achievement of his tenure but what showed his mettle was how he rose to the no-confidence motion against him. Due to ill health, he could not attend parliament sessions including the budget session, which was perhaps a first in the history of Hindu College's parliament.[21]

Dr Sarup Singh

Once Jawaharlal Nehru University (JNU) was set up, many of the great teachers like Dr Bipin Chandra got attracted to it and virtually the entire cream of the History department left

19 *In Retrospect*, pp. 44–49.

20 Ibid., p. 78.

21 *The Indraprastha*, 1983.

for the rocky campus of the newly created university. Among the students in the 1960s and 1970s, perhaps the most recalled names are of Principal B.M. Bhatia, Professor Nand Lal, Harish Khare, R.P. Kaushik, Dr N.N. Aggarwal, Mr V.M. Misra and Dr R.S. Rawat.

Old Students' Association

As early as June 1933 *The Indraprastha* talked of an Old Boys' Association although the first registered Old Students' Association (OSA) was formed in 1958 when a group of inspired young Hinduites came together to provide a platform for the alumni to meet periodically. Mr Tara Chand Mathur was elected the first president of OSA. He had been the moving spirit of the Old Boys' Association as far back as 1933 when N.V. Thadani and S. Sen were the principals of Ramjas and Commercial College respectively. Over 100 old students attended. Not a single one was over thirty-five years of age! The principal at that time was S.K. Sen and the Executive Committee included:

Mr Adishwar Lal Jain	President
Mr Madan Mohan Andley	Senior Vice President
Mr Chiranji Lal Paliwal	Vice President
Professor Raj Narain Mathur	Secretary
Professor Shambhu Dayal	Jt Secretary
Principal S.K. Sen	Ex-officio Treasurer
Mr Kedar Nath	Asst Treasurer
Mr Tara Chand Mathur	
Mr Mangat Rai	

In 1958, Mr Tara Chand Mathur along with Professor D.S. Mathur, N.K. Nigam, Rajeshwar Dayal, Santosh Nath, J.N. Kapur and V.M. Mishra, all eminent people in their respective vocations, and some other leading businessmen of Delhi, laid the foundation for OSA.

OSA started with a monthly membership fee of Re 1, Rs 3 as annual subscription and Rs 50 for life membership. After the sad demise of Tara Chand Mathur in 1965, Professor Dr Govind Rai Chaudhary, an eminent educationist took over the affairs of the OSA.

In 1977-78, Principal Dr B.M. Bhatia, took personal interest in attempting to bring the alumni and the college closer and to streamline the activities of the Association for playing a more active role. A team worked towards updating and increasing its membership. A Hinduites' directory was compiled in 1978-79, which had articles from several members. OSA participated in the 80th Founder's Day celebrations quite enthusiastically.

Lala Bhiku Ram Jain was elected the next president with Mr Lalit Bhasin as the vice president, R.K. Oberoi the secretary, Dr R.S. Rawat the treasurer, with fifteen members on the Executive Committee. OSA's activities grew. It organised a cricket match between Hinduites and the College Eleven at the college grounds every year.

Below: *Dr Govind Rai Chaudhary took over the affairs of the OSA after the sad demise of Tara Chand Mathur in 1965*

Mr Tara Chand Mathur was elected the first president of OSA

In April 1979, OSA organised a function to bid farewell to Professor Prem Chand, who retired after forty-three years as a teacher and thity-six years as Speaker of the college parliament. Prominent Hinduites and former prime ministers who attended the function included Mr Kanwar Lal Sharma, the first elected prime minister of the college, Mr D.K. Syal, Professor N.K. Nigam, Mr Lalit Bhasin, Mr Inder Sharma, Mr S.P. Aggarwal, Professor G.R. Choudhary, Professor B.M. Bhatia, Professor P.C. Sood, Professor V.M. Mishra, Mr V.P. Punj and Mr Som Benegal.

Below: *OSA celebrates 75th birthday of Professor Prem Chand, 18 April 1986*

Lala Bhiku Ram Jain

The year 1980 was memorable for the college and OSA. For the first time, six college alumni were members of the Indian Parliament: Lala Bhiku Ram Jain, Mr Charanjit Singh, Mr Hari Kishan Shastri, Dr Subramanian Swamy, Mr Kanwar Lal Gupta and Mr Vishwabandhu Gupta. Mr Gajraj Bahadur Nagar, Mr K.L. Poswal and Rao Inderjeet Singh were inducted as ministers in the Haryana government and Shri Kanwar Lal Sharma became a member of the Metropolitan Council of Delhi. OSA honoured these personalities in the college auditorium where Mr N.K. Nigam and Amitabh Verma, then prime minister of the college parliament presided.

OSA has always tried to felicitate alumni and honour their achievements. When Professor P.L. Malhotra, an alumnus of the college became the Dean of Colleges, it felicitated him. It also bid a grateful farewell to principals B.M. Bhatia and P.C. Verma on their retirement. OSA celebrated the 75th birthday of Professor Prem Chand on 18 April 1986 in the college.

The demise of great cricketer Gulshan Rai Kashyap in May 1986 at the age of fifty was a tremendous loss. As a tribute to him, the OSA started a 'Gulshan Rai Memorial Trophy' under the chairmanship of Shri Hari Kishan Shastri (MP). In November 1986, a cricket match between the Hinduites XI and St. Stephen's College XI was inaugurated by Mrs Gulshan Rai and Mr Bishen Singh Bedi, India's cricket captain. Dr A.K. Mittal, a faculty member, donated the trophy.

The appointment of Dr Kavita Sharma in January 1998, an alumnus of the college, as principal created history. The old students, among whom many were her friends, seniors and teachers, were quick to felicitate her and ask her to spell out her vision for the college.

OSA felicitated another old student, Mr Omang Apang from Arunachal Pradesh, when he was inducted as Minister of State for Tourism in the Union Cabinet in 1999 and honoured Surender Khanna when he was selected for the Indian cricket team.

The Centenary celebrations were a memorable day in the history of the college. Anand Saurabh was the prime minister of the college and Waquar Haidar, the leader of opposition. The Chief Guest, Prime Minister Atal Behari Vajpayee, remarked jokingly how could there be two prime ministers in the same place simultaneously! Shri Vajpayee released a commemorative postage stamp of the college on 17 February 1999; the road in front of the teachers' houses was named after Dr N.V. Thadani; Narendra Kumar, an alumnus of the college helped publish the Hindu alumni directory and a book of reminiscences *In Retrospect* which was also released on this occasion; and Deepak Singh, made a beautiful film on the college. A highlight of the Centenary was a grand cultural programme where eminent producer, director and music maestro, Vishal Bhardwaj together with Rekha Bhardwaj and Sudeep Bannerji, all alumni of the college, gave a performance. That evening was born the beautiful song, '*Hindu tu hai mera dil*'. This was followed by a bonfire dinner on the front lawns of the college culminating in an impromptu dance by old and current students which was sportingly joined by Principal Dr Kavita A. Sharma. The Centenary celebrations concluded with the Valedictory function the following year in which the chief guest was the Vice President of India, Shri Krishna Kant. Throughout the year, eminent speakers addressed the students as part of the Centenary Lecture series. Notable among them were Shri Shyam Benegal and Mr P. Chidambaram.

January 2000 brought a radical turn-of-the-century change in the OSA as it expanded its activities attracting a substantial number of old students into its fold. With the newly elected present President, Mr Lalit Bhasin, a new beginning was made when OSA decided to recognise and felicitate distinguished alumni every year. The modalities were worked out by a committee consisting of members of the Governing Body under Dr Bharat Ram, who was then the chairman.

Below: *Shri Atal Behari Vajpayee addressing the audience. Anand Saurabh, then prime minister of the college seated on the table (first from left)*

Shri A.B. Vajpayee (centre) releases the Centenary brochure. Left to right—Shri Bharat Ram, Dr Kavita A. Sharma and Shri Jagmohan

The first Distinguished Alumni Awards were presented as part of the Centenary celebrations of the college. A special award was given to Jivan Lal Seth, an advocate, the oldest living alumnus who was ninety-nine years of age at that time. The other awardees were eminent heart surgeon, Dr Naresh Trehan; well-known academician and scholar, Dr Kapila Vatsyayan; the first Test captain from Delhi to play for the country, Mr Prakash Bhandari; former Home secretary and a senior bureaucrat, Mr Raj Bhargava; Mr Inder Sharma, one of the senior-most entrepreneurs in tourism and later in the hospitality industry; renowned Kathak and Odissi dancer, Ms Rani Karnaa; and retired Lt General, Mr V.K. Nayar.

This practice is now a prestigious annual feature as eminent people from virtually all walks of life have been honoured by OSA. Besides this, OSA has diversified its activities and now has sports events for the alumni like annual golf and cricket matches between Hindu and St. Stephen's. The latest feather in OSA's cap was the revival of a debating culture involving not only these two colleges but there are also plans of including other colleges of the university. It has also organised film shows to raise funds for various student causes.

OSA also honours teachers whose wisdom, sagacity and knowledge helped give students the capacity to succeed in life. Apart from principals Bhatia and Verma, eminent scholars of Economics and English and some outstanding teachers who have been honoured are

Hindu College lit up for the Centenary celebrations

Pankaj Udhas given a boquet of flowers by Principal Kavita Sharma

A section of the audience during a programme in the Centenary celebrations

Vishal and Rekha Bhardwaj performing on 'Hindu tu hai mera dil' *song with Sudeep Bannerji*

Hindu College cultural programme on Founder's Day

Impromptu dance by the guests during the Centenary celebrations

Hindu College Centenary celebrations in which Dr K.P. Sarabhai (centre) played a pivotal role

Shri P. Chidambram visiting the college to deliver the Centenary lecture

Shyam Benegal coming to deliver the Centenary lecture

Shri Sat Pal Singh Chauhan, a firm administrator, was loved by the sportspersons

Lt Gov. V.K. Kapoor also attended the Centenary celebrations

The Hinduites *book was released in the Valedictory Function in 2000 by the Vice President Shri Krishan Kant*

Jivan Lal Seth, the oldest living alumnus, gets a Special Award in 2000

Justice J.S. Verma giving the Distinguished Alumni Award to actor Manoj Kumar in 2000

K.K. Birla getting the award from Justice J.S. Verma in 2000

First Distinguished Alumni Awards function, 2000

First Distinguished Alumni Award winners, 2000

Lalit Bhasim getting the Distinguished Alumni Award from Manish Tewari

Dr K.P. Sarabhai, Dr Mandhata Ojha, Professor V.M. Misra and Professor Bipin Chandra.

Dr K.P. Sarabhai, honoured in 2010, served the college for thity-seven years in the Chemistry department and is remembered for his great contribution to the corporate life of the college as well as the university. He was the speaker of the college parliament and also officiated as the principal of the college. Known for his administrative acumen he was involved in the examination work of many prestigious bodies like the Council of Indian School Certificate Examinations, UPSC and the universities of Kanpur, Agra, Gorakhpur, Meerut and Delhi. He was also involved in various social service camps organised by the university, college and DUSU. Former president, V.V. Giri invited Dr Sarabhai and some students to Rashtrapati Bhavan to felicitate them for their social work.

Dr Mandhata Ojha, also honoured in 2010, was a post-graduate in both English and Hindi. He started teaching in 1957 but joined the faculty of the college in 1959. Son of illustrious Professor of Hindi, Dr Dashrath Ojha (himself an alumnus), who had also been the head of the Department of Hindi in the college, Dr Mandhata Ojha had great credentials of his own. He authored five books on different aspects of theatre and Hindi drama and wrote critical analyses of several literary textbooks, which are recommended by universities for consultation. A very popular teacher, he was a wonderful human being to whom both the students and teachers turned for guidance and succour.

Professor V.M. Misra was a student of the college for BSc (Honours) in Physics and thereafter for MSc in Physics. He then accepted a job as lecturer in the Physics department of the college and joined in 1947 when the college was still located in Kashmere Gate. Under his stewardship the college's hockey team won several prestigious inter-collegiate championships. Professor V.M. Misra was closely associated

Previous page:
Distinguished Alumni Awards:
Inder Sharma receiving the award from Dr Karan Singh (top); Gulzar Dehlvi receiving the award from Shri Somnath Chatterjee (middle); Dr S.K. Saxena (teacher and alumni) gets a Lifetime Achievement Award from Shekhar Gupta (bottom)

with the Scout movement in India. He was awarded the Silver Elephant, the highest honour in scouting for his meritorious services and dedication to the movement. During his long stint until his retirement in February 1990, he also officiated as the principal of the college for some time.

The entire Misra family has strong bonds with the college as they all studied here. The eldest brother, Justice V.D. Misra, rose to the position of chief justice of the Himachal High Court; younger brothers, O.P. Misra and S.K. Misra, were in service while his sister, Dr (Miss) Sneh Lata Misra, after finishing her pre-medical from Hindu College, joined the Lady Hardinge Medical College for Women for her MBBS and eventually retired as Professor and head of Department of Gynaeology & Obstetrics from there.

Professor Bipin Chandra, one of the foremost historians of modern India, taught at Hindu College for eighteen years from 1951–69 and was one of the architects of the Department of History. He then joined the Department of History at the University of Delhi but almost immediately left to become Professor of Modern History at Jawaharlal Nehru University, New Delhi where he is currently Professor Emeritus. Professor Chandra has extensively worked on modern Indian history, particularly on the nature of colonialism and the struggle for Independence. He was also the UGC National Lecturer in 1973-74. Widely read, his works have been translated into many Indian languages. A National Research Professor, Professor Bipin Chandra has served in many honorary positions including President, Indian History Congress and Member, UGC. He has delivered many important lectures including the Kosambi Memorial lecture, the K.P. Jaiswal Memorial lecture, the V.D. Mahajan Memorial lecture, the Heras Memorial lecture and the Inaugural address at the first EMS Namboodiripad Memorial seminar. He was also one of the editors of the journal *Enquiry*. He is currently the chairman of the National Book Trust, India.

The credit for shouldering the responsibility of OSA and making it grow especially after 2000 goes to Lalit Bhasin, the president and Raj Kumar Oberoi who till recently served as its secretary. Lalit Bhasin is a distinguished lawyer and an eminent public figure who has made tremendous contributions and left his mark in many fields. In Lalit Bhasin, the OSA has an illustrious person who has distinguished himself as an eminent public figure. He started his law practice in 1962 and has developed Bhasin and Co. as one of the largest law firms in North India with a wide range of specialisations. Lalit Bhasin himself leads in many spheres being the chairman of the Film Certification Appellate Tribunal, Chartered Institute of Arbitrators, PhD Chamber of Commerce, Council of Industry Committee on Corporate Affairs, Services Export Promotion Council and the CII National Committee on Dispute Resolution. He is the president of the Society of Indian Law Firms, Inter Pacific Bar Association and Indian Society for Afro-Asian Studies, to name just a few. Recently he was also honoured by the Supreme Court Bar Association for completing fifty years in the legal profession in the presence of the Law minister and the chief justice of India on the occasion of National Law Day.

Raj Kumar Oberoi retired from Canara Bank. He was the prime minister of the college in 1973-74. He was also a member of the Executive Council of Delhi University and the University Court. He was a special invitee to the Delhi University Library Committee. His encyclopaedic knowledge of the college and its alumni has played a key role in keeping the vitality of the OSA up to date. He has also been felicitated by the association.

What Makes the Fragrance Unique

OSA, teachers and all who have been associated with Hindu College have imbibed the unique fragrance of the college. They have been completely committed to it and have tried to help not only whenever called upon to do so but have also taken the initiative. As has already been described by Principal P.C. Verma, one big endeavour was to gift the college with a new canteen and sports complex. Later, Jivat Thadani, son of Principal N.V. Thadani, himself an alumnus of the college, helped to make the Student's Common Room in the Students' Centre which was named after his father as the N.V. Thadani Room. Professor Rastogi, Emeritus Professor of Mathematics at the Ohio State University, contributed a computer lab. Sneh Thadani created a small corpus to publish outstanding short stories written by undergraduates in the college. In addition, many old students and teachers or their families have instituted scholarships and prizes in different subjects. In a few cases the college also finds itself as one of the beneficiaries in the wills of old students.

Jivan Lal Seth, an advocate and the oldest alumnus of the college at the age of ninety-nine when the college celebrated its Centenary in 1999, was so moved that he gave an endowment of Rs 1.5 lakh instituting a prize for the best student in Mathematics. Nostalgically recalling his years in the college he remembered how his father had given one floor of his four-storeyed house at Dufferin Bridge to Principal Thadani to run a hostel for Hindu College students. No trace of the building remains as it was burnt down by rioters in 1942.

The flavour of most of the writings by old students is that the years spent in Hindu College were the most precious, useful, important and perhaps the happiest of their lives. The time spent in the college lingers as a precious fragrance. For some it is even more precious as they found their life partners in the college—Inder Sharma, Govind Rai Chaudhary, N.K. Nayak, Lalit Bhasin, D.N. Gupta, Anju Srivastava, Reena Jain, Vishal Bhardwaj and K.J. Singh, to name just a few. People make trips to the college years after they have left, to show their families the hostel room they stayed in, the classrooms they studied in and the cricket grounds. They peep into the staff room to meet teachers or those who have not yet retired from among the non-teaching staff who taught them ways to compensate for lack of attendance or rescued them from their peccadilloes, the canteen where they ran a debt, often still unpaid. These feelings ignite when two Hinduites meet. They may never have known each other or they may be separated by time and space, but when they come together, even for a while by chance or by desire, the warmth of the embrace is savoured for days and months. The days in the college are recalled with great enthusiasm, animation and laughter.

Raj Kumar Oberoi

HINDU COLLEGE

Present Hindu College main building

What makes Hindu College so precious to those who come to it as students, teachers or support staff? The college's Centenary in 1999 gave an opportunity to take stock. Dr Tapan Basu who joined the Department of English as a teacher after spending five years as a student at St. Stephen's, did a thoughtful analysis. As he crossed to the '*Paatshala* across the road from the college,' he found that this image so purposefully developed was not too far away from reality. The staff room seemed rather casual with its armchairs and sofas instead of the 'high' chairs that he was accustomed to. While tea and coffee in his alma mater was a time bound 11 o'clock affair, at Hindu it was available all morning for the asking, making the atmosphere seem like that of a club. Teachers too could be seen sitting with their students in the staff room sipping tea with them as they engaged in academic and extra-academic discussions. There was no segregation of space to separate the 'senior members' of the faculty from the 'junior members' and decorum and ceremony were largely missing in staff meetings. The debates were free and frank and the voice of authority was not of the Chair alone. The student and *karamchari* bodies were equally assertive and even rather aggressive. It seemed chaotic and he soon discovered that at times even a hardcore Hinduite would long for the order of a Stephanian. Even the Governing Body, chaired by Dr Bharat Ram, himself a Stephanian, was only interested in measuring the performance of Hindu by comparing and contrasting it with that of St. Stephen's. Surely there was a fault in this mode of thinking. 'Hindu,' as he very discerningly says, 'was not St. Stephen's.' It was never meant to be. It was set up in 1899 not as an imitation of St. Stephen's College, but as a critique of it.[22]

Principal Dr Vinay Srivastava (sitting 3rd from left), Dr Pradumn Kumar (sitting 2nd from left) and the staff of Hindu College in 2010

With its history and heritage, Hindu College did not need to emulate any other college, least of all one which had always sought to avoid 'desecration' from the popular and the political.

The strength of Hindu College lies in its democratic ethos, in the environment and the encouragement that it provides to articulate their rights and wrongs, not merely as a self-centred exercise, but in time with the broader concerns of society at large.

22 Dr Tapan Basu, 'The Hindu-St. Stephen's Interface: Some Personal Observations', *Centenary Souvenir*, Hindu College, Delhi.

Dr Kapila Vatsyayan took a panoramic view as she looked back to connect her time at the college with the present to see what the college had meant to its students and said that what it had accomplished still holds dozens of years later. As she said, the twin compulsions or attractions that played out in every aspect of college life were the struggle for freedom and political independence and simultaneously the attraction for all that was English/European in thought and intellectual disciplines. There was no awareness of this but looking back on those times when she was a student, she thoughtfully remarked:

> We aspired for one and were immersed in the other. We did not carry either as burden. It was only later, much later that it dawned upon us that the aspirations for a free India were not matched by an equal or adequate comprehension of the complexities of our present. We were also not fully informed or equipped to know or realize the full implications of our being members of the complex plural society.[23]

Her contemporaries became the first generation of educationists, administrators, legislators and politicians in independent India. As they grappled with the challenges of a newly independent nation they slowly and gradually learnt that the very education that had prepared them to meet those challenges had also distanced them intellectually from the very soil of their land. As she said, 'We did not realize that we were both the children of Macaulay and of the Orientalist discourse.' This disjuncture has perhaps not been fully comprehended even today and is still being played out.

For those who embarked on the adventure of shaping India it became a long and tiring path of unlearning. But Dr Vatsyayan gives credit to the healthy, hardy education of Hindu College that not only educated them but more importantly also prepared them for this unlearning. Its robust and free atmosphere facilitated a mental attitude of embarking upon adventures of mind and action. So what happened to the teachers and students of this generation? In their journeys lies the triumph of the college as it succeeded in opening new vistas for the 'janta' it undertook to educate rather than those who were elite by birth or social position.

Dr Indra Sen, a teacher in Philosophy left Hindu College to join Aurobindo Ashram, Dr S.K. Saxena went to join the University of Hawaii, to return in part to Indian Philosophy. Dr Daya Krishna, a senior contemporary took journeys in many directions on intellectual traditions. Dr Raj Krishna became a national economist and Giri Lal the propounder of Swadeshi causes. Lakshmi Jain travelled via cooperative movements to Vinoba Bhave. These were circuitous paths to roots but it was Hindu College and its intellectual atmosphere that made these possible. In this sense, the college did not cater to the high elite. It helped the ordinary middle class to tread new paths and make small beginnings in the by-lanes and highways of life.

---

23 *In Retrospect*, p. 74.

A recent message to *The Indraprastha* by Leela Gandhi might give a clue on why the college is so important for so many of its former students:

> Why has the College been so important to me? With hindsight I realize that at the time I joined Hindu, it was really not a fully made or fully constituted institution (with traditions, and rituals and set styles) unlike so many other colleges on campus. Rather its appeal and sometimes its lack thereof lay in the fact that all of us—students, faculty, workers, staff—were granted the freedom collaboratively to call into being, to give it the shape we wanted. As with any scene of wish-fulfillment, with this freedom came a heavy responsibility to summon the best sort of place: egalitarian, radical, tolerant, ecumenical, democratic, unpretentious, generous, experimental, improvisational and so on. Yet this created space would disappear once we had gone, to be reinvented by succeeding generations. I really don't know if we were always true to our bit of the bargain. What I do know is that precisely in granting us the prerogative thus to give it shape, the college made us mindful of our own best selves and so too of the fragile, precious and oftentimes occasional nature of such selves. I believe that all of us Hinduites have gained a wonderful if complex inheritance: the understanding that we are made, intricately, by the things we make.

It is a wonderful and precious legacy to have: to have the capacity and fluidity to make our destiny as a collective and to assert our will in making it. This lies in our very foundation; in surmounting all odds to survive and grow; to have the courage to defy colonial oppression; to understand and refuse to take the easy way out in accepting the colonial agenda of education; and to participate in the shaping of not only Hindu College as a nationalist institution but through it, of the nation. Higher education today is at the crossroads. While there are deep fault lines in the system, there are also significant positives: students are brighter, more aware, career conscious and competitive. With increasing integration into the world economy, expansion of communication and information technology, rapid transportation which has made the world a global neighbourhood and a rise in expectations and impatience with conventional obstacles, change is bound to occur. But it has to come from within and in keeping with its own values, cultural and ethical ethos. Otherwise there will be an irreparable rupture. Hindu College with its legacy has the capacity to play a significant role.

Continuity and change, change and continuity—this is deeply ingrained in the Indian psyche. Its genius lies in its capacity to absorb, adapt, assimilate and integrate. Hindu College is truly a product of that psyche. It is after all a people's movement which has had the capacity to absorb, adapt, assimilate and integrate in spite of opposition and meagre resources by its sheer determination and resilience. It must now reawaken to think outside of the system to reach excellence by looking ahead without losing its moorings and take the lead in becoming a significant player in shaping policy and thereby the course of events.

Distinguished Alumni Awardees

Here is a list of all those who have been felicitated by the OSA:

2000-2001
Dr K.K. Birla
Manoj Kumar
Justice Y.K. Sabharwal (Retd)
Dr J.S. Bajaj
Prof. J.N. Kapur
Khub Chand
H.K. Dua
Jivan Lal Seth

2001-2002
Kapila Vatsyayan*
(also awarded Lifetime Achievement Award in 2011-12)
Dr Naresh Trehan
Prakash Bhandari
Raj Bhargava
Inder Sharma*
(also awarded Lifetime Achievement Award in 2007-08 and Special Award in 2011-12)
Lt Gen. V.K. Nayar
Rani Karnaa

2002-2003
Bhiku Ram Jain
Justice B.P. Singh
S. Rajgopal
Air Marshal S.K.C. Gupta
V.P. Punj
Narendra Kumar
Manjit Dua
L.C. Jain
Ajay Bijli
Soni Sangwan

2004-2005
Kamal Kashyap
Dinesh Mathur
Kuldeep Dhingra
Mahesh Rangarajan
Bal Swarup Rahi
Man Mohan Sood
Arun Bhagat
Murali Karthik
Akash Chopra
Gautam Gambhir*
(also awarded Special Award in 2009-10)
Rahul Sanghvi
S.P.S. Chauhan
Jai Inderpal Singh
(Director Physical Education to represent the outstanding sportspersons down the years)

2005-2006
Gulzar Dehlvi
Prem Prakash
Kapil Batra
Vishal Bhardwaj
A.K. Bhattacharya
Suchitra Gupta
Surender Khanna
Justice Mukul Mudgal (Retd)*
(also awarded Lifetime Achievement Award in 2009-10)
Kavita A. Sharma
P.P. Sawhney
Zorawar Singh
Late Prof. Amba Prasad (Posthumous Award)

2006-2007
Kanwar Rajender Singh
Vinay Lamba
Ranjeet Kumar
K.C. Mehra
Dr Jaiveer Agarwal
Prof. S.K. Saxena
Vinod Kumar Khanna
Madhup Mudgal
T.C.A. Rangachari
Deeksha Suri
Shradha Suri Marwah
Kunwar Sachdev

2007-2008
Pratap Khanna
L.K. Malhotra
Reva Nayyar
Sandeep Parekh
Savita Datta
Col Anil Shorey*
(also awarded Lifetime Achievement Award posthumously in 2010-11)
Justice Rabindra Bhat
Prof. Hema Sharda
Prem Behl
Satya Narain Gupta

2008-2009
Arjun Rampal
Imtiaz Ali
Loveleen Tandon
Tisca Chopra
Vinod Rai*
(also awarded Lifetime Achievement Award in 2010-11)
Justice G.S. Sistani
Hardeep Singh Puri
Asha Swarup
Viresh Pratap Chaudhry
Sreenivasan Jain
Syed Saba Karim
Sunil Valson
Prof. B.M. Bhatia
Prof. Bipan Chandra

2009-2010
Samir Modi
Dr Parvez Ahmed
Justice Mukta Gupta
Justice Siddharth Mridul
Pradeep Puri
C. Balakrishnan
Rajinder Pal
Dr Sudarshana Sabharwal
Justice Manmohan
Narendra Singh Rathore
W.D. Mathur
Pradeep Jain
Justice S.K. Mishra
Rudra Gangadharan
Prof. R.W. Desai
Gursharan Singh
Sapna Rana
Prof. P.C. Verma

2010-2011
Vikramjit Singh
Rao Inderjit Singh
Ranjan Chatterjee
Ashok Trivedi
Dr Subramanian Swamy
V.P. Singh
Hari Gidwani
Suneeta Trivedi
Anju Srivastava
Raj Vikash Verma
R.K. Oberoi
Prof. V.M. Misra
Late R.S. Jassal (Posthumous Award)

2011-2012
Lalit Bhasin
Prof. Satish Kumar
Naval K. Anand
Anil Goswami
Alok Joshi
Yashowardhan Azad
I.V.S. Juneja
Brij Bhardwaj
Deepak Verma
Sidharth Luthra
Akash Lal
Muktesh Pardeshi
D.S. Bains
Latika Thukral
Sunaina Jerath
Sanjay Sehgal
Late Giri Lal Jain (Posthumous Award)

Bibliography

Basu, Aparna, ed. *University of Delhi 1922–1997, Platinum Jubilee*. Delhi: University of Delhi, 1998.

Bayly, C.A. *Empire and Information: Intelligence Gathering and Social Communication in India, 1780–1870*. Cambridge: Cambridge University Press, 1996.

________. 'Local Control in Indian Towns—the Case of Allahabad 1880–1920'. *Modern Asian Studies* 5 (4) (1971): 292-293.

________. *Origins of Nationality in South Asia: Patriotism and Ethical Government in the Making of Modern India*. New Delhi: Oxford University Press, 1998.

________. *Rulers, Townsmen and Bazaars: North Indian Society in the Age of British Expansion 1770–1870*. Cambridge: Cambridge University Press, 1983.

________. *The Local Roots of Indian Politics: Allahabad 1880–1920*. London: Oxford University Press, 1975.

Bayly, Susan. *Caste, Society and Politics in India from the Eighteenth Century to the Modern Age*. In *The New Cambridge History of India*, IV.3. Cambridge: Cambridge University Press, 1999.

Centenary Souvenir. Hindu College: University of Delhi, 1999.

Chand, Tara. *History of the Freedom Movement in India*, Vol. II. New Delhi: Publications Division, Ministry of Information and Broadcasting, 1967, rpt 1974.

Chenoy, Shama Mitra. *Shahjahanabad: A City of Delhi, 1638–1857*. New Delhi: Munshiram Manoharlal Publishers, 1998.

Confidential Letter (no. 263, 19 February 1921). Department of Education. New Delhi: National Archives of India.

Correspondence between Mahatma Gandhi and N.V. Thadani as given by Shri Jivat Thadani.

Dar, S. L, and S. Somaskandan. *History of Banaras Hindu University*. Varanasi: Banaras Hindu University Press, 1966.

Dayal, Maheshwar. *Rediscovering Delhi: The Story of Shahjahanabad*. New Delhi: S. Chand, 1976.

Gallagher, John, Gordon Johnson and Anil Seal. *Locality, Province and Nation: Essays on Indian Politics, 1870–1940*. London: Cambridge University Press, 1973.

Garrett, H.L.O. *The Trial of Bahadur Shah Zafar*. Reprinted with an introduction by M.J. Akbar. New Delhi: Roli Books, 1932, rpt 2007.

Goenka, K.K. *Premchand Vishwakosh*, Vol. 1. New Delhi: Prabhat Prakashan, 1981.

Gupta, Manmath Nath. *History of the Indian Revolutionary Movement*. Bombay, New Delhi: Somaiya Publications Pvt. Ltd., 1972.

Hardas, Balshastri. *Armed Struggle for Freedom: Ninety Years War of Independence—1857 to Subhash*. Translated by S.S. Apte. Poona: Kal Prakashan, 1958.

Haynes, Douglas E. 'From Tribute to Philanthropy: The Politics of Gift Giving in a Western Indian City'. *The Journal of Asian Studies* 46 (2) (May 1987): 339–360.

Holman, Dennis. *Sikander Sahib: The Life of Colonel James Skinner, 1778–1841*. London: Heinemann, 1961.

Jaitly, Ashok. *St. Stephen's College: A History*. New Delhi: Lotus Collection, Roli Books, 2006.

Joshi, Arun. *Lala Shri Ram: A Study in Entrepreneurship and Industrial Management*. New Delhi: Orient Longman, 1975.

Joshi, Arun, ed. *Remembering Lala Shri Ram: Reminiscences on his 100th Birthday*. Delhi: DCM Limited, 1983.

Kamath, Shanti. *The Saga of Indraprastha College for Women*. New Delhi: Indraprastha Educational Trust, 2000.

Kapur, J. N. *A Life with Mathematics and Education: An Autobiography*. New Delhi: Mathematical Sciences Trust Society, 1997.

Khatri, Durgaprasad. *Balidan*. Varanasi: Kamlapati Khatri Lahri Books, 1964.

Kumar, Usha. *Yogeshwar Dayal Aur Dilli*. New Delhi: Bani Publications, 2005, 2nd edn 2006.

Letter (No. D813/33, Pol. February 1933) from the Home Department, Government of India to the Chief Commissioner, Delhi 1931.

Letters from Confidential Branch, Chief Commissioner's office to the Vice Chancellor (D.C. No. F-123/42) August and September 1942.

Letter (No. 1752 of September, 1942) from the Honorary Secretary, Committee of Management, Hindu College, Delhi to the superintendent of Education.

Mahajan, V. D. *Nationalist Movement in India*. New Delhi: Sterling, 1976.

Memorandum of Association, Hindu College, Delhi, 15 May 1901.

Minutes of Meetings of Board of Trustees, Hindu College, Delhi.

Minutes of Meetings of Executive Council, University of Delhi.

Monk, F.F. *A History of St. Stephen's College, Delhi*. Calcutta: YMCA Publishing House, 1935.

Naregal, Veena. *Language Politics, Elites, and the Public Sphere*. New Delhi: Permanent Black, 2001.

Nigam, Nand Kishore. *Balidan: Chandrashekhar Azad ki Romanchkari Jeevani*. New Delhi: Nand Kishore Nigam.

Newsletters of Old Students' Association.

Oberoi, Raj K., ed. *The Hinduites, Biographical Directory*. Delhi: Old Students' Association, Hindu College, February 1979.

Oldenburg, Veena Talwar. *The Making of Colonial Lucknow, 1856–1877*. Princeton: Princeton University Press, 1984.

Oral interview of Prof. N.K. Nigam, recorded on 1 March 1968. Oral History Transcript No. 70. New Delhi: Nehru Memorial Museum and Library.

Photocopy of the full file containing the the documents when Hindu College, University of Delhi, was registered under the Societies Registration Act XXI of 1860 on 24 October 1945 that was obtained via a letter under the Right to Information Act, 2005.

Pradhan, Ram Chandra. *Bhagavadgita, A Primer and Life-Sketch of Karmayogi Lala Rai Kedarnath*. Noida: Bhagvadgita International Foundation, 1995, 4th edn, 2004.

Punjab District Gazeteers, Vol.V A (Delhi District).

Ram, Bharat. *Reminiscences and Reflections*. New Delhi: Vikas Publishing House, 1990.

Rana, S., ed. *Sarup Singh: A Living Legend*. New Delhi: National Publishing House, 1998.

Renold, Leah. *A Hindu Education: Early Years of the Banaras Hindu University*. New Delhi: Oxford University Press, 2005.

Report of the Commission on Christian Higher Education in India: An Enquiry into the Place of the Christian College in Modern India. London: Oxford University Press, 1931.

Sanatan Dharma College magazine 1928-29 Lahore, brought out in the memory of Raghubar Dayal Shastri after his death on 13 April 1929.

Seal, Anil. *The Emergence of Indian Nationalism: Competition and Collaboration in the Later Nineteenth Century*. Cambridge: Cambridge University Press, 1968.

Secret Letter from the Vice Chancellor to the Chief Commissioner of Delhi from Hindu Rao Hospital, 13 September 1942.

Sharan, Brij Behari. *Ek Shatabdi*. New Delhi, April 2003.

________. *Lala Lachhman Dass Garg: Atmakatha*. New Delhi, 1991.

Sharma, Manudutt, ed. *36th no. of Agrawal Itihas Granth Samuchchay*. Hissar: Shri Durbar Karyalaya, 2001.

Sharma, R.S. *Perspectives in Social and Economic History of Early India*. New Delhi: Munshiram Manoharlal Publishers, 1983.

Shri Hansraj Gupta ki Bahumukhi Sevaon ke Uplakshya Mein Samarpit Abhinandan Granth. New Delhi: Shri Hansraj Gupta Abhinandan Granth Samaroh Smriti Prakashan, 1972.

Singh, Bhai Nahar. *Struggle for Free Hindustan*. New Delhi: Atlantic Publishers, 1988.

Singh, Khushwant, and Arun Joshi. *Shri Ram: A Biography*. New York: Asia Publishing House, 1968.

Singh, Khushwant, and Syeda Saiydain Hameed, eds. *A Dream Turns Seventy Five: The Modern School 1920–1995*. New Delhi: Allied Publishers, 1995.

Singh, Sangat. *Freedom Movement in Delhi: 1858–1919*. New Delhi: Associated Publishing House, 1972.

Souvenir on the Occasion of the Diamond Jubilee of Hindu College, Delhi (1899–1959).

Stalk, Ulrike. *An Empire of Books: The Naval Kishore Press and the Diffusion of the Printed Word in Colonial India*. Ranikhet: Permanent Black, 2007.

The Indraprastha. Delhi: Hindu College.

University of Delhi Calendar, 1922–1923.

Unpublished notes of Shri Jivat Thadani.

Vatsyayan, Kapila, Kavita A. Sharma, Suroopa Mukherjee, Tapan Basu and Sunil Dua, eds. *In Retrospect*. New Delhi: Har-Anand Publications, 2000.

Acknowledgements

Finding information for a prestigious institution like Hindu College, Delhi, which is now 114 years old, was a gigantic job. We visited several libraries, met several people whose ancestors were involved with the formation and running of the college, went through hundreds of documents and we managed to finally complete the book—yet far from complete.

We are grateful to many people who have been generous with their time and support in making available information as well as some rare pictures. We have not been able to carry all the pictures that we would have liked to because the requirements of the text overtook everything else. We would also like to thank our publisher Mr Bikash D. Niyogi and our editor Mr Shaurya Shaukat Sircar for their infinite patience and hard work.

It is near impossible to acknowledge everyone's help individually. Yet we must acknowledge the contribution of the following institutions, people and well-wishers for their great help. If we have inadvertently left out some names we seek your indulgence and forgiveness.

Delhi Archives – Sanjay Garg, Ravindra Singh
National Archives of India
Nehru Memorial Museum and Library
Delhi Public Library
Hardayal (Harding) Library
Hindu College, Delhi
Mr Sushil Gupta
Mr Harsh Agarwal
Mr Ashok Pratap Singh
Mr Raj Kumar Gupta
Late Mr S.P. Agarwal
Mr Tejpal Gadodia
Col Brij Behari Sharan
Gurwala family
Mr Lalit Bhasin
Prof. R.W. Desai
Mr Sharif Bharti
Mr Raj Kumar Oberoi
Mr Sondeep Shankar
Dr Majumdar, Chief Librarian, India International Centre (IIC)
Ms Rajesh Sharma, Hindu College
Mr Sanjeev Dutt Sharma, Librarian, Hindu College
Mr Rana Sen
Dr Malashri Lal
Mr Deepak Singh
Mr Manish Karnwar
Mr Daljit Singh
Mr Desh Raj Gupta
Mr Mahendra Gupta
Late Mr Satya Narain Gupta
Mr B.D. Saini
Mr Desh Deepak
Ms Sandhya Jain
Ms Shruti Gupta
Mr P.C. Verma
Mr Ajay Verma
Mrs Usha Kumar
Mr Bhawani Shankar
Mr Ashwini Shankar
Mr Ashok Kumar
Mr K.P. Sarabhai
Ms Nirmala Hari, IIC
Mr N.C. Mathur
Mr Suresh Mathur
Mr Bhadra Puri
Central Secretariat Library
Mr Amitabh Sengupta
Dr Kapila Vatsyayan
Mr Ambarish Ganesh
Dr Meena Gautam
Mr G.S. Moondhra, Ramjas Foundation
Mr K.L. Kamat
Mr Rukun Advani
Ms Shrinkhla Sahai
Mr Asif Azmi
Lucknow Literary Festival
Mr Praful Thakkar
Mr Rahul Chug
Ms Devaki Jain
Delhi University Archives

Index

J

K

L

M

T

REGISTRAR OF JOINT STOCK COMPANIES • PUNJAUB •

[illegible]

Boshesharnath

Shri Krishna Das

Secretary

Hukam Ram

Chairman

Din Dayal Sharma

[illegible]

Jaganath

Sat Narain Gurwala

Kedar Nath

Kanhaiya Lal

President

19/3/12

Hukam Ram

Shri Krishna Das

Secretary

Chairman

Sultan Singh

Chairman

Raj Narayan

Chairman

REGISTRAR OF JOINT STOCK CO[MPANIES] • PUNJAUB •

Hari Chand

for L. Raghubir Singh

[illegible]

Registered this ... day of June 1901 ... provisions of ac[t] ... 1860.

S. K. Sen

Shri Krishna Das

Secretary

[illegible]

Krishna Lal

Registrar Joint [Stock Companies]

Mannmal

Mannmal

Krishna Lal

[illegible]

Chandu Lal

Mathra Das